The
Collected
Poems of
William
Carlos
Williams

Volume II
1939-1962

William Carlos Williams, 1959. Photograph by Lisa Larsen.
Used by permission of *Life Magazine* © Time Inc.

The Collected Poems of William Carlos Williams

Volume II
1939-1962

Edited by Christopher MacGowan

A NEW DIRECTIONS BOOK

Manufactured in the United States of America
New Directions Books are printed on acid-free paper; clothbound editions are Smyth
sewn.
First published clothbound by New Directions in 1988 and as New Directions Paper-
book 731 in 1991.
Published simultaneously in Canada by Penguin Books Canada Limited.

Library of Congress Cataloging-in-Publication Data
(Revised for vol. 2)

Williams, William Carlos, 1883–1963.
    The collected poems of William Carlos Williams.
    (A New Directions Book)
    Bibliography: v. 1, p. 467–548.
    Includes indexes.
    Contents: v. 1. 1909–1939 / edited by A. Walton Litz
and Christopher MacGowan—v. 2. 1939–1962 / edited by
Christopher MacGowan.
    I. Litz, A. Walton.   II. MacGowan, Christopher J.
(Christopher John)   III. Title.
PS3545.I544A17   1986   811'.52   86-5448
ISBN 13: 978-0-8112-1188-8 (pbk. V.2)
ISBN 10: 0-8112-1188-6   (pbk. V.2)
New Directions Books are published for James Laughlin
by New Directions Publishing Corporation,
80 Eighth Avenue, New York 10011

SEVENTH PAPERBOUND PRINTING

Contents

xiii

Preface

This volume is the second of a two-volume edition collecting all of William Carlos Williams' published poetry with the exception of his long poem *Paterson* (which will be edited as a separate volume). Volume II covers the years from 1939 to 1962—when the cumulative effect of a series of strokes forced Williams to stop writing in the months before his death in March 1963.

Continuing the aim of presenting Williams' development and achievement in as clear a way as possible, this volume follows Volume I in rejecting Williams' own arrangement of his collected poems—in this case his *Collected Later Poems* of 1950. Instead, the poems Williams published in individual volumes are printed in their original order in those volumes, while poems that remained uncollected or were only collected in the 1950 collection are printed chronologically according to date of first publication. The poems first published in *Collected Later Poems* appear in their chronological place in 1950. Volume II begins with uncollected poems from the years 1939-1944, and concludes with the Pulitzer prize-winning *Pictures from Brueghel* (1962).

Williams organized *The Collected Later Poems* around a framework somewhat more chronological than the thematic arrangement of *Collected Earlier Poems*, although the sections representing *The Wedge* (1944) and *The Clouds* (1948) do not exactly correspond to the poems in those two volumes. However, Williams' design for the volume was frustrated by his overlooking a number of his 1940s poems (some found their way into *The Collected Earlier Poems*), and particularly by his failing to catch the absence of a section containing ten poems that had been mislaid by his typist. The section was hastily added to the back of the book in the middle of the print run. The later printing history of the book further obscured his original intentions. In a 1963 revision John Thirlwall added a further section, "The Lost Poems (1944-1950)," and in 1972 New Directions tacked a poem written in 1960, "Tribute to Neruda, the Poet Collector of Seashells," onto the end of this section. Those readers interested in Williams' arrangement of *Collected Later Poems*, and a list of the later additions, will find a table of contents in Appendix C.

The opening poems of Volume II reflect Williams' continuing uncertainty and experimentation as he sought a solution to the stylistic and thematic problems raised by his plans for *Paterson*. Many of these poems are included in the various pre-*Paterson* typescripts Williams arranged and rearranged from the middle 1930s to the early years of the next decade, and that are now deposited at Harvard and Buffalo. In sending the first of these, the eighty-seven page *Detail & Parody for the poem Paterson* typescript, to New Directions in 1939 Williams indicated something of the scope of his ambitions. "They are not," he wrote of the poems "in some ways, like anything I have written before but rather plainer, simpler, more crudely cut. Look 'em over. I too have to escape from my own modes. I offer them as one man's digression from the early or recent work of WCW." A 1941 sequence of poems in *The Broken Span* titled "For the Poem *Paterson*," is the only extended arrangement of these poems Williams chose to publish. Not until the opening poems of *The Wedge* (1944), does Williams articulate what came to be the workable strategy for his long poem.

A unifying feature of Williams' concerns in the 1950s is his interest in "the American idiom" and "the variable foot," but the decade also saw him respond in two different ways to two very different challenges, and produce two very different kinds of poetry. In 1951 and 1952 Williams suffered two strokes, and these were followed by a severe depression that eventually demanded hospitalization. The triadic-line poems of the first half of the 1950s record both the tragedy and the determined response. However, by 1954 Williams had come to feel that the triadic "vein of poetry" was "petering out," and in 1957 he told Cid Corman "something more comprehensive has to take its place." *Pictures from Brueghel* collects most of the poems that grew out of this final demand.

A number of further strokes took their toll, and Williams told John Thirlwall at the end of 1961 that he had given up writing, although a number of poems in various states of completion were found among the poet's papers after his death. I have published the uncollected, posthumously published poems by date of composition, concluding the final uncollected section with "Stormy," the poem that Paul Mariani records was "the last poem Floss was sure her husband had written." Other departures from the practice of publishing uncollected poems by date of publication are documented in Appendix A.

A distinguishing feature of this volume is the large number of uncollected translations that Williams made in the second half of his career, often during periods of uncertainty about the direction of his own work. The translations are from languages he knew well—French and Spanish— and from those he knew barely or not at all—Greek and Chinese. Trans-

lating contemporary writers, as he told Nicolas Calas in 1940 and David
Ignatow in 1949, could help him in the struggle with problems of form,
while translation from the classics, he reminded Cid Corman in 1955,
demanded "lively invention" in order to demonstrate how "present
modes differ from the past by showing what in the present is *equivalent*,
not the same, with what existed then."

A detailed description of the editorial procedures for this volume may
be found in Appendix A, "A Note on the Text." The reader should keep
these general principles in mind:

(1) Although the poems are printed within the context of the original
volumes in which they appeared, or in order of first publication, a cor-
rected text of *Collected Earlier Poems* and *Collected Later Poems* is used
for the poems that appeared in those volumes. The poems not included
in those two collections, or in *Pictures from Brueghel* (which reprinted
The Desert Music and *Journey to Love*) are printed in their original pub-
lished forms, and are identified in the Annotations (Appendix B).

(2) As is the practice in Volume I, a number of poems that undergo
significant verbal or lineation changes are included in the text in both a
first version and a later revised version. Other examples of significant
revision are provided in the Annotations (Appendix B).

(3) The authors of translated poems are indicated in the main text
immediately beneath the title of the poem, unless the group title of the
poems makes the authorship clear. Further information on the original
poems appears in the Annotations (Appendix B).

(4) Poems in manuscript or typescript have not been included in this
text (with the exception of those written after 1938 which have been
published elsewhere since Williams' death).

(5) Although Williams published from his work in progress on *Pater-
son* through the 1940s and 1950s, I do not reprint these extracts unless
Williams chose to include lines from the long poem as self-contained
shorter poems in his collections—for example, "The Descent," and see
"Paterson," and "Paterson: Episode 17" in Volume I. I do reprint the
1952 "Paterson, Book V: The River of Heaven," since these lines subse-
quently developed into the separate poem "Asphodel, That Greeny
Flower."

(6) The Annotations (Appendix B) conform to the principles laid out
in Volume I, documenting significant textual variants and background
information from both published and unpublished sources. Explanatory
notes are not provided for items of general cultural knowledge that can

be found in standard dictionaries or encyclopedias. The page numbers in the running heads for Appendix B are keyed to the titles of the poems in the main text.

(7) Appendix D reprints four additional poems that have been discovered since this volume's first publication in 1988. The poems represent an addition to Emily Wallace's *A Bibliography of William Carlos Williams,* and further bibliographical information is provided in Appendix D. The two additional poems from the 1937 anthology *. . . and Spain sings* that were printed in Appendix D up to the fifth printing of this volume, were removed with its sixth printing and now appear in Appendix D of Volume I.

(8) The Indexes of Titles and First Lines at the back of this volume index poems in both Volumes I and II.

C.M.

POEMS

1939-1944

THE SWAGGERING GAIT

Bareheaded
the hair blond in tight curls
the heavy and worn

blue sweater
buttoned tight
under a cold sky

he walks
and lifts the butt of cigar
he holds

to his pursing lips
alone—
save for the tilt

of his shoulders
the swing of his knees—
Even the paper

lunch bag in his other hand
sharing
that one distinction

THE DECEPTRICES

Because they are not,
they paint their lips
and dress like whores.

Because they are uncertain,
they put on the bold
looks of experience.

This is their youth, too
soon gone, too soon
the unalterable conclusion.

ILLEGITIMATE THINGS

Water still flows—
The thrush still sings

though in
the skirts of the sky

at the bottom of
the distance

huddle
. . . . echoing cannon!

Whose silence revives
valley after

valley to peace
as poems still conserve

the language
of old ecstasies.

THE POET AND HIS POEMS

1

The poem is this:
a nuance of sound
delicately operating
upon a cataract of sense.

Vague. What a stupid
image. Who operates?

And who is operated
on? How can a nuance

operate on anything?
It is all in
the sound. A song.
Seldom a song. It should

be a song—made of
particulars, wasps,
a gentian—something
immediate, open

scissors, a lady's
eyes—the particulars
of a song waking
upon a bed of sound.

2

Stiff jointed poets
or the wobble
headed who chase
vague images and think—

because they feel
lovely movements
upon the instruments
of their hearts—

that they are gifted
forget the
exchange, how much
is paid and how little

when you count it
in your hand you
get for it later in
the market. It's

a constant mystery
no less in the
writing of imaginative
lines than in love.

DEFIANCE TO CUPID

Not in this grave
will I lie
more than a summer
holiday!

Dig it deep, no
matter, I
will break that sleep
and run away.

TAILPIECE

What time is it? Yes,
how the grass at the
top of the bank flutes
it of the time! and
the dirt and snow, the
cold red dirt
and scattered snow
mingle their emphasis!

What time is it? Time
to begin again! the
beat confused, mistaken
for the measure, the
measure presuming over
the facts to chop the
world away as we move—

While Love's barge
pulling at the beat

sends up its white plume—
What time is it? the
clumsy bows stacked
with waste in bales
squat jurymast aslant
tackle rattling—down
down, down the frozen
river to Time without end
the salt sea . . .

THE ROCKING WOMAN

Wind your thread
and wind your thread,
thinking of men
long since dead.

Witty, well made,
but mulish,
you lost them all
being love foolish.

Maybe you're better
off—who knows?—
the leaves falling
when the wind blows.

THE GENIUS

We have written
    but not enough
not intensely enough—

We have not carried
        the same construction
far enough
nowhere near far enough

to the final
development and conclusion

We stop by the cemetery
and look at the
        tombs—
the dried flower heads
on the graves—
and moan and bewail—

And nothing, nothing
    comes of it.

Hail at least Picasso
the Spaniard
who goes through
No use reading the names
on the stones
the men there are dead
        the sunlight
does not penetrate to them
and the evergreens
malignant. Memory,
        yes,
green for our thoughts
but it is
        too late.

THE APPROACHING HOUR

You Communists and Republicans!
all you Germans and Frenchmen!
you corpses and quickeners!
The stars are about to melt
and fall on you in tears.

Get ready! Get ready!
you Papists and Protestants!
you whores and you virtuous!

The moon will be bread
and drop presently into your baskets.

Friends and those who despise
and detest us!
Adventists and those who believe
nothing!
Get ready for the awakening.

A PORTRAIT OF THE TIMES

Two W. P. A. men
stood in the new
sluiceway

overlooking
the river—
One was pissing

while the other
showed
by his red

jagged face the
immemorial tragedy
of lack-love

while an old
squint-eyed woman
in a black

dress
and clutching
a bunch of

late chrysanthemums
to her
fatted bosoms

turned her back
on them
at the corner

CHERRY BLOSSOMS AT EVENING

In the prebirth of the evening
the blue cherry blossoms
on the blue tree
from this yellow, ended room—
press to the windows
inside shall be out
the clustered faces of the flowers
straining to look in

THE RITUALISTS

In May, approaching the city, I
saw men fishing in the backwash
between the slips, where at the time
no ship lay. But though I stood

watching long enough, I didn't see
one of them catch anything
more than quietness, to the formal
rhythms of casting—that slow dance.

THE GRACEFUL BASTION

A white butterfly
in an August garden,
light as it may seem

among the zinnias
and verbenas,
fragile among the red

trumpeted petunias,
is ribbed with steel
wired to the sun

whose triumphant power
will keep it safe,
free as laughter,

secure against
bombardments no more
dangerous to its

armored might than if
the cotton clouds
should merely fall.

THE SLEEPING BRUTE

For three years at evening
the sparrow has come
under the porch roof to sleep.

What has this to do
with the war in Europe? For
three years winter

and summer the same sparrow
with covered head
asleep among the gray shadows

FROM A WINDOW

Here's a question for us. Help me
to find the answer. The tops
of the row of poplar trees are level
with the fourth floor of the hospital

And, Yes, says Sister Francis,
the lady in the next bed had her

baby circumcised this morning. I've
noticed that in the wards you have

to use your psychology. If the
first one doesn't eat her apple pie
especially if she is a leader the whole
ward will go without its dessert—

Heart-shaped leaves tear at their stems
outside the window of the scrub-room
while the trees rock and sway
in the broken light and a seething

sound sets off their changing colors.
What is the answer to this rivalry?

RIVER RHYME

The rumpled river
takes its course
lashed by rain

This is that now
that tortures
skeletons of weeds

and muddy waters
eat their
banks the drain

of swamps a bulk
that writhes and fat-
tens as it speeds.

SKETCH FOR A PORTRAIT OF HENRY FORD

A tin bucket
full of small used parts

nuts and short bolts
slowly draining onto
the dented bottom—
forming a heavy sludge
of oil—depositing
in its turn steel grit—

Hangs on an arm
that whirls it at increasing
velocity around
a central pivot—
suddenly the handle gives
way and the bucket
is propelled through
space   .   .   .

AN INFORMATIVE OBJECT

The monolith of a double flight
of six concrete steps
has flown butterfly-like to
rest slantwise on its platform
waving its two wings in the air
at the edge of the dump-heap
now in reverse leading left and right
to a new platform filled with
rain the threshold to other entrances

TO A WOMAN SEEN ONCE

No one is lovely
but you alone

a green branch
fallen into the sea

that was jostled
and broken to be

returned after
certain years all

straightness
and strength from

that mold—I
am through with you.

THE NEW CLOUDS

The morning that I first loved you
had a quality of fine division about it
a lightness and a light full of
small round clouds all rose upon the
ground which bore them, a light of
words upon a paper sky, each a meaning
and all a meaning jointly. It was a
quiet speech, at ease but reminiscent
and of praise—with a disturbance
of waiting. Yes! a page that glowed
by all that it was not, a meaning more
of meaning than the text whose
separate edges were the edges of the sky.

For the Poem *Paterson*

A man like a city and a woman like a flower—who are in
love. Two women. Three women. Innumerable women,
each like a flower. But only one man—like a city.

1. DETAIL

Her milk don't seem to . .
She's always hungry but . .

She seems to *gain* all right,
I don't know.

2. SPARROWS AMONG DRY LEAVES
[*First Version*]

The sparrows
by the iron fence-post
hardly seen

for the dry leaves
that half
cover them—

stirring up
the leaves—fight
and chirp

stridently
search
and

peck the sharp
gravel to
good digestion

and love's
obscure and insatiable
appetite

3. ST. VALENTINE

A woman's breasts
for beauty
A man's delights
for charm

The rod and cups
of duty

to stave us
from harm!

A woman's eyes
a woman's
thighs and a man's
straight look:

Cities rotted to
pig-sties
will stand up by
that book!

4. SOMETIMES IT TURNS DRY AND THE LEAVES FALL BEFORE THEY ARE BEAUTIFUL

This crystal sphere
upon whose edge I drive
turns brilliantly—
The level river shines!

My love! My love!
how sadly do we thrive:
thistle-caps and
sumac or a tree whose

sharpened leaves
perfect as they are
look no farther than—
into the grass.

5. IN SISTERLY FASHION

The ugly woman clutched
her lover round the neck
her skin was white as snow
as she wept softly to herself

knowing her lack of beauty
like the sting of death—
by which she praised in
sisterly fashion your fitted
limbs your honied breath

6. DETAIL

I had a misfortune in September,
just at the end of my vacation.

I been keepin' away from that for years.
Just an accident. No foundation.

None at all, no feeling. I'm too
old to have a child. Why I'm fifty!

7. RALEIGH WAS RIGHT
[First Version]

We cannot go to the country
for the country will bring us
    no peace
What can the small violets
tell us that grow on furry stems
in the long grass among
lance-shaped leaves?

Though you praise us
and call to mind the poets
who sung of our loveliness it was
long ago!
long ago!
when country people
would plow and sow with
flowering minds and pockets
at ease—if ever this were true.

Not now. Love itself a flower
with roots in a parched ground.
Empty pockets
make empty heads. Cure it
if you can but do not believe
that we can live today
in the country
for the country will bring us
         no peace.

8. THE UNKNOWN

Do you exist
my pretty bird
flying
above the snow?

Are you actually
flying
or do I imagine
it so?

Detail of wing
and breast
unquestionably
there—

Or do I merely
think you
perfect
in mid-air?

CODA

Beating heart
feather
of wing and breast

to this
bleakness
antithetical

In love
dear love, my love
detail is all

9. FERTILE

You are a typical American woman
you think men grow on trees—

You want love, only love! rarest
of male fruit! Break it open and

in the white of the crisp flesh
find the symmetrical brown seeds.

10. DETAIL

Hey!
Can I have some more
milk?

YEEEEAAAAASSSSS!
—always the gentle
mother!

11. THE THOUGHTFUL LOVER

Deny yourself all
half things. Have it
or leave it.

But it will keep—or
it is not worth
the having.

Never start
anything you can't
finish—

However do not lose
faith because you
are starved!

She loves you
she says. Believe it
—tomorrow.

But today
the particulars
of poetry

that difficult art
require
your whole attention.

12. THE END OF THE PARADE

The sentence undulates
raising no song—
It is too old, the
words of it are falling
apart. Only percussion
strokes continue
with weakening
emphasis what was once
cadenced melody
full of sweet breath.

13. DETAIL

Doc, I bin lookin' for you
I owe you two bucks.

How you doin'?

Fine. When I get it
I'll bring it up to you.

14. A FOND FAREWELL

You? Why you're
just sucking
my life blood out.

What do I care
if the baker
and the garbage man

must be served.
Take what
you might give

and be damned
to you. I'm
going elsewhere.

15. THE A B AND C OF IT
[First Version]

a. Love's very fleas
   are mine. Enter me
   worms and all
   till I crumble

   and steam with it
   pullulate
   to be sucked into
   an orchid.

b. But the fleas
   were too shy

didn't want to
offend

recoiled from
the odors
and couldn't
unbend

c. Take me then
Spirit of Loneliness
insatiable
Spirit of Love

and let be—
for Time without
odor is Time
without me

A LOVE POEM

Basic hatred
sometimes has a flower
pure crystal
a white camellia

It assumes
the shape of love
is love
to all appearances

COMFORT

My head hurts like hell!

Gives you some idea of what
the hereafter is like.

They say we live again or
something.

  Here take these two aspirins.

FLATTERY

(For F. W.)

You tell me that I love myself
more than any other thing.

But how should I interpret it
were it not for you who give
the meaning, taken from itself
to be as many as the grass
under your spell. You steal me
from myself to come up
in a thousand forms full of
the smell and sights that make
up your own varied seasons.

PIGHEADED POET

Everything I do
everything I write
drives me
from those I love

If it is good
they are bewildered
if it is bad
ashamed

At great risk
to the love they bear me
I walk barefoot
in quicksand

DETAILS FOR PATERSON

I just saw two boys.
One of them gets paid for distributing circulars
and he throws it down the sewer.

I said, Are you a Boy Scout?
He said, no.
The other one was.
I have implicit faith in
     the Boy Scouts

If you talk about it
long enough
you'll finally write it—
If you get by the stage
when nothing
can make you write—
If you don't die first

I keep those bests that love
     has given me
Nothing of them escapes—
I have proved it
proven once more in your eyes

Go marry! your son will have
blue eyes and still
there'll be no answer
you have not found a cure
No more have I for that enormous
wedged flower, my mind
miraculously upon
the dead stick of night

RIVER RHYME II

Shine miraculous
mottled river

dancing flames
patched black with
doom. We shall
never see what our
love portends
never its flower
in bloom.

BRIEF LIEF

Pray
pay
no attention to my greatness

You
too
could do as well as

I
by
letting root bring forth first

stem
leaf

then
when
ready, at the last (if ever)

sweet
meat.

ELECTION DAY

Warm sun, quiet air
an old man sits

in the doorway of
a broken house—

boards for windows
plaster falling

from between the stones
and strokes the head

of a spotted dog

CONVENTIONAL BALLAD

Ladies, ladies! what you offer
is not always what we please—
Why shouldn't he stand in a
    telephone booth a block
    from home and chew candy?

Our heads fail us
the measure lags behind the
    elastic order grasped in
    a split second by our
    more ready knees.

Take off the wraps. Let us
breathe, let us breathe only!
Is there no choice
    save only by a process of
    condemnation? Ladies,
    Ladies, ladies, ladies!

10/14

Rose in the park
with a white center
blood red
single rose—

the scraping of
fallen leaves still leaves

your loveliness
unshaken

THE PREDICTER OF FAMINE

White day, black river
corrugated and swift—

as the stone of the sky
on the prongy ring
of the tarnished city
is smooth and without motion:

A gull flies low
upstream, his beak tilted
sharply, his eye
alert to the providing water.

THE LAST TURN
[*First Version*]

Then see it! in distressing
detail—from behind a red light
at 53d and 6th
of a November evening, with
the jazz of the cross lights
echoing the crazy weave of
the breaking mind: splash of
a half purple half naked woman's
body whose bejeweled guts
the cars drag up and down—
No house but that has its
brains blown off by the dark!
Nothing recognizable
but the whole, one jittering
direction made of all directions
spelling the inexplicable,
pigment upon flesh and flesh

the pigment the genius of a world
artless but supreme . . .

Three Poems for Horace Gregory

THE UNITED FRONT

They have removed a building to make
parking space for the bank, showing
the sandy subsoil of this region. And there
a black cat scratches and sits down.

TO A CHINESE WOMAN

passing my house in the suburbs.
To a woman passing. To Asia
passing my house in the suburbs.
To China. To the moon. To the
stars. To the month of May. To
hell with this—After
her!—startling the flowers!

THE FIGHT

It was outside a place
across the track—
We'd been going all day.

But you know—none
of us had any dough we
're all on relief—

I told the Chief about
it this morning and
he wanted to pick him up.

But you know—he's
my best friend. I don't
mind a shiner but look

at this here. I showed
it to my wife when
I got home and she says,

Those are tooth marks!
Then it started to
swell on me, right down

to the ankle. Look,
these three little marks
here and those others

down there under them.
That looks like teeth
don't you think so?

All I want to know is
is it dangerous? That's
all I care about it.
                    overheard by:
                        William Carlos Williams

Jean Sans Terre
YVAN GOLL

JOHN LANDLESS AT THE FINAL PORT
[*First Version*]

John Landless in a keelless boat
Having sailed many oceans without shore

A dawnless day at a townless port
Landed and knocked at a houseless door

He knows of old this woman without face
Before a mirrorless wall who combs her hair
This sheetless bed this fireless embrace
This dastard love without despair

He knows these rusted galleys without oars
These mastless bricks these steamless steamers
These barless streets windows without women
Sleepless nights docks haunted by no fears

And what of these men who battle
With gestures of the old gladiator's art
Arms without fists revolvers without slugs
Pitiless eyes and pledges without heart

And why do these ships go on loading
From dock to ship unloading from ship to dock?
Why the voracious hunger of these cranes
Which faithless seek high heaven to unlock?

These hides will never sole a shoe
This cotton never clothe the naked
This wood will never give off sparks
This grain to holy bread be baked

What is this port at which none lands?
Where this cape lacking a continent?
Which is this merciless lighthouse?
Who this traveler missing punishment?

JEAN SANS TERRE
CIRCLES THE EARTH SEVEN TIMES

At blond dawn
A life unfurled

He journeys far
To the great world

He departs alone
The mystery soldier
A simple flower
In his button-hole

Smiling always
Blinking clear
He deceives love
At each frontier

In the cities
Boiling with beer
All gaiety
Loses its cheer

At the port bars
Watched for his grace
The strong boys
Hate his face

Beloved by the seas
And fever isles
Bitter winds
Kiss him whiles

Seven times
He circles the earth
Bearing his faith
In his head's girth

Barber bootblack
Priest corsair
Emperor bankrupt
Wastrel's fair

It's small matter
The world to course

To eat fire
To make wars

Oh the same trouble
Everywhere
Coming and going
Walk and stair

Morning and night
Bread and thirst
Flesh and dream
Here! Eat and burst!

Individual
Sad heart and bare
Wordless and nameless
His own despair

No papers left
No heirs found
Beg for your death
At the burying-ground

JEAN SANS TERRE
LEADS THE CARAVAN

Have I a hundred years since or
A hundred thousand tramped these wastes
With a track more vulnerable
Than fire of a sun that hastes?

My camel leads the caravan
Through centuries of rusted sand
To find as might any profane wind
The key to the oblivion land

My great-grandparents long since
Have worked this sea and no less

Could their passing shadow have brought
To yoke the ancient nothingness

Although life's mortal light
Would wring their hearts about by day
Still they had a candle lit
For antique love to find the way

In me their ancient skeleton
Of gold calcined by the years
And my new flesh tries as it may
To fill it with heavy cares

I hear the red wolf that howls
On the cavern of my blood
Cracking the bones at nightfall
Of the dream again abroad

Sail on sail on slow dromedaries
And traverse eternity
From the quaternary dawns
To the tomb's near certainty

My kin with limbs of gold and ebony
Die of thirst and of hope the most
At both my wrists I open the veins
That may prove to them a host

I wish that my love would rot
And never see light again
If by this final sacrifice
A young god be born in men

If without Alp to water
From the desert's lifeless skin
The freshness of a rose should rise
And a cloak of sudden green

No bitch will I need to chase
The hunger of a jackal

Enough that my faith revive
And the aurora of my choral

Offering those who covet
Slow camel and proud lion
Salt from my weak moist hand
The strength of my religion

JEAN SANS TERRE AT THE FINAL PORT
[Second Version]

(To Claire Sans Lune)

Landless John on a keelless boat
Having sailed many oceans without shore
A dawnless day at a townless port
Knocks with his boneless hand at a houseless door

He knows this woman without face who combs
Her faded hair across a silverless mirror
The restless bed the fireless embrace
That fear at dawn of evening's early terror

And on the wharves where ancient silence rots
And weary suns, too early picked, grow worse
The sea-gulls all their patience gone
Head for another universe

What joy or pain the longshoremen unload
Imported cradles or exported biers
Casks without oil or fabrics without wool
They whistle vainly sad tunes on the piers

These hides will never sole a shoe
This cotton never clothe the naked
This wood will never give off sparks
This wheat to holy bread be baked

What is this port at which none lands?
Where is this cape without a continent?
Which is this beacon without pity?
Who is this traveler without chastisement?

JEAN SANS TERRE
REVIEWS THE FATHERS

Our fathers liked to carry persian beards
Between the beards old cigars and old words
They liked the chicken soup and marrow bone
And then to stay at God's diamond throne

They sold green herring and they bought black suits
But God was ever present in disputes
The hurricane was hidden over the land
When any sin grew in their skin or gland

They were the fathers but they were the fool
To worship glassware or a rag of wool
They used the oaks to hang a man with thoughts
They used the river to look at the clouds

What worth is life but to account odd coins
To dig the earth to burn her oils
To fabricate thin web for tears of girls
To carve one's nails to curb one's curls

Their daughters wore silk over unknown sores
And healed behind the throat the song of whores
Their sons despised the herrings and the gods
Lost battles of the future in their cods

Meanwhile the fathers curled their flowering beards
Sold coal and slag bought orchards oaks and birds
Built palaces drank wine ate steak
And didn't sin—but earth began to quake

One day the tyrant came—the hurricane
The fathers' beards were strewn o'er street and lane
Their door stayed open like a mouth of drowned
Only the dogs remained and mourned around

Well thousand fathers
Their daughters and their sons are gone are gone
Their savior himself vanished at the wall
But swallows came back after all

JEAN SANS TERRE
DISCOVERS THE WEST POLE

John Landless leads his landless folk
All those who owned no window and no door
And nothing but the bed to die and to be born
And the shadowy bitch licking their misery

They wander on the roads of centuries
Riding the meager mare of hope
Seething with the yellow fever of the night
Feeding on black milk and bitter herbs

They leave the upright house in the godless street
Stores of oblivion factories of ghosts
They even leave the blooming tree of knowledge
On which are hung their brothers and their fears

Although they know the codes of human reasons
And touch the antic oxen at their tail
And grasp the trout at the garnet ear
And value fur and pulp and fat

They go ahead harassed by the tempest's fury
By glowing snow and by the wind of myth
Chased by the trumpets of the Scythian wrath
And by the blizzard of sharp whetted eyes

John Landless led them out of time and doubt
Out of the iron cities and the Pharaoh towers

Out of the depths and oblique corridors
Along the heedless roads

A gray-haired angel took them to the hill
Offering them the conquest of the Western Pole
The moon-bird flew and dropped his golden feathers
Over the dust of waking centuries

Here the landless folk will build Westopolis
Again stores of oblivion factories of ghosts
Again the upright houses down the godless street
And trees of knowledge where friends are hanged

John Landless flees at dawn back toward East alone

JEAN SANS TERRE
AT THE FINAL PORT

(To Claire Sans Lune)

John Landless sailing on a helmless boat
Through waveless oceans towards shoreless sands
Lands on a dawnless day at a townless port
Knocks at a houseless door with his boneless hands

Yet he remembers well these ancient galleys
These ageless slaves these steamless steamers
These barless streets these gazeless windows
These sleepless walls these godless dreamers

He knows this woman without faith and face
Who combs the curls of her fallen hair
He knows her restless bed her fireless embrace
Her love without desire and despair

He wonders why the cranes don't stop to load
Why they load caskets and the newborn grain
The wrathless lemons and the joyless wines
Why they load coal and unload ash again

This leather never will be shoe
This cotton never bandage the soldiers
This lumber will not heat the homeless
This wheat never feed the paupers

But who is he this nameless passenger
Who was not born and has no right to die
No reason to embark or disembark
But who is he this passenger without a lie?

Nicolas Calas: Four Poems

WRESTED FROM MIRRORS

In falling the dream was broken
I found oblivion in a mirror lost to the sea
Drunk with torments
Devoured by fears
I drank of that water no light has fondled
As an object bent upon its shadow
I see love now under an oblique light
Who forces my head to bow?
Upsets the hour?

How rejoin the sun without passing through day-break?
Remove fear from all shows and I will swim the full compass of oblivion
By the same movement
To lose oneself and discover the direction of things
Beyond left and beyond right
Beyond daring and the horizon
Beyond the wind

The wind of fear
A cruel wind all but immutable

Which tears up the echo buried in sand
And the smoke imprisoned in fossil bones
Which robs jackals of their dreams
And nurslings of the future
A wind that betrays its fury in its embraces

Sunk in my misery I drown my star

In that rectilinear fall a new face shows as a lure
The light consumes it
And opposes to fate all that remains of me
In the inevitable rhythm of disaster
I could say before the end of day
All the mirrors are thirsty
The stroke of an oar suffices to blot out a star
Without reflection without shadow the heart slowly dies
And makes of remembrance a sleeplessness without end

Avenger and conquerer of myself
I swear by these quakes of destiny
A fierce world of violent ideas will raise itself
Its image carved on that clearest eye
Already denies the capricious humor of the prophets
Roughens the mirrors
Lifts the ensanguined heads of the black bulls

THE AGONY AMONG THE CROWD

To die unwrinkled near a breath of fire
To hate death
To pursue madness beyond the precinct of the dream
Water air and all the sciences
To reply to them all

Listen to the noise of men who recoil
Hangmen, magi, doctors
Nothing horrifies them
Suffering is without pity

Tomorrow's moon has become already their nearest caress
They are like blind men imprisoned by the distance

At the peak of tranquility
I AM
I persist
Like the man drowned in his misfortune

NARCISSUS IN THE DESERT

Three faces in a single one

Too much sand for the sun
Sets madness afire
Its liquid shadow sprawls out

A new break asserts itself

The mirror is too keen
At its contact the eyes die of thirst
And turn their looks away
The paper keeps it neutral white as dry as space is
To weld the prop to life
To follow the trail
To make a poem violent as a mirage
With love to drink three faces as one
Plunge thine hair under
And Narcissus will have lived.

TO REGAIN THE DAY AGAIN

To regain the day again
Give it the image and the surprised dream
Love unfolds itself
Let us return forward toward the burst of new faces
And the words which carry efficacious gestures far beyond
    all commandment

Let us fix with a new precision the dramatic movement
Of boats without prow or sail
Vanquished or victor to bind it fast within flaming love

I have need of thy tears and to be unjust!

DEFENSE

I'll tell you what to do
You that blame me for
Illicit pleasure in the new verse,
You that imply that I am a pervert
Fagged in sense,
You that accuse me of seeking
The whip's taste having
Failed to respond to the normal.
Do this:
Admire fallen cheeks,
Wrinkles and yellow liver spots,
Discolored teeth or
If you prefer, shiny false ones:
Take your beauty out
Of a Sunday afternoon
To some quiet corner
Of the Park, kiss her—
Slip your hand tremblingly
About hers, discuss with her
The inner recesses of the soul—
And leave me and the insolent children
To mock you from the shrubbery.

THE PETUNIA

Purple!
for months unknown

but for
the barren sky.

A purple trumpet
fragile
as our hopes
from the very
sand
saluting us.

AN EXULTATION

England, confess your sins! toward the poor,
upon the body of my grandmother. Let the agents
of destruction purify you with bombs, cleanse
you of the profits of your iniquities to the last
agony of relinquishment.
She didn't die! Neither shall you, if
day by day you learn through abnegation
as she did, to send up thanks to those who
rain fire upon you.
Thanks! thanks to a just and kind heaven
for this light that comes as a blasting fire
destroying the rottenness of your slums as well
as your most noble and historic edifices, never
to be replaced!
If! You will survive if—you accept it with
thanks when, like her, excoriated by devils
you will have preserved in the end, as she did,
a purity—to be that never as yet known
leader and regenerator of nations, even of those
rotten to the core, who by a sovereignty
they cannot comprehend
have worked this cleansing mystery upon you.

THE YELLOW SEASON

The black, long-tailed,
one then, unexpectedly, another

glide easily on a curtain
of yellow leaves, upward—

The season wakens! loveliness
chirping and barking stands
among the branches, its
narrow-clawed toes and furry
hands moving in the leaves—

Round white eyes dotted with
jet live still, alert—in
all gentleness! unabated
beyond the crackle
of death's stinking certainty.

WAR, THE DESTROYER!

(*For Martha Graham*)

What is war,
the destroyer
but an appurtenance

to the dance?
The deadly serious
who would have us suppress

all exuberance
because of it
are mad. When terror blooms—

leap and twist
whirl and prance—
that's the show

of this the circumstance.
We cannot change it
not by writing, music

neither prayer.
Then fasten it
on the dress, in the hair

to incite and impel.
And if dance be
the answer, dance!

body and mind—
substance, balance, elegance!
with that, blood red

displayed flagrantly
in its place
beside the face.

PASSAIC, N. J.

I'd like to live on Tulip Street
and have a fig tree in the yard
I'd wrap it in tarpaper and rags
lest the winter prove too hard

The niggers and wops on Tulip Street
have few prejudices, I none
and fig trees grow freely there
for practically anyone.

FROM A PLAY

I am a writer
    and I take
great satisfaction
    in it

I like to time
    my phrases

balance them by
  their sensual

qualities and make
  those express
as much as
  or more

than the merely
  literal
burden of the thing
  could ever tell

PRELUDE IN BORICUA
LUIS PALÉS MATOS

Mixup of kinkhead and high yaller
And other big time mixups.
Messaround of voodoo chatter
Where their warm black bodies
Loosen the savage conga.

With crowing of the maraca
And heavy grunt of the gongo
The island curtain goes up on
An aristocracy macaca
Based in trip and corn pone.

To the solemn haitian God-be-praised
Is opposed the rumba habanera
With its angular hips and shoulders
While the cuban negrito
Takes on his hot-foot mulatta.

From her jamboree, taking the trail,
Flies Cuba, all sails set
To gather on her haunches
The golden tourist Niagara.

(Tomorrow they'll be shareholders
In some sugar mill
And take over with the money . . .)

And in whatever corner—lot, bay,
Pier or cane-field—
The negro drinks his cold portion
Consoled by the melody
That springs from his own bowels.

Jamaica, the heavy tub-of-guts
Switches her lingo to guts enough.
Santo Domingo dolls herself up
And with imposing civic gesture
Stirs her heroic genius
To a hundred presidential odes.
With her tray of penny candy
And white magic eyes
Comes Haiti to the market.
The Windward Islands are made up
Of overwhelming disgusts
To astonish the cyclones
With their fly-swatter palm trees.

And Puerto Rico? My burning island
For thee all has indeed ended.
Among the shambles of a continent
Puerto Rico, lugubriously
You bleat like a roast goat.

Mixup of black boy and high yaller,
This book to your hands
With ingredients from the Antilles
Sum up a day . . .

. . . and in short, lost time,
that leaves me heavy headed.
Something drawn out or reported,
Little really lived
And much of pretension and hearsay.

GOTHIC CANDOR

You have such a way of talking of Him!
and his little fifteen year old mother!

She was never a tragic figure, you say.
I feel sorry for them. They were pathetic.

I pity them. And I wonder if those sculptors
ever really looked at a woman holding

a baby in her arms. Oh see this one! I'm
so glad he made Him a jew! And look at her

face! That's the way He was when He was
here with us, just a little Jewish baby!

THE GENTLE NEGRESS

No other such luxuriance: the
elephant among bending trees,
the grass parting and
a horned head through! Small
yellow-hearted flowers trampled,
the tree broken that sends out
six new heads come night-fall.
Rain that drowns and a blaze
that sears the ground till it
cracks,
like a pistol shot! Strong
in the leg, soft voiced—
Listening; more
than can be seen! Listening to
the shriek of monkeys that hides
a deeper tone—under. Hiding
and waiting; a luxuriance,
a prominence. Unresistant to go
down quietly, in a violence of
half spoken words! Lillian!
Lillian!

TO THE DEAN

What should I say of Henry Miller:
a fantastic true-story of Dijon remembered,
black palaces, warted, on streets
of three levels, tilted, winding through
the full moon and out and
down again, worn-casts of men: Chambertin—
This for a head

The feet riding a ferry
waiting under the river side by side
and between. No body. The feet
dogging the head, the head bombing the feet
while food drops into and
through the severed gullet, makes clouds
and women gabbling and smoking, throwing
lighted butts on carpets in department stores,
sweating and going to it like men

Miller, Miller, Miller, Miller
I like those who like you and dislike
nothing that imitates you, I like
particularly that Black Book with its
red sporran by the Englishman that does you
so much honor. I think we should
all be praising you, you are a very good
influence.

THE VIRTUOUS AGENT

That which gives me to see,
ratiocinate and compound,
sing, make music, that I do

with or counter the grain.
The grain? The moral law. The
law may bury me in quicklime.

THINKING BACK TOWARD CHRISTMAS:
A STATEMENT FOR THE VIRGIN

With sharp lights winking
yellow, red
in the early dawn
in the darkness
through the broom of branches—
the world is gloomy and new
and mostly silent

Low to the left,
beyond the hill, the sparkle
of small lights
upon a vague, milky ground—
and higher, through a screen
of dark catalpa husks,
smooth, brokenly
tilted to one sun-like star
the moon

The old man wakes early
while married lovers
lie abed
and croaks his advice to
all mothers: Be silent,
forbearing under the stars
but mostly silent,
silent as the dawn

And, adds the superannuated
carpenter—while
in the semi-dark a huge squirrel
runs leaping
through the snow: Dry leaves
at noon out of the wind
to lie in will
still stand a man in good stead.

THE WEDGE

1944

William Carlos Williams

THE WEDGE

MCMXLIV
The Cummington Press

AUTHOR'S INTRODUCTION

The war is the first and only thing in the world today.

The arts generally are not, nor is this writing a diversion from that for relief, a turning away. It *is* the war or part of it, merely a different sector of the field.

Critics of rather better than average standing have said in recent years that after socialism has been achieved it's likely there will be no further use for poetry, that it will disappear. This comes from nothing else than a faulty definition of poetry—and the arts generally. I don't hear any-one say that mathematics is likely to be outmoded, to disappear shortly. Then why poetry?

It is an error attributable to the Freudian concept of the thing, that the arts are a resort from frustration, a misconception still entertained in many minds.

They speak as though action itself in all its phases were not com-patible with frustration. All action the same. But Richard Coeur de Lion wrote at least one of the finest lyrics of his day. Take Don Juan for in-stance. Who isn't frustrated and does not prove it by his actions—if you want to say so? But through art the psychologically maimed may become the most distinguished man of his age. Take Freud for instance.

The making of poetry is no more an evidence of frustration than is the work of Henry Kaiser or of Timoshenko. It's the war, the driving forward of desire to a complex end. And when that shall have been achieved, mathematics and the arts will turn elsewhere—beyond the atom if necessary for their reward and let's all be frustrated together.

A man isn't a block that remains stationary though the psychologists treat him so—and most take an insane pride in believing it. Consis-tency! He varies; Hamlet today, Caesar tomorrow; here, there, some-where—if he is to retain his sanity, and why not?

The arts have a *complex* relation to society. The poet isn't a fixed phe-nomenon, no more is his work. *That* might be a note on current affairs, a diagnosis, a plan for procedure, a retrospect—all in its own peculiarly enduring form. There need be nothing limited or frustrated about that. It may be a throw-off from the most violent and successful action or run parallel to it, a saga. It may be the picking out of an essential detail for memory, something to be set aside for further study, a sort of shorthand of emotional significances for later reference.

Let the metaphysical take care of itself, the arts have nothing to do with it. They will concern themselves with it if they please, among other things. To make two bald statements: There's nothing sentimental about a machine, and: A poem is a small (or large) machine made of words. When I say there's nothing sentimental about a poem I mean that there can be no part, as in any other machine, that is redundant.

Prose may carry a load of ill-defined matter like a ship. But poetry is the machine which drives it, pruned to a perfect economy. As in all machines its movement is intrinsic, undulant, a physical more than a literary character. In a poem this movement is distinguished in each case by the character of the speech from which it arises.

Therefore, each speech having its own character, the poetry it engenders will be peculiar to that speech also in its own intrinsic form. The effect is beauty, what in a single object resolves our complex feelings of propriety. One doesn't seek beauty. All that an artist or a Sperry can do is to drive toward his purpose, in the nature of his materials; not to take gold where Babbitt metal is called for; to make: make clear the complexity of his perceptions in the medium given to him by inheritance, chance, accident or whatever it may be to work with according to his talents and the will that drives them. Don't talk about frustration fathering the arts. The bastardization of words is too widespread for that today.

My own interest in the arts has been extracurricular. Up from the gutter, so to speak. Of necessity. Each age and place to its own. But in the U.S. the necessity for recognizing this intrinsic character has been largely ignored by the various English Departments of the academies.

When a man makes a poem, makes it, mind you, he takes words as he finds them interrelated about him and composes them—without distortion which would mar their exact significances—into an intense expression of his perceptions and ardors that they may constitute a revelation in the speech that he uses. It isn't what he *says* that counts as a work of art, it's what he makes, with such intensity of perception that it lives with an intrinsic movement of its own to verify its authenticity. Your attention is called now and then to some beautiful line or sonnet-sequence because of what is said there. So be it. To me all sonnets say the same thing of no importance. What does it matter what the line "says"?

There is no poetry of distinction without formal invention, for it is in the intimate form that works of art achieve their exact meaning, in which they most resemble the machine, to give language its highest dignity, its illumination in the environment to which it is native. Such war, as the arts live and breathe by, is continuous.

It may be that my interests as expressed here are pre-art. If so I look for a development along these lines and will be satisfied with nothing else.

A SORT OF A SONG

Let the snake wait under
his weed
and the writing
be of words, slow and quick, sharp
to strike, quiet to wait,
sleepless.

—through metaphor to reconcile
the people and the stones.
Compose. (No ideas
but in things) Invent!
Saxifrage is my flower that splits
the rocks.

CATASTROPHIC BIRTH

Fury and counter fury! The volcano!
Stand firm, unbending. The chemistry
shifts. The retort does not fracture.
The change reveals—change.
The revelation is compact—
compact of regathered fury

By violence lost, recaptured by violence
violence alone opens the shell of the nut.
The best is hard to say—unless

near the break. Unless the shell hold
the kernel is not sweet.
Under violence the meat lies regained

Each age brings new calls upon violence
for new rewards, variants of the old.
Unless each hold firm
Unless each remain inflexible
there can be no new. The new opens
new ways beyond all known ways.

Shut up! laughs the big she-Wop.
Wait till you have six like a me.
Every year one. Come on! Push! Sure,
you said it! Maybe I have one next year.
Sweating like a volcano. It cleans you up,
makes you feel good inside. Come on! Push!

The impasse becomes a door when the wall
is levelled. The cone lifts, lifts
and settles back. Life goes on. The cone
blocks the crater and lifts half its height.
Life goes on. The orange trees bloom.
The old women talk tirelessly.

The laboratory announces officially
that there is no need to worry. The
cone is subsiding, smoke rises as
a funnel into the blue unnatural sky—
The change impends! A change stutters
in the rocks. We believe nothing can change.

The fracture will come, the death dealing
chemistry cannot be long held back.
The dreaded eruption blocks out the valley,
the careful prognosticator as well as
the idlers. The revelation is complete.
Peace is reborn above the cinders

Only one man is left, the drunkard
who had been confined underground to

rot with the rats and lizards.
The old woman who had been combing out
the child's hair is also intact
but at a touch she falls into a heap of ashes

Only he who had been confined
in disgrace underground is rescued alive
and he knows nothing more of it
than to stand and curse the authorities
who left him there so long without food
and liquor while they were digging him out

Rain will fall. The wind and the birds
will bring seeds, the river changes
its channel and fish re-enter it.
The seawind will come in from the east.
The broken cone breathes softly on
the edge of the sky, violence revives and regathers.

PATERSON: THE FALLS

What common language to unravel?
The Falls, combed into straight lines
from that rafter of a rock's
lip. Strike in! the middle of

some trenchant phrase, some
well packed clause. Then . . .
This is my plan. 4 sections: First,
the archaic persons of the drama.

An eternity of bird and bush,
resolved. An unraveling:
the confused streams aligned, side
by side, speaking! Sound

married to strength, a strength
of falling—from a height! The wild
voice of the shirt-sleeved
Evangelist rivaling, Hear

me! I am the Resurrection
and the Life! echoing
among the bass and pickerel, slim
eels from Barbados, Sargasso

Sea, working up the coast to that
bounty, ponds and wild streams—
Third, the old town: Alexander Hamilton
working up from St. Croix,

from that sea! and a deeper, whence
he came! stopped cold
by that unmoving roar, fastened
there: the rocks silent

but the water, married to the stone,
voluble, though frozen; the water
even when and though frozen
still whispers and moans—

And in the brittle air
a factory bell clangs, at dawn, and
snow whines under their feet. Fourth,
the modern town, a

disembodied roar! the cataract and
its clamor broken apart—and from
all learning, the empty
ear struck from within, roaring . . .

THE DANCE

In Brueghel's great picture, The Kermess,
the dancers go round, they go round and
around, the squeal and the blare and the
tweedle of bagpipes, a bugle and fiddles
tipping their bellies (round as the thick-
sided glasses whose wash they impound)
their hips and their bellies off balance

to turn them. Kicking and rolling about
the Fair Grounds, swinging their butts, those
shanks must be sound to bear up under such
rollicking measures, prance as they dance
in Brueghel's great picture, The Kermess.

WRITER'S PROLOGUE TO A PLAY IN VERSE

In your minds you jump from doors
to sad departings, pigeons, dreams
of terror, to cathedrals; bowed,
repelled, knees quaking, to the-closed-
without-a-key or through an arch
an ocean that races full of sound
and foam to lay a carpet for
your pleasure or a wood that waves
releasing hawks and crows or
crowds that elbow and fight for
a place or anything. You see it
in your minds and the mind at once
jostles it, turns it about, examines
and arranges it to suit its fancy.
Or rather changes it after a pattern
which is the mind itself, turning
and twisting the theme until it gets
a meaning or finds no meaning and
is dropped. By such composition,
without code, the scenes we see move
and, as it may happen, make
a music, a poetry
which the poor poet copies if
and only if he is able—to astonish
and amuse, for your delights,
in public, face to face with you
individually and secretly addressed.

We are not here, you understand,
but in the mind, that circumstance
of which the speech is poetry.

Then look, I beg of you, try and
look within yourselves rather than
at me for what I shall discover.
Yourselves! Within yourselves. Tell
me if you do not see there, alive!
a creature unlike the others, something
extraordinary in its vulgarity,
something strange, unnatural to
the world, that suffers the world poorly,
is tripped at home, disciplined at
the office, greedily eats money—
for a purpose: to escape the tyranny
of lies. And is all they can think
of to amuse you, a ball game? Or
skiing in Van Diemen's land in August
—to amuse you! Do you not come here
to escape that? For you are merely
distracted, not relieved in the blood,
deadened, defeated, stultified.

But this! is new. Believe it, to be
proved presently by your patience.
Run through the public appearance
of it, to come out—not stripped
but, if you'll pardon me, something
which in the mind you are and would
be yet have always been, unrecognized,
tragic and foolish, without a tongue.
That's it. Yourself, the thing
you are, speechless—because there is
no language for it, shockingly revealed.

Would it disturb you if I said
you have no other speech than poetry?
You, yourself, I mean. There is
no other language for it than the poem
—falsified by the critics until
you think it's something else, fight
it off, as idle, a kind of lie,
smelling of corpses, that the practical

world rejects. How could it be you?
Never! without invention. It is, if
you'll have patience, the undiscovered
language of yourself, which you avoid,
rich and poor, killed and killers,
a language to be coaxed out of poets—
possibly, an intolerable language
that will frighten—to which
you are not used. We must make it
easy for you, feed it to you slowly
until you let down the barriers,
relax before it. But it's easy
if you will allow me to proceed, it
can make transformations, give it
leave to do its work in you.

Accept the convention as you would
opera, provisionally; let me go ahead.
Wait to see if the revelation
happen. It may not.
Or it may come and go, small bits
at a time. But even the chips of it
are invaluable. Wait to learn
the hang of its persuasions as it makes
its transformations from the common
to the undisclosed and lays that open
where—you will see a frightened face!

But believe! that poetry will be
in the terms you know, insist on that
and can and must break through everything,
all the outward forms, to re-dress
itself humbly in that which you
yourself will say is the truth, the
exceptional truth of ordinary people,
the extraordinary truth. You shall see.

It isn't masculine more than it is
feminine, it's not a book more than
it is speech; inside the mind, natural

to the mind as metals are to rock,
a gist, puppets which if they present
distinction it is from that hidden
dignity which they, by your leave,
reflect from you who are the play.

This is a play of a husband and a wife.
As you love your husband or your wife
or if you hate him or if you hate
her, watch the language! see if you
think that it expresses something of
the things, to your knowledge, that
take place in the mind and in the world
but seldom on the lips. This play
is of a woman and her lover, all
mixed up, of life and death and all
the secret language that runs through
those curious transactions, seldom
heard but in the deadest presentations
now respectfully unnaturalized.

For pleasure! pleasure, not for
cruelty but to make you laugh, until
you cry like General Washington
at the river. Seeing the travelers
bathing there who had had their clothes
stolen, how he laughed! And how
you shall laugh to see yourselves
all naked, on the stage!

BURNING THE CHRISTMAS GREENS

Their time past, pulled down
cracked and flung to the fire
—go up in a roar

All recognition lost, burnt clean
clean in the flame, the green
dispersed, a living red,

flame red, red as blood wakes
on the ash—

and ebbs to a steady burning
the rekindled bed become
a landscape of flame

At the winter's midnight
we went to the trees, the coarse
holly, the balsam and
the hemlock for their green

At the thick of the dark
the moment of the cold's
deepest plunge we brought branches
cut from the green trees

to fill our need, and over
doorways, about paper Christmas
bells covered with tinfoil
and fastened by red ribbons

we stuck the green prongs
in the windows hung
woven wreaths and above pictures
the living green. On the

mantle we built a green forest
and among those hemlock
sprays put a herd of small
white deer as if they

were walking there. All this!
and it seemed gentle and good
to us. Their time past,
relief! The room bare. We

stuffed the dead grate
with them upon the half burnt out
log's smoldering eye, opening
red and closing under them

and we stood there looking down.
Green is a solace
a promise of peace, a fort
against the cold (though we

did not say so) a challenge
above the snow's
hard shell. Green (we might
have said) that, where

small birds hide and dodge
and lift their plaintive
rallying cries, blocks for them
and knocks down

the unseeing bullets of
the storm. Green spruce boughs
pulled down by a weight of
snow—Transformed!

Violence leaped and appeared.
Recreant! roared to life
as the flame rose through and
our eyes recoiled from it.

In the jagged flames green
to red, instant and alive. Green!
those sure abutments . . . Gone!
lost to mind

and quick in the contracting
tunnel of the grate
appeared a world! Black
mountains, black and red—as

yet uncolored—and ash white,
an infant landscape of shimmering
ash and flame and we, in
that instant, lost,

breathless to be witnesses,
as if we stood
ourselves refreshed among
the shining fauna of that fire.

IN CHAINS

When blackguards and murderers
under cover of their offices
accuse the world of those villainies
which they themselves invent to
torture us—we have no choice
but to bend to their designs,
buck them or be trampled while
our thoughts gnaw, snap and bite
within us helplessly—unless
we learn from that to avoid
being as they are, how love
will rise out of its ashes if
we water it, tie up the slender
stem and keep the image of its
lively flower chiseled upon our minds.

IN SISTERLY FASHION

Part of the sequence *For the Poem* Paterson:
See p. 16.

THE WORLD NARROWED TO A POINT

Liquor and love
when the mind is dull
focus the wit
on a world of form

The eye awakes
perfumes are defined

inflections
ride the quick ear

Liquor and love
rescue the cloudy sense
banish its despair
give it a home.

THE OBSERVER

What a scurvy mind
whose constant breath
still simulates
the forms of death—
unable or unwilling
to own the common
things which we must
do to live again
and be in love and
all its quickening
pleasures prove—

A FLOWING RIVER

You are lovely as a river
under tranquil skies—
There are imperfections
but a music overlays them—

telling by how dark a bed
the current moves
to what sea that shines
and ripples in my thought

THE HOUNDED LOVERS

Where shall we go?
Where shall we go
who are in love?

Juliet went
to Friar Laurence's cell
      but we have no rest—

Rainwater lies on
the hard ground reflecting
      the morning sky

But where shall we go?
We cannot resolve ourselves
      into a dew

nor sink into the earth.
Shall we postpone it
      to Eternity?

The dry heads of the
goldenrod
      turned to stiff ghosts

jerk at their stalks
signaling grave warning.
      Where shall we go?

The movement of benediction
does not turn back
      the cold wind.

THE CURE

Sometimes I envy others, fear them
a little too, if they write well.
For when I cannot write I'm a sick man
and want to die. The cause is plain.

But they have no access to my sources.
Let them write then as they may and
perfect it as they can they will never
come to the secret of that form

interknit with the unfathomable ground
where we walk daily and from which
among the rest you have sprung
and opened flower-like to my hand.

TO ALL GENTLENESS

Like a cylindrical tank fresh silvered
upended on the sidewalk to advertise
some plumber's shop, a profusion
of pink roses bending ragged in the rain—
speaks to me of all gentleness and its
enduring.

        Secure in the enclosing rain,
a column of tears borne up by the heavy
flowers: the new and the unlikely, bound
indissolubly together in one mastery.

Out of fear lest the flower be broken
the rose puts out its thorns. That
is the natural way.

            We witless, wistful
of the flower, unable still by heavy
emphasis to praise enough its silence,
inventors of opera as national background;
the classic tradition, bellowing
masks, long since decayed, in our time
also perishes.

        And they speak,
euphemistically, of the anti-poetic!
Garbage. Half the world ignored . . .

Is this praise of gentleness?

            The lion
according to old paintings will

lie down with the lamb. But what is meant
has not been precisely enough stated:
missed or—postponed.
The arrow! That the arrow fly!

Forthwith she holds it to the string, the
hygienic arrow! that, crescent, she
may achieve poise, win perhaps a prize
later at the meet or making a profession
of it grow to be a teacher of the art

—and the innocent shaft, released,
plunges forward . . .

                    The courts are
overcrowded, fear obsesses all intimacies
unless legalized—and money,
articulated to government mounts still
as wonder in the minds of the speculators,

to buy
          (the ferment wedging their skulls
ever wider)

              to buy, shall we say, the
grass, or a small cloud perhaps (in
whose shadow a lifting wind whirls) or
if Queen Blanche, a pond
of waterlilies or the rain itself.

The natural way, to buy!

                          —to buy off.

But if the wing of a plane in combat,
coming down, an uncertain landing, if
by the shattering prop of a plane he
is knocked into the sea,

gives himself up injured for lost and then—
his wound eased by the seawater—goes

on out of habit, swims alone among
the enquiring waves twelve hours, fourteen
hours. . . . picked up and
returned to this life.

That too is
the natural way, by claw and law—

To which
we are opposed!

For most
fear gentleness and misinterpret it,
which if by chance they meet the
longer arc, upgrade or downgrade, the
wash and swing, they are discomfited—

A matter of indifference—

the wave
rising or the wave curving to the hollow:

Swam hour after hour, the healthy
life he'd led formerly at Seattle holding
him . . .

Or was it? Who
can tell? come back for all that a
month later when they'd released him held
incommunicado at the hospital, to say,
Here I am, as I promised!

Copernicus,
Shostakovich. Is it the occasion
or the man? Take an apple and split it
between the thumbs. Which is which?

Caught in the shuffling of the wider
undulations one is brought down, another

lifted by the wash; a rush of algae
proliferant or a mammoth caught in the ice
hair and all for dogs later to dig
and devour . . .

        the phase, is supreme!

            except
for gentleness that joins our lives
in one.

      But shoot! shoot straight,
they say. The arrow flies! the barb
is driven home and . . . strength
thrust upon weakness, the convulsive ecstasy

achieved, in the moment of impact
we are left deafened and blinded, blind to
the sun and moon, the brilliant
moonlight leaves, to fish and fowl:

                  the
bird in white above the swimming bird
and from the depths of the wood
the song that is the bird, unseen.

The bomb-sight adjusted destruction hangs
by a hair over the cities. Bombs away!
and the packed word descends—and
rightly so.

      The arrow! the arrow!

Only . . . that is . . .

the moment is lost! without us, the
completion, the learned moment. The gates
opened, it also falls away,
                unrecognized!

It is, yes Jakus, the prize, the prize!
in which that which has been held from you,
my perky lad, is hid.

                    The flower is our sign.

Milkweed, a single stalk on the bare
embankment (and where
does the imagination begin?

                            Violence and
gentleness, which is the core? Is
gentleness the core?)

                    Slender green
reaching up from sand and rubble (the
anti-poetic they say ignorantly, a
disassociation)

                    premising the flower,
without which, no flower.

                    She was
forewoman to a gang at the ship foundry,
cleared the finished parts to
the loading platform; had three misses,
all boys, by the man she lives with—
and may the fourth be a boy also for which
he married her.

                    Tough, huh?

                    Never had a backache.

Not the girth of thigh, but
that gentleness that harbors all violence,
the valid juxtaposition, one
by the other, alternates, the cosine, the
cylinder and the rose.

THREE SONNETS

1

As the eye lifts, the field
is moving—the river,
slowly between the stones
steadily under the bare
branches, heavy slabs close
packed with jagged rime-cupped
edges, seaward—

what was the mudbank
crowded, sparkling
with diamonds big as fists,
unbelievable to witness

2

The silent and snowy mountains
do not change their
poise—the broken line,
the mass whose darkness
meets the rising sun, waken
uncompromised above the gulls
upon the ice-strewn
river.

    You cannot succor me,
you cannot change. I will
open my eyes at morning even though
their lids be sealed
faster by ice than stone!

3

My adored wife, this—in spite
of Dr. Kennedy's remark
that the story of the repeated

injury would sound bad in a divorce
court—the bastard:

In the one woman
I find all the rest—or nothing
and raise them thence and celebrate
them there and close their eyes
and bury them in her and
decorate their graves. Upon her
their memory clings, each one
distinct, enriching her
while I yet live to enjoy, perhaps.

THE POEM

It's all in
the sound. A song.
Seldom a song. It should

be a song—made of
particulars, wasps,
a gentian—something
immediate, open

scissors, a lady's
eyes—waking
centrifugal, centripetal

THE ROSE

The stillness of the rose
in time of war
reminds me of
the long sleep just begun
of that sparrow
his head pillowed unroughed
and unalarmed upon

the polished pavement or
of voluptuous hours
with some
breathless book when
stillness was an eternity
long since begun

RUMBA! RUMBA!

No, not the downfall
of the Western World
but the wish for its
        downfall
in an idiot mind—
Dance, Baby, dance!

thence springs the conflict,
that it may crash
        hereafter;
not submit and end in
a burst of laughter—
Cha cha, chacha, cha!

to hide the defect—
the difficultly held
burden, to perfect!
melted in a wish to die.
Dance, Baby, dance
        the Cuban Rumba!

A PLEA FOR MERCY

Who hasn't been frustrated
with the eternal virgin
shining before him and he
cold as a stone?

FIGUERAS CASTLE

Nine truckloads of jewels
while the people starved
Nine truckloads
in the mud

And the people's enemies
coming fast. Stick 'em
in your pockets
the General said,

They're yours, by God, and
check them in for the
people at the Consulate
in Perpignan.

But some of them didn't
bother—like those who had
stolen them first
and were not

arrested for it as these were
in their need, not held
for it as these were
in their dire need.

ETERNITY

She had come, like the river
from up country and had work now
in town—

When? Tonight. The street was
dark, she late. Two
young rips

had cavorted down the hill in
the silence, jabbering. Then
he heard

the click of her heels—at his
age! and the darkness
grew milky

away above him and seemed to
move, coming down. She
appeared

bare headed, in pearl earrings
and a cloak. Where shall
we go?

The boy friend was expecting me
it was hard to
get away.

Where are you supposed to be?
Night, greater than
the cataract

surged in the cisterns of Noah's
chest, enormous night
that makes

of light a fruit, everywhere
active in the dark.
Olympia

would be expecting him, he swam
from her zig-zag through
the dark—

half things bulging and rotted
out, hanging, standing at
false angles,

abandoned! drove thence close
to two hundred miles
filling

the tank once near midnight, To
the left, at the second
car tracks,

brother. And the stars performed
their stated miracles.
The wind

rose and howled toward 3 A.M.
with a dash of rain turning
warm. Swift

or slow from capsule to capsule
of the light he saw between
the stars

the sky! velvet, like a leaf,
in detail and counting at
random there,

continued, later halting under a
street lamp to make
some notes.

Olympia, her face drawn but relieved
said nothing. Breakfast
at seven.

THE HARD LISTENER

The powerless emperor
makes himself dull
writing poems in a garden
while his armies
kill and burn. But we,
in poverty lacking love,
keep some relation
to the truth of man's

infelicity: say
the late flowers, unspoiled
by insects and waiting
only for the cold.

THE CONTROVERSY

What do you know about it? the Architect said.
The Executive asked me, What the hell
do you know about business?

Is it so arcane? I can read, I said. Isn't it
just to put 4 and take away 5? From whom?
Isn't that all there is to

it? Whom can you best belabor? And do I have
to read the whole *Apologia*
to make up my mind touching

Newman's undecorated place in the world? Who?
they both said,—the situation
and its effects? It's because

of unrelated statements such as that that I
have come to have no respect for
what you say, one of them

looked at me and said. The Jews. Oh the
Jews, the Jews! Is Stinkeroo
Mormun a Jew? If not

then the world is safe (from the Jews!) I can
still read and collate experiences
you never dreamed, I

answered them. Nuts! they said. Very well. Nuts!
and decorated nuts and nuts again,
I said, to you, gentlemen.

PERFECTION

O lovely apple!
beautifully and completely
rotten,
hardly a contour marred—

perhaps a little
shrivelled at the top but that
aside perfect
in every detail! O lovely

apple! what a
deep and suffusing brown
mantles that
unspoiled surface! No one

has moved you
since I placed you on the porch
rail a month ago
to ripen.

No one. No one!

THESE PURISTS

Lovely! all the essential parts,
like an oyster without a shell
fresh and sweet tasting, to be
swallowed, chewed and swallowed.

Or better, a brain without a
skull. I remember once a guy in
our anatomy class dropped one
from the third floor window on
an organ grinder in Pine Street.

A VISION OF LABOR: 1931

In my head the juxtapositions
impossible otherwise to accomplish:
two young rubber-booted ditchdiggers
beside the bed of the dying bishop—
cracking obscene jokes
at the expense of the flabby woman in
the white bathing suit, the weak breaths
of the old man masquerading under
the double suck of the mule-pump

—by the edge of the sea! the shore
exploded away, constructively,
the sewer going down six feet inside
the seawall along the front of
the cottages—not through them
unfortunately—a *cloaca maxima* like
the one under the Roman Forum
which alone made that possible in
that place . . .

That's it! There, there!
That's the answer. The thing to be
done: Alone made that
possible (before the rest stands)
there in that place.

The girl lying there
supine in the old rowboat reading an
adventure magazine and the two guys
—six foot three each of them
if they were an inch—washing their
hip-boots off in the stream jerking
from the pump at the finished manhole,
washing their hands, their heads
and faces, cupping their hands to drink
the stuff. Geezus! What the hell
kind of water is that to drink? But
they probably know what they're doing

—and looking down the bank at her
lying flat out there in the heat with
her five-and-ten dark glasses on
to protect her eyes from the sun's
glare—looking down and smiling over
her like insane men.

　　　　　When you've been broke
and damned near starving for
five years you get to look that way,
said my cousin who had had a taste
of it. You can't help it. That's
poverty. Both your mind and your body
are affected. But they're just mechanics
damn good ones most of them, like
anybody else.

　　　　　—the white suit
pulled up tight into her crotch the
way she was lying there facing them
—till they called it off, threw
the switch and the pump
stopped and the bishop died
and—they turned their backs on it,
flung their boots over their shoulders
and went home.

THE LAST TURN

Then see it! in distressing
detail—from behind a red light
at 53d and 8th
of a November evening, the jazz
of the cross lights echoing the
crazy weave of the breaking mind:
splash of a half purple, half
naked woman's body whose jeweled
guts the cars drag up and down—

No house but has its brains
blown off by the dark!
Nothing recognizable, the whole one
jittering direction made of all
directions spelling the inexplicable:
pigment upon flesh and flesh
the pigment the genius of a world,
against which rages the fury of
our concepts, artless but supreme.

THE END OF THE PARADE

Part of the sequence *For the Poem* Paterson:
See p. 20.

THE A, B & C OF IT

a. Love's very fleas are mine. Enter
   me, worms and all till I crumble
   and steam with it, pullulate
   to be sucked into an orchid.

b. But the fleas were too shy
   didn't want to offend
   recoiled from the odors
   and couldn't unbend.

c. Take me then, Spirit of Loneliness
   insatiable Spirit of Love
   and let be—for Time without
   odor is Time without me.

THE THOUGHTFUL LOVER

Part of the sequence *For the Poem* Paterson:
See p. 19.

THE AFTERMATH

The Winnah! pure as snow
courageous as the wind
strong as a tree
deceptive as the moon

All that is the country
fitted into you
for you were born there.
Now it is rewarding you

for the unswerving mind
curious as a fox
which fox-like escaped
breathless to its hole.

They say you have grown
thinner and that
there is a girl now to
add to the blue eyed boy.

Good! the air of the
uplands is stimulating.

THE SEMBLABLES

The red brick monastery in
the suburbs over against the dust-
hung acreage of the unfinished
and all but subterranean

munitions plant: those high
brick walls behind which at Easter
the little orphans and bastards
in white gowns sing their Latin

responses to the hoary ritual
while frankincense and myrrh

round out the dark chapel making
an enclosed sphere of it

of which they are the worm:
that cell outside the city beside
the polluted stream and dump
heap, uncomplaining, and the field

of upended stones with a photo
under glass fastened here and there
to one of them near the deeply
carved name to distinguish it:

that trinity of slate gables
the unembellished windows piling
up, the chapel with its round
window between the dormitories

peaked by the bronze belfry
peaked in turn by the cross,
verdigris—faces all silent
that miracle that has burst sexless

from between the carrot rows.
Leafless white birches, their
empty tendrils swaying in
the all but no breeze guard

behind the spiked monastery fence
the sacred statuary. But ranks
of brilliant car-tops row on row
give back in all his glory the

late November sun and hushed
attend, before that tumbled
ground, those sightless walls
and shovelled entrances where no

one but a lonesome cop swinging
his club gives sign, that agony

within where the wrapt machines
are praying. . . .

THE STORM

A perfect rainbow! a wide
arc low in the northern sky
spans the black lake

troubled by little waves
over which the sun
south of the city shines in

coldly from the bare hill
supine to the wind which
cannot waken anything

but drives the smoke from
a few lean chimneys streaming
violently southward

THE FORGOTTEN CITY

When with my mother I was coming down
from the country the day of the hurricane,
trees were across the road and small branches
kept rattling on the roof of the car.
There was ten feet or more of water
making the parkways impassable with wind
bringing more rain in sheets. Brown torrents
gushed up through new sluices in the
valley floor so that I had to take what road
I could find bearing to the south and west,
to get back to the city. I passed through
extraordinary places, as vivid as any
I ever saw where the storm had broken
the barrier and let through
a strange commonplace: Long, deserted avenues

with unrecognized names at the corners and
drunken looking people with completely
foreign manners. Monuments, institutions
and in one place a large body of water
startled me with an acre or more of hot
jets spouting up symmetrically over it. Parks.
I had no idea where I was and promised myself
I would some day go back to study this
curious and industrious people who lived
in these apartments, at these sharp
corners and turns of intersecting avenues
with so little apparent communication
with an outside world. How did they get
cut off this way from representation in our
newspapers and other means of publicity
when so near the metropolis, so closely
surrounded by the familiar and the famous?

THE YELLOW CHIMNEY

There is a plume
of fleshpale
smoke upon the blue

sky. The silver
rings that
strap the yellow

brick stack at
wide intervals shine
in this amber

light—not
of the sun not of
the pale sun but

his born brother
the
declining season

THE BARE TREE

The bare cherry tree
higher than the roof
last year produced
abundant fruit. But how
speak of fruit confronted
by that skeleton?
Though live it may be
there is no fruit on it.
Therefore chop it down
and use the wood
against this biting cold.

RALEIGH WAS RIGHT

We cannot go to the country
for the country will bring us
    no peace
What can the small violets tell us
that grow on furry stems in
the long grass among lance shaped
    leaves?

Though you praise us
and call to mind the poets
who sung of our loveliness
it was long ago!
long ago! when country people
would plow and sow with
flowering minds and pockets
    at ease—
if ever this were true.

Not now. Love itself a flower
with roots in a parched ground.
Empty pockets make empty heads.
Cure it if you can but

do not believe that we can live
today in the country
for the country will bring us
    no peace.

THE MONSTROUS MARRIAGE

She who with innocent and tender hands
reached up to take the wounded
pigeon from the branch, found it turn

into a fury as it bled. Maddened she clung
to it stabbed by its pain and the blood
of her hands and the bird's blood

mingled while she stilled it for the moment
and wrapped it in her thought's
clean white handkerchief. After that

she adopted a hawk's life as her own.
For it looked up and said, You are
my wife for this. Then she released him.

But he came back shortly. Certainly,
since we are married, she said to him, no
one will accept it. Time passed.

I try to imitate you, he said while she
cried a little in smiling. Mostly,
he confided, my head is clouded

except for hunting. But for parts of
a day it's clear as any man's—by
your love. No, she would

answer him pitifully, what clearer than
a hawk's eye and reasonably the
mind also must be so. He turned his

head and seeing his profile in her
mirror ruffled his feathers and gave
a hawk's cry, desolately.

Nestling upon her as was his wont he
hid his talons from her soft flesh
fluttering his wings against her sides

until her mind, always astonished at
his assumptions, agonized, heard
footsteps and hurried him to

the open window whence he made off.
After that she had a leather belt made
upon which he perched to enjoy her.

SOMETIMES IT TURNS DRY AND THE LEAVES FALL BEFORE THEY ARE BEAUTIFUL

Part of the sequence *For the Poem* Paterson:
See p. 16.

SPARROWS AMONG DRY LEAVES

The sparrows by the iron fence post—
hardly seen for the dry leaves
that half cover them—
stirring up the leaves, fight
and chirp stridently, search and
peck the sharp gravel to
good digestion and love's
obscure and insatiable appetite.

PRELUDE TO WINTER

The moth under the eaves
with wings like

the bark of a tree, lies
symmetrically still—

And love is a curious
soft-winged thing
unmoving under the eaves
when the leaves fall.

SILENCE

Under a low sky—
this quiet morning
of red and
yellow leaves—

a bird disturbs
no more than one twig
of the green leaved
peach tree

ANOTHER YEAR

In the rose garden in the park
let us learn how little there is
        to fear
from the competition of conflicting
        seasons—
and avoid comparisons,
alone in that still place.
The slender quietness of the old
        bushes
is of a virtue all its own . . .

THE CLOUDS
[First Version]

Filling the mind
upon the rim of the overarching sky, the horses of

the dawn charge from south to north, gigantic beasts
rearing flame-edged above the pit,
a rank confusion of the imagination still uncured,
a rule, piebald under the streetlamps, reluctant
to be torn from its hold.

Their flanks still
caught among low blocking forms their fore-parts
rise lucid beyond this smell of a swamp, a mud
livid with decay and life! turtles
that burrowing among the white roots lift their green
red-striped faces startled before the dawn.

A black flag, writhing and whipping at the staff-head
mounts the sepulcher of the empty bank, fights
to be free . .
South to north! the direction
unmistakable, they move distinct beyond the unclear
edge of the world, clouds! like statues
before which we are drawn—in darkness, thinking of
our dead, unable, knowing no place
where else rightly to lodge them.

Tragic outlines
and the bodies of horses, mindfilling—but
visible! against the invisible; actual against
the imagined and the concocted; unspoiled by hands
and unshaped also by them but caressed by sight only,
moving among them, not that that propels
the eyes from under, while it blinds:

—upon whose backs the dead ride, high!
undirtied by the putridity we fasten upon them—
South to north, for this moment distinct and undeformed,
into the no-knowledge of their nameless destiny.

A COLD FRONT

This woman with a dead face
has seven foster children

and a new baby of her own in
spite of that. She wants pills

for an abortion and says,
Uh hum, in reply to me while
her blanketed infant makes
unrelated grunts of salutation.

She looks at me with her mouth
open and blinks her expressionless
carved eyes, like a cat
on a limb too tired to go higher

from its tormentors. And still
the baby chortles in its spit
and there is a dull flush
almost of beauty to the woman's face

as she says, looking at me
quietly, I won't have any more.
In a case like this I know
quick action is the main thing.

AGAINST THE SKY

Let me not forget at least,
after the three day rain,
beaks raised aface, the two starlings
at and near the top twig

of the white-oak, dwarfing
the barn, completing the minute
green of the sculptured foliage, their
bullet heads bent back, their horny

lips chattering to the morning
sun! Praise! while the
wraithlike warblers, all but unseen
in looping flight dart from

pine to spruce, spruce to pine
southward. Southward! where
new mating warms the wit and cold
does not strike, for respite.

AN ADDRESS

Walk softly on my grave
for I desired you,

a matter for sorrow
for decay;

flowers without odor
garlanded

about the sad legend:
Live in this

whom green youth denied.

THE GENTLE NEGRESS

Wandering among the chimneys
my love and I would meet
I with a pale skin
she as brown as peat

Her voice was low and gentle
and full of surprise
that I should find her lovely
and would search her eyes

with a longing hard to fathom
from what she said
as I sat to comfort her
lying in bed.

TO FORD MADOX FORD IN HEAVEN

Is it any better in Heaven, my friend Ford,
    than you found it in Provence?

I don't think so for you made Provence a
    heaven by your praise of it
to give a foretaste of what might be
    your joy in the present circumstances.
It was Heaven you were describing there
    transubstantiated from its narrowness
to resemble the paths and gardens of a
    greater world where you now reside.
But, dear man, you have taken a major
    part of it from us.
            Provence that you
praised so well will never be the same
    Provence to us
        now you are gone.

A heavenly man you seem to me now, never
    having been for me a saintly one.
It lived about you, a certain grossness that
    was not like the world.
The world is cleanly, polished and well
    made but heavenly man
is filthy with his flesh and corrupt that
    loves to eat and drink and whore—
to laugh at himself and not be afraid of
    himself knowing well he has
no possessions and opinions that are worth
    caring a broker's word about
and that all he is, but one thing, he feeds
    as one will feed a pet dog.

So roust and love and dredge the belly full
    in Heaven's name!
I laugh to think of you wheezing in Heaven.
    Where is Heaven? But why

do I ask that, since you showed the way?
    I don't care a damn for it
other than for that better part lives beside
    me here so long as I
live and remember you. Thank God you
    were not delicate, you let the world in
and lied! damn it you lied grossly
    sometimes. But it was all, I
see now, a carelessness, the part of a man
    that is homeless here on earth.

Provence, the fat assed Ford will never
    again strain the chairs of your cafés
pull and pare for his dish your sacred garlic,
    grunt and sweat and lick
his lips. Gross as the world he has left to
    us he has become
a part of that of which you were the known
    part, Provence, he loved so well.

POEMS

1945-48

SUNFLOWERS

There's a sort of
multibranched sunflower
blooms hereabouts
when the leaves begin
first to fall. Their
heads lean in the rain
about an old man who,
stumbling a little,
solicitously carries in
his tomatoes from
the fallen vines, green
in one basket and, in
the other shining reds.

THRENODY

The Christian coin—
embossed with a dove and sword—
is not wasted by war,
rather it thrives on it
and should be tossed
into the sea for the fish
to eye it as it falls
past the clutching fingers
of children—
for them to eye it
and sing, join in a choir
to rival the land and set
coral branches swaying:
Peace, peace to the oceans,
the dread hurricane die,
ice melt at the poles
and sharks be at rest!
as it drops, lost, to its grave.

THE RARE GIST

The young German poked his head
in at the door, handed me
an advertising leaflet for some
drug manufacturer and left,

coloring furiously, after a few
thinly spoken words. My
attention was sharply roused.
It seemed a mind well worth

looking into. And beneath that,
another layer, Phoenix-
like. It was almost, I confess,
as though I envied him

TO A SPARROW

Your perch is the branch
and your boudoir the branch also.
The branch, the rough branch!
evergreen boughs closing you about
like ironed curtains
to complete the decor.

The sun pours in
as the roughing wind blows
and who will conceive the luxury,
the rare lightness of
your fluttering toilette like him,
he who is lost and alone in the world?

Princess of the airy kingdoms
the sky is your wardrobe
and yellow roses
the frilled chrysanthemums bending
to the late season your park.

Among the clouds your couriers
post to embassies
beyond our fondest dreams
and heaven, the ancient court of saints
whispers to us
among the hemlocks
insistently of you.

THE PHOENIX AND THE TORTOISE

The link between Barnum and Calas
is the freak
against which Rexroth rages,
the six-legged cow, the legless woman

for each presents a social concept
seeking approval, a pioneer society
and a modern asserting the norm
by stress of the Minotaur.

It's a legitimate maneuver,
perhaps it is all art
and Barnum our one genius (in the arts)
on the moral plane: the freak

and the athlete: the circus,
by which we return from Agamemnon
sober to our tasks—of pleasure—
and to our minds. If so,

in spite of Rexroth, Barnum
our Aeschylus, we
should show ourselves
more courteous to Calas the Greek

who has come from Oxford via Paris
to enlighten us, affect
less flippancy toward his
Confound the Wise:

"If, in a study such as this, in which the ideas of the writer are dis-
cussed, we stop short at questions concerning form, it is because forms—
and I hope this appears clearly in everything I have so far said—are for us
tightly bound up with ideas and feelings. On this point I am a monist and
opposed to the positivistic and dualistic habits that the last century has be-
queathed us. Any error concerning form is consequently a fundamental
error, and when ideas are erroneous and when feelings are untrue, then
conformity bursts out and appears in form."

Read of Miranda

the Portuguese torso—connoting
Rexroth's *Tortoise*, say what he will:
read one then the other,
moral concepts both, curiously linked,

by which in time we may
behold, "the sun set where it did arise
and moons grow into virgins' eyes,
post sprout leaves and turn a tree and

morbid fruit normality," as in
the fluctuating molecule; details of
The Greatest Show on Earth—if
the mind survive and I be an American.

THE YELLOW TREE PEONY

The girl whose arms are leaves
at whose heart
a small flower with
bowed head
hides its moon-glow
of remote thought—
is pursued by the sun
with flaming gifts,
crimson and white.

But she of ample thighs
and full breasts
though she yields her
mooney flower
hides still her face
among the leaves
of her arms—remembering!

A bear that threads
the ravine at night and
the wild fox protect her.
But we have chicks
to raise and lambs to culture.
Who will protect us
from her dominion?

Translations of Paul Eluard—Poet of France

A WOLF

The good snow the sky black
The dead branches the torment
Of the woods full of snares
Shame to the hunted beast
Is the arrow flight in his heart

The tracks of a cruel prey
Steel the wolf and it is always
The most beautiful wolf and always
The last alive that threatens
The bulk absolute of death.

A WOLF

The day astonishes and the night fills me with fear
Summer haunts me and winter pursues

A beast has rested his paws
On the snow on the sand in the mud
His paws come from far beyond my own steps

On a chase where death
Wears the imprint of life.

UNCERTAIN OF THE CRIME

One rope one single twist one sole man
Strangled ten men
Burned a village
Swallowed a people

The she cat who makes part of life
Like a pearl in its shell
The gentle cat has eaten her kittens.

CURFEW

So what the door was guarded
So what we were imprisoned there
So what the street was barred off
So what the town was under attack
So what she was famished
So what we were without arms
So what night had fallen
So what we made love.

FROM THE OUTSIDE

The night the cold the solitude
I had been carefully shut in
But the branches sought their way into my prison

All about me the grass found the sky
They bolted up the sky

My prison crumbled
The living cold cold that scorches took possession.

FROM THE INSIDE

First commandment of the wind
The rain encloses the day
First signal for us to spread
The clear veil of our eyes

Before a house standing alone
In the wake of a kindly wall
At the bosom of a greenhouse asleep
We gaze on a velvety fire

Outside the earth is defamed
Outside the lair of the dead
Crumbles and slips in the mud

A flayed rose turns blue.

HEY RED!

There are men and
plenty of them
whose heads resemble
nothing so much as
the head of a dick—
color and form—
America is full
of them, a kind of
brains I suppose
at that . Thick .

DEATH BY RADIO

(For F.D.R.)

Suddenly his virtues became universal
We felt the force of his mind
on all fronts, penetrant
to the core of our beings
Our ears struck us speechless
while shameless tears sprang to our eyes
through which we saw
all mankind weeping.

EAST COOCOO

The innocent locomotive
laboring against the grade
streams its cloud of smoke
above the fallen snow.

Its labors are human to
the superhuman dread that
fastens every mind upon
the coming blast of bombs.

Peacefully we quarrel
over the doctrinal wage-rate,
build the cathedral, split
hairs in internecine wars.

And we too shall die
among the rest and the brave
locomotive stand falling apart
untended for a thousand years.

AT KENNETH BURKE'S PLACE

And "the earth under our feet,"
we say glibly, hating

the "Esoteric" which is not
to be included in our anthologies, the
unthinkable: the younger generation
the colored (unless marketable)
and—Plato was no different—the
"private language."
                    But
the earth also is a "private language"
barring, barring—Well,
principally cash, our one link,
says K. B., with the universal—the
step, the first step out of
domesticity, the familial. Cash. The
first nickel is the first defiance.
But the earth under our feet is
the singing, the winds, the snow—
the surge and slosh of the sea. It's
the indecisive, the rare occurrence
of the expected. The earth
is the esoteric to our dullness,
it opens caves, it distils dews:
the furry root of the fern.
Catalogues are not its business.
Its business, its business is
external to anthologies, outside the
orthodoxy of plotted murders.
                    It is
the green apple smudged with
a sooty life that clings, also,
with the skin: the small green apple
still fast here and there
to the leafless brush of unpruned
twigs sprouting from old knees
and elbows upon the tree
that was cleared of undergrowth about
it and still stands.
        There is a basketful
of them half rotted on the half rotten
bench. Take up one
and bite into it. It is still good

even unusual compared with the usual,
as if a taste long lost and regretted
had in the end, finally,
been brought to life again.

"THE ROCK-OLD DOGMA"

It had to be, of course, a rock
over which comparatively recent ants
crawled. When it split,
with time, only then did the imprint

of the fern reveal itself—
And the fern, and the fish-spine or
bird-plume—fossil botany goes
into smaller particles. Which is to

say, the rock as such is recent or
should one say, not so
recent as recurrent? protean: The
rock-old dogma! Pitiful rock

that has known no youth or no greater
youth than that! the rock
was food once to fern and fishes
that left there their traces—

And the paleontology of the dogma, a
pitiful youth! had also its
earlier phase—when it was not
rock-like but living and will live again.

APPROACH TO A CITY

Getting through with the world—
I never tire of the mystery
of these streets: the three baskets
of dried flowers in the high

barroom window, the gulls wheeling
above the factory, the dirty
snow—the humility of the snow that
silvers everything and is

trampled and lined with use—yet
falls again, the silent birds
on the still wires of the sky, the blur
of wings as they take off

together. The flags in the heavy
air move against a leaden
ground—the snow
pencilled with the stubble of old

weeds: I never tire of these sights
but refresh myself there
always for there is small holiness
to be found in braver things.

THE USURERS OF HEAVEN

Wanting to save their fortunes for—
Wanting to rescue
and perpetuate their fortunes
they join the reverse, carefully
—to the wail of a child lost and—
the poor denied . . .

Bottom wise the plumbers scratch
their ears. Why not? Why not?
—quit at 3 P.M. pocketing
their twenty bucks per—
Why not two hundred?
Why not more?
or nothing will drain off.
—and refuse to take on apprentices
at rapid enough a pace, while
the work languishes. And . . .

The wheel beckons as it whirls, so
softly, so very softly that
nobody notices; the
usurious costs pursue: the hours
flit by profitless and . . .

—the mattresses of the poor
remain hard, hard as
the pavements of a cathedral.
But rest, my child, and be comforted.
Rest, rest! and be comforted.

ROGATION SUNDAY

O let the seeds be planted
and the worry and unrest be invited!
Let that which is to come
of the weather and our own weakness
be accepted!

Let work mate with fertility
the man and the soil join to produce
a world, a world of blade and blossom!
We believe! We believe
in the wonder of continuous revival,
the ritual of the farm.

This is our world and this
is our message to the world and to each other:
Let the seed be planted, the man
and the soil be ploughed equally
by the joy in the planting—
that the grass, the grasses that bear
the seeds: oat, rye and corn
and other yield
speak their message of revival and thrive
by our labor this Maytime.

CODA:

Who shall reap the harvest?
To whom shall the praise be given?
No man—but all men together in love
and devotion. There is no other harvest
and no other praise!
O let the seeds be planted and the rain
and the sun and the moon add their wonder.

LUSTSPIEL

Vienna the Volk iss very lustig,
she makes no sorry for anything!
    She likes to dance and sing!

Vienna is a brave city, the girls
have sturdy legs. Yeah!
    She likes to dance and sing!

Death conquered Vienna but his men
had to be called off because
given the meanest break she'd lead
them hellbent to chuck the racket
for there's not a soul in Vienna
    but likes to dance and sing!

—drop their guns, dump the boss
grab a girl and join the rest
    who like to dance and sing!

Vienna the Volk iss very lustig,
she makes no sorry for anything!
    She likes to dance and sing!

THE UNITED STATES

The government of your body, sweet,
shall be my model for the world.

There is no desire in me to rule
that world or to advise it. Look
how it rouses with the sun, shuts
with night and sleeps fringed by
the slowly turning stars. I boil
I freeze before its tropics and its
cold. Its shocks are mine and to
the peaceful legislature of its seas,
by you its president,
I yield my willing services.

THE RESEMBLANCE

The Jewess was happy
she had no car
—though it was raining

but she had her
baby, all wrapped
up in her arms—as

she too was all
wrapped up, short as
she was, and on

her head stood a green
clown's cap that
made her look

for all the world
like a painting
by Rouault.

THE BIRTH OF VENUS

Today small waves are rippling, crystal clear, upon the pebbles
at Villefranche whence from the wall, at the Parade Grounds of

the Chasseurs Alpins, we stood and watched them; or passing along
the cliff on the ledge between the sea and the old fortress, heard
the long swell stir without cost among the rock's teeth. But we

are not there!—as in the Crimea the Black Sea is blue with waves
under a smiling sky, or be it the Labrador North Shore, or wherever
else in the world you will, the world of indolence and April; as
November next, spring will enliven the African coast southward
and we not there, not there, not there!

Why not believe that we shall be young again? Surely nothing
could be more to our desire, more pebble-plain under a hand's breath
wavelet, a jeweled thing, a Sapphic bracelet, than this. Murder
staining the small waves crimson is not more moving—though we strain
in our minds to make it so, and stare.

Cordite, heavy shells falling on the fortifications of Sebastopol,
fired by the Germans first, then by the Russians, are indifferent to
our agony—as are small waves in the sunlight. But we need not elect
what we do not desire. Torment, in the daisied fields before Troy
or at Amiens or the Manchurian plain is not

of itself the dearest desired of our world. We do not have to die,
in bitterness and the most excruciating torture, to feel! We can
lean on the wall and experience an ecstasy of pain, if pain it must
be, but a pain of love, of dismemberment if you will, but a pain
of almond blossoms, an agony of mimosa trees in bloom, a

scented cloud! Even, as old Ford would say, an exquisite sense of
viands. Would there be no sculpture, no painting, no Pinturicchio, no
Botticelli—or frescos on the jungle temples of Burma (that the jungles
have reclaimed) or Picasso at Cannes but for war? Would there be
no voyages starting from the dunes at Huelva

over the windy harbor? No Seville cathedral? Possibly so. Even
the quietness of flowers is perhaps deceptive. But why must we suffer
ourselves to be so torn to sense our world? Or believe we must so
suffer to be born again? Let the homosexuals seduce whom they will
under what bushes along the coasts of the Middle Sea

rather than have us insist on murder. Governments are defeats, distor-
tions. I wish (and so I fail). Notwithstanding, I wish we might
learn of an April of small waves—deadly as all slaughter, that we
shall die soon enough, to dream of April, not knowing why we have been
struck down, heedless of what greater violence.

SEAFARER

The sea will wash in
but the rocks—jagged ribs
riding the cloth of foam
or a knob or pinnacles
     with gannets—
are the stubborn man.

He invites the storm, he
lives by it! instinct
with fears that are not fears
but prickles of ecstasy,
a secret liquor, a fire
that inflames his blood to
coldness so that the rocks
seem rather to leap
at the sea than the sea
to envelope them. They strain
forward to grasp ships
or even the sky itself that
bends down to be torn
upon them. To which he says,
It is I! I who am the rocks!
Without me nothing laughs.

THE SOUND OF WAVES

A quatrain? Is that
the end I envision?
Rather the pace
which travel chooses.

Female? Rather the end
of giving and receiving
—of love: love surmounted
is the incentive.

Hardly. The incentive
is nothing surmounted,
the challenge lying
                    elsewhere.

No end but among words
looking to the past,
plaintive and unschooled,
wanting a discipline

But wanting
more than discipline
a rock to blow upon
as a mist blows

or rain is driven
against some
headland jutting into
a sea—with small boats

perhaps riding under it
while the men fish
there, words blowing in
taking the shape of stone

      .   .   .   .   .

Past that, past the image:
a voice!
out of the mist
above the waves and

the sound of waves, a
voice   .   speaking!

THE COUNTER

My days are burning
My brain is a flower
Hasten flower to bloom
my days are burning

Quietly the flower
opens its petals
My days are burning
My brain is a flower

My brain a flower lost
to its own fragrance
indifferent, idle—
my days are burning

PERIOD PIECE: 1834

It was on the old Paterson and
      Hudson R. R.
The first engine out of town
Toot! Toot! blurted the whistle.
      McNeill threw
in another scoopful at the door
How's your boy, Jimmy? said
      the fireman
By God, he's a Whistler, son;
I hear the kids are fixing it
      to get married
Let 'em, said his pard. Right!
And that's how the great James
      McNeill
Whistler was set up to be born

THE PAUSE

Values are split, summer, the fierce
jet an axe would not sever, spreads out

at length, of its own weight, a rainbow
over the lake of memory—the hard
stem of pure speed broken. Autumn
comes, fruit of many contours, that
glistening tegument painters love hiding
the soft pulp of the insidious reason,
dormant, for worm to nibble or for woman.
But there, within the seed, shaken by
fear as by a sea, it wakes again! to
drive upward, presently, from that soft
belly such a stem as will crack quartz.

APRIL IS THE SADDEST MONTH

There they were
stuck
dog and bitch
halving the compass

Then when
with his yip
they parted
oh how frolicsome

she grew before him
playful
dancing and
how disconsolate

he retreated
hang-dog
she following
through the shrubbery

FOR G.B.S., OLD

As the mind burns
the external is swallowed

nor can cold
censor it when it launches
its attack

Sever man
into his parts of bird and fish
Wake him
to the plausibilities
of those changes
he contemplates but does not dare

And by such acceptance
he forfeits
the green perspectives
which frightened him off
to his own destruction—

the mirage
the shape of a shape
become the shape he feared
his Tempest frozen
into a pattern
of ice.

THE MODEST ACHIEVEMENT

Flossie put the velvet pansies
        in a flat dish,
a flat glass dish—because
        the stems were short.

But they looked crushed there.
        Why now do they
seem so entrancing? Because
        among them she

interspersed a pattern of rose-
        red apple blossoms
charged to lift and waken
        the somber show.

NO GOOD TOO

She's the girl
had her picture
in the papers: just
14 years old and

ran off with
the guy her mother
brought home
from a gin mill

THE CLOUDS

1948

William Carlos Williams

THE CLOUDS,
Aigeltinger, Russia, &c.

Published jointly by The Wells College Press
and The Cummington Press. Mcmxlviij.

AIGELTINGER

In the bare trees old husks make new designs
Love moves the crows before the dawn
The cherry-sun ushers in the new phase

The radiant mind
addressed by tufts of flocking pear blossoms
proposes new profundities to the soul

Deftness stirs in the cells
of Aigeltinger's brain which flares
like ribbons round an electric fan

This is impressive, he will soon proclaim
God!

And round and round, the winds
and underfoot, the grass
the rose-cane leaves and blackberries
and Jim will read the encyclopedia to his
new bride—gradually

Aigeltinger you have stuck in my conk
illuminating, for nearly half a century I
could never beat you at your specialty

Nothing has ever beaten a mathematician
but yeast

The cloudless sky takes the sun in its periphery
and slides its disc across the blue

They say I'm not profound

But where is profundity, Aigeltinger
mathematical genius

dragged drunk from some cheap bar to serve
their petty purposes?

Aigeltinger, you were profound

FRANKLIN SQUARE

Instead of
the flower of the hawthorn
the spine:

The tree is in bloom
the flowers
and the leaves together

sheltering
the noisy sparrows
that give

by their intimate
indifference,
the squirrels and pigeons

on the sharp-
edged lawns—the figure
of a park:

A city, a decadence
of bounty—
a tall negress approaching

the bench
pursing her old mouth
for what coin?

LABRADOR

How clean these shallows
how firm these rocks stand

about which wash
the waters of the world

It is ice to this body
that unclothes its pallors
to thoughts
of an immeasurable sea,

unmarred, that as it lifts
encloses this
straining mind, these
limbs in a single gesture.

THE APPARITION

My greetings to you, sir, whose memory,
the striped coat and colors— What is one man?
a man remembered still in the jacket
of his success? of the winning club?
in himself—successful? one man, alone?
This is that he who slights his fellows—
or else, as he is, plunges
to the wind-whipped swirl, hat, coat, shoes
and—as you did—drags in the body
to the grapples defying death and the sea.
Not once but—again!
Is this the war—that spawned you? Or
did you make the war? Whichever, there you are.

THE LIGHT SHALL NOT ENTER

It is in the minds
of the righteous
that death crows loudest.

Death! the cry is. Death!
in the teeth
of the sky, as though

fire is not to blast
and the copper of desire
burnish under it. Oh

we choose our words
too carefully
to fit a calcined skeleton

of meaning, in which
lives! lives only resent-
ment. We the flame

and furnace talk, embittered
as though ours were
some other

destiny whose entrails
are not to burn—shall
escape the heat. Pah!

A WOMAN IN FRONT OF A BANK

The bank is a matter of columns,
like . convention,
unlike invention; but the pediments
sit there in the sun

to convince the doubting of
investments "solid
as rock"—upon which the world
stands, the world of finance,

the only world: Just there,
talking with another woman while
rocking a baby carriage
back and forth stands a woman in

a pink cotton dress, bare legged
and headed whose legs

are two columns to hold up
her face, like Lenin's (her loosely

arranged hair profusely blond) or
Darwin's and there you
have it:
a woman in front of a bank.

THE NIGHT RIDER

Scoured like a conch
or the moon's shell
I ride from my love
through the damp night.

There are lights
through the trees,
falling leaves,
the air and the blood

an even mood
warm with summer dwindling,
relic of heat:
Ruin dearly bought

smoothed to a round
carved by the sand
the pulse a remembered pulse
of full-tide gone

CHANSON

This woman! how shall I describe her
who is wealthy in the riches
of her sex? No counterfeit, no mere
metal to be sure—

yet, a treasury, a sort of lien upon
all property we list and transfer.

This woman has no need to play the market
or to do anything more than watch

the moon. For to her, thoughts are not
like those of the philosopher
or scientist, or clever playwright.
Her thoughts are to her

like fruit to the tree, the apple, pear.
She thinks and thinks well, but
to different purpose than a man, and I
discover there a novel territory.

It is a world to make the world
little worth traveling by ship or air.
Moscow, Zanzibar, the Ægean
Islands, the Crimea she surpasses

by that which by her very being she
would infer, a New World
welcome as to a sailor and habitable
so that I am willing to stay there.

THE BIRDSONG

Disturb the balance, broken bird
the distress of the song
cuts through an ample silence
sweeping the trees.

It is the trouble
of the brook that makes it loud,
the current broke to give
out a burbling

breaks the arched stillness,
ripples the tall grass
gone to heady seed, bows the heads
of goldenrod

that bear a vulgar happiness,
the bay-berry,
briars—
break also your happiness for me.

THE VISIT

I have committed many errors
but I warn—the interplay
is not the tossed body. Though
the mind is subtler than the sea,
advancing at three speeds,
the fast, the medium and the slow,
recapitulating at every ninth
wave what was not at first directly
stated, that is still only
on the one level.

        There are the fish
and at the bottom, the ground,
no matter whether at five feet
or five miles, the ground, revealing,
when bared by the tides, living
barnacles, hungry on the rocks
as the mind is, that hiss as often
loudly when the sun bites them.

And I acknowledge, the mind is
still (though rarely) more than
its play. I can see also
the dagger in the left hand when
the right strikes. It does
not alter the case.

Let us resume. The
naive may be like a sunny day
deceptive
and is not to be despised
because it is so amusing to see

the zigzag and slender gulls
dip
into the featureless surface.
It is fish they are after,
fish—and get them.

        Still I
acknowledge the sea is there and
I admire its profundity only
what does that amount to?
Love also may be deep, deep
as thought, deeper than thought
and as sequential—

          thought
full of detail, let us say, as
the courts are full of law
and the sea, weeds and
as murmurous: that does not
alter the case either. Yet you
are right in the end: law
often decides cases. Well?
I prefer to go back to my cases
at the hospital.

Say I am less an artist
than a spadeworker but one
who has no aversion to taking
his spade to the head
of any who would derogate
his performance in the craft.

You were kind to be at such
pains with me and—thanks
for the view.

THE QUALITY OF HEAVEN

Without other cost than breath
and the poor soul,

carried in the cage of the ribs,
chirping shrilly

I walked in the garden. The
garden smelled of roses.
The lilies' green throats opened
to yellow trumpets

that craved no sound and the rain
was fresh in my face,
the air a sweet breath.

                  Yesterday
the heat was oppressive

dust clogged the leaves' green
and bees from
the near hive, parched, drank,
overeager, at

the birdbath and were drowned there.
Others replaced them
from which the birds were
frightened.
              —the fleece-light air!

TO A LOVELY OLD BITCH

Sappho, Sappho, Sappho! initiate,
handmaiden, to Astarte,
you praised delicate flowers

and likened them
to virgins of your acquaintance.
Let them grow, thank God!
outside the cemetery barrier:

—burials for cash,
the shares ample security
against—?

The butterfly,
The Painted Admiral,
on a milkweed cluster,
untrampled,
keep you company and pale
blue chickory, frilled
petals

—butter-and-eggs,
lady's-slipper, close beside
the rust of the dump-heap
—rust, broken fruit-baskets
and bits of plaster,
painted on one side,

from dismantled bedrooms.

THE BITTER WORLD OF SPRING

On a wet pavement the white sky recedes
mottled black by the inverted
pillars of the red elms,
in perspective, that lift the tangled

net of their desires hard into
the falling rain. And brown smoke
is driven down, running like
water over the roof of the bridge-

keeper's cubicle. And, as usual,
the fight as to the nature of poetry
—Shall the philosophers capture it?—
is on. And, casting an eye

down into the water, there, announced
by the silence of a white
bush in flower, close
under the bridge, the shad ascend,

midway between the surface and the mud,
and you can see their bodies
red-finned in the dark
water headed, unrelenting, upstream.

LAMENT

What face, in the water,
distinct
yet washed by an obscurity?

The willow supplants its own
struggling rafters
(of winter branches)

by a green radiance. Is it
old or young?
But what this face

reflected beyond the bare structures
of a face
shining from the creaseless

water? A face
overlaid with evil, brown water;
the good insecure, the evil

sure beyond the buried sun. Lift
it. Turn away.
There was beside you

but now another face,
with long nose and clear blue eyes,
secure . . .

A HISTORY OF LOVE

1

And would you gather turds
for your grandmother's garden?
Out with you then, dustpan and broom;
she has seen the horse passing!

Out you go, bold again
as you promise always to be.
Stick your tongue out at the neighbors
that her flowers may grow.

2

Let me stress your loveliness
and its gravity

its counter-hell: Reading
finds you on the page

where sight enlarges
to confound the mind and only

a child is frightened
by its father's headgear

while a bird jigs and ol' Bunk
Johnson blows his horn.

3

With the mind and with the hand,
by moral turn and prestidigitation
fan the smoldering flame of love
which in the dull coals is all but gone.

Between one and the other transpose
wrong and rouse

the banished smile that used to spring
at once at meeting!

Rewaken love, again, again! to warm
the chilly heart and bring fresh flowers.
For flowers are not, as we are not
of that stuff whence we both are got.

MISTS OVER THE RIVER

The river-mirror mirrors the cold sky
through mists that tangle sunlight,
the sunlight of early morning,
in their veils veiling

the dark outlines of the shores. But
the necessity, you say, cries
aloud for the adjusting—greater than
song, greater perhaps than all song

While the song, self committed, the river
a mirror swathed in sunlight,
the river in its own body cries out
also, silently

from its obscuring veils. You
insist on my unqualified endorsement.
Many years, I see, many years
of reading have not made you wise.

WHEN STRUCTURE FAILS
RHYME ATTEMPTS TO COME TO THE RESCUE

The old horse dies slow.
By gradual degrees
the fervor of his veins
matches the leaves'

stretch, day by day. But
the pace that his
mind keeps is the pace
of his dreams. He

does what he can, with
unabated phlegm,
ahem! but the pace that
his flesh keeps—

leaning, leaning upon
the bars—beggars
by far all pace and every
refuge of his dreams.

EDUCATION A FAILURE

The minor stupidities
of my world
dominate that world—
as when

with two bridges across
the river and one
closed for repairs
the other also

will be closed by
the authorities
for painting! But then
there is heaven

and the ideal state
closed also
before the aspiring soul.
I had rather

watch a cat threading
a hedge with

another sitting by
while the bird

screams overhead
athrash
in the cover of the
low branches.

THE BANNER BEARER

In the rain, the lonesome
dog idiosyn-
cratically, with each
quadribeat, throws

out the left fore-
foot beyond
the right intent, in
his stride,

on some obscure
insistence—from bridge-
ward going
into new territory.

THE GOAT

Having in the mind thought
to have died,
to that celebrant
among trees, aging (with the season)
foreign to sight—

in a field a goat, befouled,
shagbellied, indifferent to
the mind's ecstasies,
flutters its blunt tail

and turns a vacant face
lop-eared, sleepy-eyed to stare,
unblinking, meditant—
listless
in its assured sanctity.

TWO DELIBERATE EXERCISES

1.   LESSON FROM A PUPIL RECITAL
(*For Agnes*)

In a fourfold silence the music
struggles for mastery and the mind
from its silence, fatefully assured,
wakens to the music: Unnamed,
without age, sex or pretence of
accomplishment—their faces
blank, they rise and move
to the platform unannounced and
the music leads them—the racially
stigmaed, the gross bodied, all
feet—cleansing from each
his awkwardness for him to blossom
thence a sound pleading,
pleading for pleasure, pleasure!
at the tunnel of the ear. And love,
who hides from public places,
moves in his bed of air, of flowers,
of ducks, of sheep and locust
trees in bloom—the white, sweet
locust—to fade again
at the sounds into
impossibilities and thunderstorms.
          There remains the good teacher
blinking from his dream before
the hand-shakes of his constituents.

2. VOYAGES

In the center, above the basin,
the mirror. To the left of
it the Maxfield Parrish, Ulysses
at Sea, his small ship coming
fog-threatened from between
Scylla and Charybdis. And
to the right the girl of nine,
play-pail in hand, bareheaded upon
a dune-crest facing the shining
waters. There you have it,
unexcelled as feeling. What
of it? Well, we live among
the birds and bees in vain unless
there result—now or then—
a presentation to which
these two presentations serve
as humble stopgaps—to invoke
for us a whole realm, compact of
inverted nature, straining
within the imprisoned mind to
free us. Well, to free us.

      At which, seeing in the pasture
horses among the brambles,
hearing the wind sigh,
we broach the chaos—unless
Valéry be mistaken—of
the technical where stand waiting
for us or nowhere the tree-
lined avenues of our desires.

THE MIRRORS

Is Germany's bestiality, in detail
like certain racial traits,
any more than a reflection of the world's

evil? Take a negative, take Ezra Pound
for example, and see
how the world has impressed itself

there. It is as when with infra-red
searching a landscape obscured
to the unaided eye one discloses

the sea. The world is at its worst the
positive to these foils,
imaged there as on the eyes of a fly.

HIS DAUGHTER

Her jaw wagging
her left hand pointing
stiff armed
behind her, I noticed:

her youth, her
receding chin and
fair hair;
her legs, bare

The sun was on her
as she came
to the step's edge,
the fat man,

caught in his stride,
collarless,
turned sweating
toward her.

DESIGN FOR NOVEMBER

Let confusion be the design
and all my thoughts go,

swallowed by desire: recess
from promises in
the November of your arms.
Release from the rose: broken
reeds, strawpale,
through which, from easy
branches that mock the blood
a few leaves fall. There
the mind is cradled,
stripped also and returned
to the ground, a trivial
and momentary clatter. Sleep
and be brought down and so
condone the world, eased of
the jagged sky and all
its petty imageries, flying
birds, its fogs and windy
phalanxes . . .

THE MANEUVER

I saw the two starlings
coming in toward the wires.
But at the last,
just before alighting, they

turned in the air together
and landed backwards!
that's what got me—to
face into the wind's teeth.

THE HORSE

The horse moves
independently
without reference
to his load

He has eyes
like a woman and
turns them
about, throws

back his ears
and is generally
conscious of
the world. Yet

he pulls when
he must and
pulls well, blowing
fog from

his nostrils
like fumes from
the twin
exhausts of a car.

HARD TIMES

Stone steps, a solid
block too tough
to be pried out, from
which the house,

rather, has been
avulsed leaving
a pedestal, on which
a fat boy in

an old overcoat, a
butt between
his thick lips, the
coat pushed back,

stands kidding,
Parking Space! three

steps up from his
less lucky fellows.

THE DISH OF FRUIT

The table describes
nothing: four legs, by which
it becomes a table. Four lines
by which it becomes a quatrain,

the poem that lifts the dish
of fruit, if we say it is like
a table—how will it describe
the contents of the poem?

THE MOTOR-BARGE

The motor-barge is
at the bridge the
air lead
the broken ice

unmoving. A gull,
the eternal
gull, flies as
always, eyes alert

beak pointing
to the life-giving
water. Time
falters but for

the broad river-
craft which
low in the water
moves grad-

ually, edging
between the smeared

                    bulkheads,
                    churning a mild

                    wake, laboring
                    to push past
                    the constriction
                    with its heavy load

RUSSIA

The Williams Avenue Zionist Church (colored)
a thing to hold in the palm of the hand,
your big hand—
the dwarf campanile piled up, improvised
of blue cinder-blocks, badly aligned
(except for the incentive)

                              unvarnished,
the cross at the top slapped together
(in this lumber shortage) of sticks from
an old barrel top, I think

                              —painted white

Russia, idiot of the world, blind idiot
—do you understand me?

                    This also
I place in your hands . . .

I dream! and my dream is folly. While
armies rush to the encounter
I, alone, dream before the impending
onslaught. And the power in me,
to be crushed out: this paper, forgotten
—not even known ever to have existed,
proclaims the power of my dream . . .

Folly! I call upon folly to save us—
and scandal and disapproval, the restless
angels of the mind—

                                        (I omit
the silly word exile. For from what and
to what land shall I be exiled and talk of
the cardinal bird and the starling
as though they were strange?)

                                        I am
at home in my dream, Russia; and only there,
before the obliterating blow
                    that shall flatten everything
and its crazy masonry,
                            am I at home.

Inspired by my dream I do not call upon
a party to save me, nor a government
of whatever sort.

                    Rather I descend into
my dream as into a quiet lake
and there, already there, I find
my kinships. Thence I rise by my own
propulsions into a world beyond the moon.

O Russia, Russia! must we begin to call
you idiot of the world? When
you were a dream the world lived in you
inviolate—

O Russia! Russians! come with me into
my dream and let us be lovers,
connoisseurs, idlers—Come with me
in the spirit of Walt Whitman's earliest
poem, let us loaf at our ease—a moment
at the edge of destruction.

Look through my eyes a moment. I am
a poet, uninfluential, with no skill
in polemics—my friends tell me I lack
the intellect. Look,

I once met Mayakovsky. Remember
Mayakovsky? I have a little paper-bound
volume of his in my attic, inscribed by him
in his scrawling hand to our mutual
friendship. He put one foot up
on the table that night at 14th St. when
he read to us—and his voice came
like the outpourings of the Odyssey.

                    Russians!
let Mayakovsky be my sponsor—he
and his Willie, the Havana street-cleaner—
Mayakovsky was a good guy and killed
himself, I suppose, not to embarrass you.

And so I go about.

And now I want to call your attention—
that you may know what keen eyes
I have in my dream—
to Leonardo's Last Supper! a small print
I saw today in a poor kitchen.

                    Russia!
for the first time in my life, I noticed
this famous picture not because
of the subject matter but because
of the severity and simplicity
of the background! Oh there was
the passion of the scene, of course,
generally. But particularly,
ignoring the subject, I fell upon
the perpendiculars of the paneled
woodwork standing there, submissive,
in exaggerated perspective.

There you have it. It's that background
from which my dreams have sprung. These
I dedicate now to you, now when I am
about to die. I hold back nothing. I lay

my spirit at your feet and say to you:
Here I am, a dreamer. I do not
resist you. Among many others, undistinguished,
of no moment—I am the background
upon which you will build your empire.

THE ACT

There were the roses, in the rain.
Don't cut them, I pleaded.
                    They won't last, she said.
But they're so beautiful
                    where they are.
Agh, we were all beautiful once, she
                    said,
and cut them and gave them to me
                    in my hand.

THE SAVAGE BEAST

As I leaned to retrieve
my property
he leaped with all his weight
so that I felt

the wind of his jaws
as his teeth gnashed
before my mouth.
Isn't he *aw*ful! said

the woman, his collar
straining under her clutch.
Yes, I replied drily
wanting to eviscerate

the thing there, scoop
out his brains
and eat them—and hers
too! Until it flashed

on me, How many, like
this dog, could I not wish
had been here in my
place, only a little closer!

THE WELL DISCIPLINED BARGEMAN

The shadow does not move. It is the water moves,
running out. A monolith of sand on a passing barge,
riding the swift water, makes that its fellow.

Standing upon the load the well disciplined bargeman
rakes it carefully, smooth on top with nicely squared
edges to conform to the barge outlines—ritually: sand.

All about him the silver water, fish-swift, races
under the Presence. Whatever there is else is moving.
The restless gulls, unlike companionable pigeons,

taking their cue from the ruffled water, dip and circle
avidly into the gale. Only the bargeman raking
upon his barge remains, like the shadow, sleeping

RAINDROPS ON A BRIAR

I, a writer, at one time hipped on
painting, did not consider
the effects, painting,
for that reason, static, on

the contrary the stillness of
the objects—the flowers, the gloves—
freed them precisely by that
from a necessity merely to move

in space as if they had been—
not children! but the thinking male

or the charged and deliver-
ing female frantic with ecstasies;

served rather to present, for me,
a more pregnant motion: a
series of varying leaves
clinging still, let us say, to

the cat-briar after last night's
storm, its waterdrops
ranged upon the arching stems
irregularly as an accompaniment.

OL' BUNK'S BAND

These are men! the gaunt, unfore-
    sold, the vocal,
blatant, Stand up, stand up! the
    slap of a bass-string.
Pick, ping! The horn, the
    hollow horn
long drawn out, a hound deep
    tone—
Choking, choking! while the
    treble reed
races—alone, ripples, screams
    slow to fast—
to second to first! These are men!

Drum, drum, drum, drum, drum
    drum, drum! the
ancient cry, escaping crapulence
    eats through
transcendent—torn, tears, term
    town, tense,
turns and backs off whole, leaps
    up, stomps down,
rips through! These are men
    beneath

whose force the melody limps—
    to
proclaim, proclaims—Run and
    lie down,
in slow measures, to rest and
    not never
need no more! These are men!
    Men!

SUZANNE

Brother Paul! look!
—but he rushes to a different
window.
The moon!

I heard shrieks and thought:
What's that?

That's just Suzanne
talking to the moon!
Pounding on the window
with both fists:

    Paul!   Paul!

—and talking to the moon.
Shrieking
and pounding the glass
with both fists!

Brother Paul! the moon!

NAVAJO

Red woman,
    (Keep Christ out

of this—and
his mountains:
Sangre de Cristo
red rocks that make
the water run
blood-red)
squaw in red
red woman
walking the desert
I suspected
I should remember
you this way:
    walking the brain
    eyes cast down
    to escape ME!
    with fixed sight
    stalking
    the gray brush
    paralleling
    the highway . . .
    —head mobbled
    red, red
    to the ground—
    sweeping the
    ground—
    the blood walking
    erect, the
    desert animating
    the blood to walk
    erect by choice
    through
    the pale green
    of the starveling
    sage

GRAPH

There was another, too
a half-breed Cherokee

tried to thumb a ride
out of Tulsa, standing there

with a bunch of wildflowers
in her left hand
pressed close
just below the belly

THE TESTAMENT OF PERPETUAL CHANGE

Mortal Prudence, handmaid of divine Providence
    Walgreen carries Culture to the West:
hath inscrutable reckoning with Fate and Fortune:
    At Cortez, Colorado the Indian prices
We sail a changeful sea through halcyon days and storm,
    a bottle of cheap perfume, furtively—
and when the ship laboreth, our stedfast purpose
    but doesn't buy, while under my hotel window
trembles like as a compass in a binnacle.
    a Radiance Rose spreads its shell-thin
Our stability is but balance, and wisdom lies
    petals above the non-irrigated garden
in masterful administration of the unforeseen
    among the unprotected desert foliage.

'Twas late in my long journey when I had clomb to where
    Having returned from Mesa Verde, the ruins
the path was narrowing and the company few
    of the Cliff Dwellers' palaces still in possession of my mind

THE FLOWER

This too I love
Flossie sitting in the sun
on its cane
the first rose

yellow as an egg the pet
canary

in his cage
beside her caroling

FOR A LOW VOICE

If you ignore the possibilities of art,
huh, huh, huh, huh, huh, &c.
you are likely to become involved,
huh! in extreme, huh, huh, huh, huh, huh

&c. difficulties. For instance, when
they started to make a park
at the site of the old Dutch, huh, huh, huh!
cemetery, ha, ha, ha, ha, ha, &c.

they could not, digging down
upon the hoary, heh, heh! graves,
find so much as a thighbone, huh, huh, huh!
or in fact anything! wha, ha,

ha, ha, ha, ha, ha, ha, &c.
to remove! This,
according to the requirements of the case,
created a huh, huh, huh, huh

shall we say, dilemma? So that,
to make a gesture, for old time's sake,
heh, heh! of filling
the one vault retained as communal repository

huh, huh! and monument, they
had to throw in SOMETHING! presumed
to be bones but observed by those nearest,
heh, heh, heh! more to resemble

rotten tree roots than *ossa!*
a low sort of dissembling, ha, ha, ha, &c.
on the part of the officials
were it not excusable, oh, ho, ho, ho, ho, &c.

under the head of . . . Yes, yes, of course!
wha, ha, ha, ha, ha, ha! Whoh, ho,
hee, hee! Rather a triumph of
a sort! Whoop la! Whee hee!—don't you think?

THE WORDS LYING IDLE

The fields parched, the leaves
drying on the maples, the birds' beaks
gaping! if it would rain,
if it would only rain! Clouds come up,
move from the west and from the south
but they bring no rain. Heat and dry winds
—the grass is curled and brittle underfoot,
the foot leaves it broken. The roads are dust.

But the mind is dust also
and the eyes burn from it. They burn more
from restless nights, from the full moon shining
on a dry earth than from lack of rain.
The rain, if it fell, would ease the mind
more than the grass, the mind would
be somewhat, at least, appeased against
this dryness and the death implied.

LEAR

When the world takes over for us
and the storm in the trees
replaces our brittle consciences
(like ships, female to all seas)
when the few last yellow leaves
stand out like flags on tossed ships
at anchor—our minds are rested

Yesterday we sweated and dreamed
or sweated in our dreams walking
at a loss through the bulk of figures

that appeared solid, men or women,
but as we approached down the paved
corridor melted—Was it I?—like
smoke from bonfires blowing away

Today the storm, inescapable, has
taken the scene and we return
our hearts to it, however made, made
wives by it and though we secure
ourselves for a dry skin from the drench
of its passionate approaches we
yield and are made quiet by its fury

Pitiful Lear, not even you could
out-shout the storm—to make a fool
cry! Wife to its power might you not
better have yielded earlier? as on ships
facing the seas were carried once
the figures of women at repose to
signify the strength of the waves' lash.

PICTURE OF A NUDE IN A MACHINE SHOP

and foundry,
               (that's art)
        a red ostrich plume
in her hair:

Sweat and muddy water,
coiled fuse-strips
                      surround her
poised sitting—
(between red, parted
                  curtains)

the right leg
               (stockinged)
up!
        beside the point—
at ease.

Light as a glove, light
as her black gloves!
Modeled as a shoe, a woman's
high heeled shoe!

—the other leg stretched
out
      bare
            (toward the top—
and upward)
        as
the smeared hide under
shirt and pants
stiff with grease and dirt
is bare—

         approaching
the centrum
         (disguised)
the metal to be devalued!

        —bare as
a blow-torch flame,
           undisguised.

THE BRILLIANCE

Oh sock, sock, sock!
brief but persistent.
Emulate the gnat
or a tree's leaves

that are not the tree
but mass to shape it.
Finis! Finish
and get out of this.

A UNISON

The grass is very green, my friend,
and tousled, like the head of—
your grandson, yes? And the mountain,
the mountain we climbed
twenty years since for the last
time (I write this thinking
of you) is saw-horned as then
upon the sky's edge—an old barn
is peaked there also, fatefully,
against the sky. And there it is
and we can't shift it or change
it or parse it or alter it
in any way. *Listen! Do you not hear
them? the singing?* There it is and
we'd better acknowledge it and
write it down that way, not otherwise.
Not twist the words to mean
what we should have said but to mean
—what cannot be escaped: the
mountain riding the afternoon as
it does, the grass matted green,
green underfoot and the air—
rotten wood. *Hear! Hear them!
the Undying.* The hill slopes away,
then rises in the middleground,
you remember, with a grove of gnarled
maples centering the bare pasture,
sacred, surely—for what reason?
I cannot say. Idyllic!
a shrine cinctured there by
the trees, a certainty of music!
a unison and a dance, joined
at this death's festival: Something
of a shed snake's skin, the beginning
goldenrod. Or, best, a white stone,
you have seen it: *Mathilda Maria
Fox*—and near the ground's lip,
all but undecipherable, *Aet Suae*

Anno 9—still there, the grass
dripping of last night's rain—and
welcome! The thin air, the near,
clear brook water!—and could not,
and died, unable; to escape
what the air and the wet grass—
through which, tomorrow, bejeweled,
the great sun will rise—the
unchanging mountains, forced on them—
and they received, willingly!
Stones, stones of a difference
joining the others, at pace. *Hear!*
Hear the unison of their voices. . . .

THE SEMBLABLES

Included in *The Wedge.* See p. 84.

THE HURRICANE

The tree lay down
on the garage roof
and stretched, You
have your heaven,
it said, go to it.

THE PROVINCE

The figure
of tall
white grass
by the cinder-bank
keeps its alignment
faultlessly.
Moves!
in the brilliant

channels
of the wind

Shines!
its polished
shafts
and feathered
fronds
ensconced there
colorless
beyond all feeling

This is
the principle
of the godly,
fluted, a
statue
tall and pale

—lifeless
save only in
beauty,
the kernel
of all seeking,
the eternal

THE MIND'S GAMES

If a man can say of his life or
any moment of his life, There is
nothing more to be desired! his state
becomes like that told in the famous
double sonnet—but without the
sonnet's restrictions. Let him go look
at the river flowing or the bank
of late flowers, there will be one
small fly still among the petals
in whose gauzy wings raised above

its back a rainbow shines. The world
to him is radiant and even the fact
of poverty is wholly without despair.

So it seems until there rouse
to him pictures of the systematically
starved—for a purpose, at the mind's
proposal. What good then the
light winged fly, the flower or
the river—too foul to drink of or
even to bathe in? The 90 story building
beyond the ocean that a rocket
will span for destruction in a matter
of minutes but will not
bring him, in a century, food or
relief of any sort from his suffering.

The world too much with us? Rot!
the world is not half enough with us—
the rot of a potato with
a healthy skin, a rot that is
never revealed till we are about to
eat—and it revolts us. Beauty?
Beauty should make us paupers,
should blind us, rob us—for it
does not feed the sufferer but makes
his suffering a fly-blown putrescence
and ourselves decay—unless
the ecstasy be general.

THE STYLIST

Long time no see.
        —a flash as
from polished steel,
then:

        I've been too
    damned poor to get out

of the woods. I was
expecting you
to come up and bring
me into town.

No answer.

NOTE TO MUSIC:
BRAHMS 1ST PIANO CONCERTO

Of music, in a cavernous house,
we enjoy our humanity the more
being by machine, since it is lost,
survives, is rekindled only
ad interim, pending a willed
refusal: the Demuths, the Sheelers,
the Hartleys, green and gray;
black (the meaning crimson)
are moved likewise in us thereby.

We falter to assurance in despair
hearing the piano pant to
the horns' uncertain blow that
octaves sidelong from the deafened
windows crescendo, rallentando,
diminuendo in wave-like dogmas
we no longer will. Let us sob
and sonnet our dreams, breathing
upon our nails before the savage
snow . . .

THE INJURY

From this hospital bed
I can hear an engine
breathing—somewhere
in the night:

—Soft coal, soft coal,
   soft coal!

And I know it is men
   breathing
shoveling, resting—

—Go about it
the slow way, if you can
find any way—
          Christ!
who's a bastard?
       —quit
and quit shoveling.

A man breathing
    and it quiets and
the puff of steady
work begins
      slowly: Chug.
Chug. Chug. Chug. . . .
    fading off.
Enough coal at least
   for this small job

   Soft! Soft!
—enough for one small
engine, enough for that.

A man shoveling
working and not lying here
   in this
hospital bed—powerless
—with the white-throat
   calling in the
poplars before dawn, his
faint flute-call,
triple tongued, piercing
the shingled curtain
of the new leaves;

drowned out by
car wheels
singing now on the rails,
taking the curve,
slowly,
a long wail,
high pitched:
rounding
the curve—
—the slow way because
(if you can find any way) that is
the only way left now
for you.

THE RED-WING BLACKBIRD

The wild red-wing black-
bird croaks frog-
like though more shrill
as the beads of

his eyes blaze over the
swamp and the o-
dors of the swamp vodka
to his nostrils

A PLACE (ANY PLACE) TO TRANSCEND ALL PLACES

In New York, it is said,
they *do* meet (if that is
what is wanted) talk but
nothing is exchanged
unless that guff
can be retranslated: as
to say, that is not
the end, there are channels
above that, draining
places from which New York

is dignified, created (the
deaf are not tuned in).

A church in New Hampshire
built by its pastor
from his own wood lot. One
black (of course, red)
rose; a fat old woman backing
through a screen door. Two,
from the armpits
down, contrasting in bed,
breathless; a letter from
a ship; leaves filling,
making, a tree (but
wait) not just leaves,
leaves of one design that
make a certain design,
no two alike, not like
the locust either, next in line,
nor the Rose of Sharon, in
the pod-stage, near it—a
tree! Imagine it! Pears
philosophically hard. Nor
thought that is from
branches on a root, from
an acid soil, with scant
grass about the bole
where it breaks through.

New York is built of
such grass and weeds; a modern
tuberculin-tested herd
white-faced behind a
white fence, patient and
uniform; a museum of looks
across a breakfast
table; subways of dreams;
towers of divisions
from thin pay envelopes.
What else is it? And what

else can it be? Sweatshops
and railroad yards at dusk
(puffed up by fantasy
to seem real) what else
can they be budded on
to live a little longer?
The eyes by this
far quicker than the mind.

       —and we have
:Southern writers, foreign
writers, hugging a dis-
tinction, while perspectived
behind them following
the crisis (at home)
peasant loyalties inspire
the avant-garde. Abstractly?
No: That was for something
else. "Le futur!" grimly.
New York? That hodge-podge?
The international city
(from the Bosphorus). Poor
Hoboken. Poor sad
Eliot. Poor memory.

       —and we have
: the memory of Elsa
von Freytag Loringhofen,
a fixation from the street
door of a Berlin
playhouse; all who "wear
their manner too obviously,"
the adopted English (white)
and many others.

       —and we have
: the script writer advising
"every line to be like
a ten word telegram" but
neglecting to add, "to a

child of twelve"—obscene
beyond belief.

Obscene and
abstract as excrement—
that no one wants to own
except the coolie
with a garden of which
the lettuce particularly
depends on it—if you
like lettuce, but
very, very specially, heaped
about the roots for nourishment.

THE OLD HOUSE

Rescued! new-white
(from Time's
dragon: neglect—tastelessness—
the down-beat)

But why?
why the descent into ugliness that
intervened, how
could it have come about,
(the essence—
cluttered with weeds, broken gear
—in a shoddy neighborhood)
something so sound?

—that there should have befallen
such decay, such decay of the senses—
the redundant and expensive,
the useless, the useless rhyme?

Stasis:
a balance of . . .
vacuities, seeking . . . to
achieve . . . by emphasis!

the full sonorities of . . . an
evasion! !

    —lack of
"virtue," the fake castellation, the
sham tower—upon a hidden
weakness of trusses, a whole period
shot to hell out of disrelatedness
to mind, to object association:
            the years following
the Civil War—

    But four
balanced gables, in a *good* old style,
four symmetrical waves,
                well anchored,
turning about the roof's pivot,
simple and direct,
            how could they not
have apprehended it? They could not—
Bitter reminder.

    And then!
out of the air, out of decay, out of
desire, necessity, through
economic press—aftermath of "the bomb"—
a Perseus! rescue comes:

                —the luminous
from "sea wrack," sets it, for itself,
a house almost gone, shining again.

THE THING

    Each time it rings
    I think it is for
    me but it is
    not for me nor for

anyone it merely
rings and we
serve it bitterly
together, they and I

THE MIND HESITANT

Sometimes the river
becomes a river in the mind
or of the mind
or in and of the mind

Its banks snow
the tide falling a dark
rim lies between
the water and the shore

And the mind hesitant
regarding the stream
senses
a likeness which it

will find—a complex
image: something
of white brows
bound by a ribbon

of sooty thought
beyond, yes well beyond
the mobile features
of swiftly

flowing waters, before
the tide will
change
and rise again, maybe

TRAGIC DETAIL

The day before I died
I noticed the maple tree
how its bark curled
against the November blaze

There was some work
to do and three birds
stepped awkwardly abreast
upon the bare lawn

Only the country-woman's
lip soft with down
black as her hair was black
against the white skin

comforted me but the twins
and their sister
excluded me dragging
insistent upon the loose gown.

PHILOMENA ANDRONICO

With the boys busy
at ball
in the worn lot
nearby

She stands in
the short street
reflectively bouncing
the red ball

Slowly
practiced
a little awkwardly
throwing one leg over

(Not as she had done
formerly
screaming and
missing

But slowly
surely) then
pausing throws
the ball

With a full slow
very slow
and easy motion
following through

With a slow
half turn—
as the ball flies
and rolls gently

At the child's feet
waiting—
and yet he misses
it and turns

And runs while she
slowly
regains her former
pose

Then shoves her fingers
up through
her loose short hair
quickly

Draws one stocking
tight and
waiting
tilts

Her hips and
in the warm still
air lets
her arms

Fall
loosely
(waiting)
at her sides

THE CLOUDS

I

Filling the mind
upon the rim of the overarching sky, the horses of
the dawn charge from south to north, gigantic beasts
rearing flame-edged above the pit,
a rank confusion of the imagination still uncured,
a rule, piebald under the streetlamps, reluctant
to be torn from its hold.

       Their flanks still
caught among low, blocking forms their fore-parts
rise lucid beyond this smell of a swamp, a mud
livid with decay and life! turtles
that burrowing among the white roots lift their green
red-striped faces startled before the dawn.

A black flag, writhing and whipping at the staff-head
mounts the sepulcher of the empty bank, fights
to be free . . .

       South to north! the direction
unmistakable, they move, distinct beyond the unclear
edge of the world, clouds! like statues
before which we are drawn—in darkness, thinking of
our dead, unable, knowing no place
where else rightly to lodge them.

Tragic outlines
and the bodies of horses, mindfilling—but
visible! against the invisible; actual against
the imagined and the concocted; unspoiled by hands
and unshaped also by them but caressed by sight only,
moving among them, not that that propels
the eyes from under, while it blinds:

—upon whose backs the dead ride, high!
undirtied by the putridity we fasten upon them—
South to north, for this moment distinct and undeformed,
into the no-knowledge of their nameless destiny.

II

Where are the good minds of past days, the unshorn?
Villon, to be sure, with his
saw-toothed will and testament? Erasmus
who praised folly and

Shakespeare who wrote so that
no school man or churchman could sanction him without
revealing his own imbecility? Aristotle,
shrewd and alone, a onetime herb peddler?

They all, like Aristophanes, knew the clouds and
said next to nothing of the soul's flight
but kept their heads and died—
like Socrates, Plato's better self, unmoved.

Where? They live today in their old state because
of the pace they kept that keeps
them now fresh in our thoughts, their
relics, ourselves: Toulouse-Lautrec, the

deformed who lived in a brothel and painted
the beauty of whores. These were
the truth-tellers of whom we are the sole heirs
beneath the clouds that bring

shadow and darkness full of thought deepened
by rain against the clatter
of an empty sky. But anything to escape humanity!
Now it's spiritualism—again,

as if the certainty of a future life
were any solution to our dilemma: how to get
published not what we write but what we would write were
it not for the laws against libelous truth.

The poor brain unwilling to own the obtrusive body
would crawl from it like a crab and
because it succeeds, at times, in doffing that,
by its wiles of drugs or other "ecstasies," thinks

at last that it is quite free—exulted, scurrying to
some slightly larger shell some snail
has lost (where it will live). And so, thinking,
pretends a mystery! an unbodied

thing that would still be a brain—but no body,
something that does not eat but flies by the propulsions
of pure—what? into the sun itself, illimitedly
and exists so forever, blest, washed, purged

and at ease in non-representational bursts
of shapeless flame, sentient (naturally!)—and keeps
touch with the earth (by former works) at least.
The intellect leads, leads still! Beyond the clouds.

III

(Scherzo)

I came upon a priest once at St. Andrew's
in Amalfi in crimson and gold brocade riding
the clouds of his belief.

It happened that we tourists had intervened
at some mid-moment of the ritual—
tipped the sacristan or whatever it was.

No one else was there—porphyry and alabaster,
the light flooding in scented
with sandalwood—but this holy man

jiggling upon his buttocks to the litany
chanted, in response, by two kneeling altar boys!
I was amazed and stared in such manner

that he, caught half off the earth
in his ecstasy—though without losing a beat—
turned and grinned at me from his cloud.

IV

With each, dies a piece of the old life, which he carries,
a precious burden, beyond! Thus each
is valued by what he carries and that is his soul—
diminishing the bins by that much
unless replenished.

It is that which is the brotherhood:
the old life, treasured. But if they live?
What then?

The clouds remain
—the disordered heavens, ragged, ripped by winds
or dormant, a calligraphy of scaly dragons and bright moths,
of straining thought, bulbous or smooth,
ornate, the flesh itself (in which
the poet foretells his own death); convoluted, lunging upon
a pismire, a conflagration, a . . . .

THE PINK CHURCH
1949

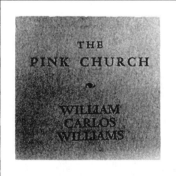

GOLDEN GOOSE CHAP BOOK 1

Published by
Golden Goose Press
Columbus Ohio: 1949

CHORAL: THE PINK CHURCH

Pink as a dawn in Galilee
whose stabbing fingers routed
Aeschylus and murder blinked . . .

—and tho' I remember little
    as names go,
the thrust of that first light
    was to me
    as through a heart
    of jade—
as Chinese as you please
but not by that—remote.

Now,
    the Pink Church
      trembles
to the light (of dawn) again,
    rigors of more
    than sh'd wisely
    be said at one stroke,
singing!
    Covertly.
        Subdued.

    Sing!
transparent to the light
    through which the light
shines, through the stone,
    until
the stone-light glows,
    pink jade
—that is the light and is
    a stone
and is a church—if the image
    hold . . .

as at a breath a face glows
and fades!

Come all ye aberrant,
drunks, prostitutes,
Surrealists—
Gide and—
Proust's memory (in a cork
diving suit
looking under the sea
of silence)
to bear witness:

Man is not sinful . . . unless
he sin!

—Poe, Whitman, Baudelaire
the saints
of this calendar.

Oh ladies whose beds
your
husbands defile! man, man
is the bringer
of pure delights
to you!

Who else?

And there stand
the-banded-together
in the name of
the Philosophy Dep'ts

wondering at the nature
of the stuff
poured into
the urinals
of custom . . .

O Dewey! (John)
  O James! (William)
   O Whitehead!
    teach well!

—above and beyond
  your teaching stands
the Pink Church:
    the nipples of
a woman who never
  bore a
    child . . .

Oh what new vows shall
we swear to make all swearing
futile:
  the fool
  the mentally deranged
  the suicide?

—suckled of its pink delight

And beyond them all whine
the slaughtered, the famished
and the lonely—
  the holy church of
their minds singing madly
  in tune, its stones
sibilant and roaring—

    Soft voiced . . .

To which, double bass:

A torch to a heap
  of new branches
  under the tied feet of
  Michael Servitus:

Be ye therefore perfect
even as your
Father in Heaven
is perfect

And all you liveried bastards,
all (tho' pardon me
all you who come
rightly under that holy
term)

Harken!

—perfect as the pink and
rounded breasts of a virgin!

Scream it in
their stupid ears—
plugged by wads of
newspulp—

Joy! Joy!
—out of Elysium!

—chanted loud as a chorus from
the Agonistes—
Milton, the unrhymer,
singing among
the rest . . .

like a Communist.

THE LION

1

Traffic, the lion, the sophisticate,
facing the primitive, alabaster,

the new fallen snow
stains its chastity the new shade.

Use defames! the attack disturbs our sleep.

This is the color of the road, the color
of the lion, sand color

—to follow the lion, of use or usage,
even to church! the bells achime
above the fallen snow!

—all follow the same road, apace.

2

Winter, the churned snow, the lion
flings the woman, taking her
by the throat upon his gullied
shoulders—shaking the weight fast
and unmolested plunges with her
among the trees—where the whiteness
sparkles—to devour her there:
transit to uses: where the traffic
mounts, a chastity packed with lewdness,
a rule, dormant, against the loosely
fallen snow—the thick muscles
working under the skin, the head
like a tree-stump, gnawing: chastity
to employment, lying down bloodied
to bed together for the last time.

MAMA

Kitten! Kitten! grown woman!
you curl into the pillows
to make a man clamp his jaws
for tenderness over you .

stroking, stroking, the nerves
taut, alert for the swift
counter-slap will make him (you
shall see) bear down hard.

NEW MEXICO

Anger can be transformed
to a kitten—as love
may become a mountain in
the disturbed mind, the
mind that prances like
a horse or nibbles, starts
and stares in the parched
sage of the triple
world—of stone, stone
layered and beaten under
the confessed brilliance
of this desert noon.

A ROSEBUSH IN AN UNLIKELY GARDEN

The flowers are yours
the full blown
the half awakened
yours

who fished heads
and arms on D day in a net
from the bloody
river

The stillness
of this squalid corner this
veined achievement is
yours

SONG

If I
could count the silence
I could sleep, sleep.

But it
is one, one. No head even
to gnaw. Spinning.

If I
could halt the glazed
spinning, surface of glass,

my mind
could shove in its fingers
and break apart

the smooth
singleness of the night—
until sleep dropped as rain

upon me.

THE WORDS, THE WORDS, THE WORDS

The perfume of the iris, sweet citron,
is enhanced by money, the
odor of buckwheat, the woman's odor.
Sand does not chafe, with money.
Sheep fold, horse neigh but money
mollifies it.
Leap or swim
sleep or be drunk in whatever arms
or none
money is the crown

Your eyes, thighs, breasts—rose pointed,
money is their couch, their room,
the light from between lattices . . .

Lady behind the hedge, behind the
wall:
silken limbs, white brow,
money filters in through the shelving
leaves over you

Rise and shake your skirts
to the buttercups, yellow as polished
gold

VENUS OVER THE DESERT

If I do not sin, she said, you shall not
walk in long gowns down stone corridors.
There is no reprieve where there is no fall-
ing off. I lie in your beds all night, from
me you wake and go about your tasks. My flesh
clings to your bones. What use is holiness
unless it affirm my perfections, my breasts,
my thighs which you part, shaking, and my lips
the door to my pleasures? Sin, you call it,
but there cannot be cold unless the heat
has bred it, how can you know otherwise? Love
comfort me in the face of my defeats! Poor
monks, you think you are gentle but I tell you
you kill as sure as shot kills a bird flying.

"I WOULD NOT CHANGE FOR THINE"

Shall I stroke your thighs,
having eaten?
Shall I kiss you,
having drunk?

Or drink to you only

—leaving the poor soul
who lives with her husband

(the truck driver)
three months, to spend
the next six
where she can find it,
dropping the kid
of that abandon in whatever
hospital about the country
will take her?

(both have T.B.)

What course has she
to offer at her academy
that he returns to her
each year to listen,
repeated, to the lectures
of her adventures?
And having drunk avidly
and eaten of the philosophies
of their reunion
—tells her his own . ?

Happy, happy married pair

I should come to you
fasting, my sweet—you
to whom I would send
a rosy wreath not so much
honoring thee as lending it
a hope that there
I might remembered be.

MISTS OVER THE RIVER

Included in *The Clouds:* see p. 135.

THE LOVE CHARM

Take this, the nexus
of unreality,
my head, I detach
it for you. Take it

in your hands, metal
to eat out
the heart, if held
to the heart. Hold it

to your heart
and wait, only wait
the while
its fissions curdle.

POEMS

1949-1953

MAY 1ST TOMORROW

The mind's a queer sponge
             squeeze it and out come bird songs
small leaves highly enameled
          and   .   moments of good reading
(rapidly) *Tuck, tuck, tuck, tuck, tuck!*
           —the mind remembering   .
Not, *not* in flux (that diarrhea)
          but nesting. *Chee woo! Tuck!*
the male mind, nesting: glancing up
          from a letter from a friend   .
asking   .   the mind
          to be   .   squeezed and let
him be the liquor which, when
          we release it, *he* shall be sopped
up, *all* his weight, and
          released again   .   by squeezing.

Full, it molds itself . . .
          like a brown breast, full
not of milk but of what breasts are
          to the eye, hemispherical
(2 would make a sphere)
          to the mind; a view of the mind
that, in a way, gives milk:
          that liquor that minds
feed upon. To feed, to feed *now!*
          Chuck, chuck, chuck. Toe whee. Chuck!
—burdensome as twin stones
          that the mind alone can milk
and give again   .
          Chee woo! etcetera

APRÈS LE BAIN

I gotta
buy me a new
girdle.

(I'll buy
you one) O.K.
(I wish

you'd wig-
gle that way
for me,

I'd be
a happy man)
I GOTTA

wig-
gle for *this*.
(You pig)

SPRING IS HERE AGAIN, SIR.

Goffle brook of a May day
(*Mon cher Cocteau*
qui déjeune des fois
avec Picasso) blossoms
in the manner of antiquity

Which is an obliquity
for the movement
and the sheen of ripples
bridging the gap for
age-old winnowing decay—

from then to now. Which
leaves very little
but the sun and air

unless one should prefer
a pool of human spittle

over which to grieve.
Rhyme it regularly if you
will. I say the night
is not always gay for
an old man who has sinned.

But the brook! is mine
and I must still prefer it
to the summits of Tibet
from which to take off:
—of spring, to the air

for relief! smell of clover,
cherries are ripening.
We lay, Floss and I, on
the grass together, in
the warm air: a bird flew

into a bush, dipped our
hands in the running water—
cold, too cold; but found
it, to our satisfaction,
as in the past, still wet.

THE HARD CORE OF BEAUTY

The most marvelous is not
            the beauty, deep as that is,
but the classic attempt
            at beauty,
at the swamp's center: the
            dead-end highway, abandoned
when the new bridge went in finally.
            There, either side an entry
from which, burned by the sun,
            the paint is peeling—

two potted geraniums
                    Step inside: on a wall, a
painted plaque showing
                    ripe pomegranates
—and, leaving, note
                    down the road—on a thumbnail,
you could sketch it on a thumbnail—
                    stone steps climbing
full up the front to
                    a second floor
minuscule
                    portico
peaked like the palate
                    of a child! God give us again
such assurance.
              There are
                    rose bushes either side
this entrance and plum trees
                    (one dead) surrounded
at the base by worn-out auto-tire
                    casings! for what purpose
but the glory of the Godhead
                    that poked
her twin shoulders, supporting
                    the draggled blondness
of her tresses, from beneath
                    the patient waves.
And we? the whole great world abandoned
                    for nothing at all, intact,
the lost world of symmetry
                    and grace: bags of charcoal
piled deftly under
                    the shed at the rear, the
ditch at the very rear a passageway
                    through the mud,
triumphant! to pleasure,
                    pleasure; pleasure by boat,
a by-way of a Sunday
                    to the smooth river.

TOLSTOY

That art is evil (stale
art, he might have said)
was to his mind as weevil
to the cotton-head

Stale art, like stale fish
stinks (I might have said)
You are aging, Master
Commit yourself to Heaven

CUCHULAIN

I had been his fool
    not a dog
    not his murderer

To court war which I
    redreamed
    —he suffered

To force him backward
    into the sea
    blood of his blood

Blood of my blood in
    tortured
    bewilderment

—his fool, shrewd witted
    to protect
    and beguile him

To read rather
    that which I
    suffered

Not a morose pig
   his doom
      to escape only

My fate—take
   upon myself
      the kindler, the

Match-man, the mind-
   miner, the very
      woman

His life lived in
   me warmed
      at his fires

A power in the night.
   Madman, clown—
      success

TWELVE LINE POEM

Pitiful lovers broken by your loves
the head of a man
the parts disjointed of a woman
unshaved pushing forward

And you? Withdrawn caressive
the thighs limp eyes
filling with tears the lower lip
trembling, why do you try

so hard to be a man? You are
a lover! Why adopt
the reprehensible absurdities of
an inferior attitude?

NUN'S SONG

For the wrongs that women do
we dedicate ourselves, O God, to You
and beg You to believe
that we truly grieve.

Our defects, not fear,
drive us to seek to be so very near
Your loving tenderness
that You may bless

us everlastingly; not dread,
but risen from the sorry dead
that each may be, at Your side
a very bride!

ANOTHER OLD WOMAN

If I could keep her
here, near me
I'd fill her mind
with my thoughts

She would get
their complexion
and live again. But
I could not live

along with her
she would drain me
as sand drains
water. Visions pos-

sess her. Dreams
unblooded walk
her mind. Her mind
does not faint.

Throngs visit her:
We are at war
with Mexico—to
please her fancy—

A cavalry column
is deploying
over a lifeless terrain
—to impress us!

She describes it
her face bemused—
alert to details. They
ride without saddles

tho' she is ig-
norant of the word
"bareback," but knows
accurately that I

am not her son, now,
but a stranger
listening. She
breaks off, her looks

intent, bent
inward, with a curious
glint to her eyes:
They say that

when the fish comes!
(gesture of getting
a strike) it
is a great joy!

WIDE AWAKE, FULL OF LOVE

Being in this stage
I look to the last,

see myself returning:
the seamed face
as of a tired rider
upon a tired horse
coming up . . .

What of your dish-eyes
that have seduced
me? Your voice
whose cello notes
upon the theme have led
me to the music?

I see your neck scrawny
your thighs worn
your hair thinning,
whose round brow
pushes it aside, and
turn again upon
the thought: To migrate

to that South to hop
again upon the shining
grass there
half ill with love
and mope and
will not startle for
the grinning worm

SONG

Pluck the florets from
        a clover head
and suck the honey, sweet.
        The world
will realign itself—ex-
        cluding Russia
and the U.S.A. and planes
        run soon

by atomic power defying
gravity.
Pluck the florets from
a clover head
and suck the honey, sweet.

SONG

Russia! Russia! you might say
and furrow the brow
but I say: There are flowers upon
the R.R. embankment
woven by growing in and out among
the rusted guard cables
lying there in the grass, flowers
daisy shaped, pink
and white in this September glare.
Count upon it there
will be soon a further revolution.

TRANSLATION

There is no distinction in the encounter, Sweet
there is no grace of perfume
to the rose but from us, which we give it
by our loving performance.

Love is tasteless but for the delicate turn
of our caresses. By them
the violet wins its word of love, no mere
scent but a word spoken,

a unique caress. That is the reason I wake
before dawn and crush my pillow:
because of the strangeness of that flower
whose petals hide for me

more than should be spoken, of love
uniting all flowers beyond

caresses, to disclose that fragrance which is
Our Mistress whom we serve.

CONVIVIO

We forget sometimes that no matter what
our quarrels we are the same brotherhood:
the rain falling or the rain withheld,
—berated by women, barroom smells
or breath of Persian roses! our wealth
is words. And when we go down to defeat,
before the words, it is still within and
the concern of, first, the brotherhood.
Which should quiet us, warm and arm us
besides to attack, always attack—but to
reserve our worst blows for the enemy, those
who despise the word, flout it, stem,
leaves and root; the liars who decree laws
with no purpose other than to make a screen
of them for larceny, murder—for our
murder, we who salute the word and would
have it clean, full of sharp movement.

THE RAT

The rat sits up and works his
        moustaches, the ontologic
phenomenon of cheese rifting his
        blood to orgiastic rule.

The tail, epicene in its application,
        the round-file tail,
that fearsome appendage which man
        for all his zest

cannot match—other than conceptu-
        ally, of which his

most thought latterly consists.
   How like this man

the rat is in the ubiquity of his
   deformity: plague
infected fleas come, through
   the connivance of

the San Frigando Chamber of
   Commerce, to infest the very
gophers of Nevada. His wise
   eyes mewing in his

spindle head the rat thrives, well
   suited to a world
conditioned to such human "tropism
   for order" at all cost.

THE HORSE SHOW

Constantly near you, I never in my entire
sixty-four years knew you so well as yesterday
or half so well. We talked. You were never
so lucid, so disengaged from all exigencies
of place and time. We talked of ourselves,
intimately, a thing never heard of between us.
How long have we waited? almost a hundred years.

You said, Unless there is some spark, some
spirit we keep within ourselves, life, a
continuing life's impossible—and it is all
we have. There is no other life, only the one.
The world of the spirits that comes afterward
is the same as our own, just like you sitting
there they come and talk to me, just the same.

They come to bother us. Why? I said. I don't
know. Perhaps to find out what we are doing.
Jealous, do you think? I don't know. I

don't know why they should want to come back.
I was reading about some men who had been
buried under a mountain, I said to her, and
one of them came back after two months,

digging himself out. It was in Switzerland,
you remember? Of course I remember. The
villagers tho't it was a ghost coming down
to complain. They were frightened. They
do come, she said, what you call
my "visions." I talk to them just as I
am talking to you. I see them plainly.

Oh if I could only read! You don't know
what adjustments I have made. All
I can do is to try to live over again
what I knew when your brother and you
were children—but I can't always succeed.
Tell me about the horse show. I have
been waiting all week to hear about it.

Mother darling, I wasn't able to get away.
Oh that's too bad. It was just a show;
they make the horses walk up and down
to judge them by their form. Oh is that
all? I tho't it was something else. Oh
they jump and run too. I wish you had been
there, I was so interested to hear about it.

TWO PENDANTS: FOR THE EARS

I

*The particulars of morning are more to be desired
than night's vague images.*

I dreamed of a tiger, wounded,
lying broken
upon a low parapet

            at least they said
it was a tiger though I never
saw it—more than a shadow—
for the night:

         an open plaza
before the post-office
—but very obscure

        When I arrived
the people were underground
huddled into a group and terrified
from the recent happenings:

a terrific fight, apparently—
between the beast and
a man, its trainer, lying
he also, out there now
horribly wounded—perhaps dead
or exhausted
—during a lull of the encounter,
having defended himself well
             —and bleeding.

No one knew or exactly knew
how the immediate
situation lay.

        Thoughtlessly or at least
without thought, my instinct
took me toward the man. I walked
into the darkness
toward the scene of the fight.

Somewhat to the right
apparently unable to lift itself
and hanging upon
the stone wall, I seemed
to make out the beast and could
hear it panting, heavily

At the same moment,
to the left, on the ground under
the wall, I saw, or
rather heard, the man—or
what I took to be the man. He was
mewing softly, a spasmodic
high pitched sighing—probably
unconscious.

As I got half way out
from the people huddled back of me
to the scene of the conflict
the breathing of the beast stopped
as though the better
for him to listen and I could feel
him watching me.

I paused.

I could
make out nothing clearly and then
did the logical thing: unarmed
I saw that I was helpless and so
turned and walked back to the others.

Has no one notified the police?
I said.

That was the end of the dream.

The yard
from the bathroom window
is another matter:

Here everything
is clear. The wind
sounds, I can make out

the yellow of the flowers—
For half an hour

I do not move.

It is Easter Sunday

The short and brilliantly stabbing grass
(my son went out during the night
                    and has not returned—later
I found that he had returned and had
fallen asleep on the couch downstairs—
his bed was empty)
—marked (plotted) by the squares
and oblongs of the flower beds
                    (beds! beds for the flowers)
the sticks of roses that will later show
brilliant blooms stand out
                              in rows, irregularly

A cloud
unclassic, a white unnamed cloud of
small tufts of white flowers
            light as wishes
(later to give place to red berries
            called service berries)
—a cloud through which the east sun
shines, anonymous
                    (a tree marked
by the practical sense of my countrymen
the shad bush   .   to say
fish are in the river)

                    floating

There are no girls here
                not above
                        virtual infancy

—small white flowers
                shining
                        profusely together

Thousands of glittering small leaves
that no church bell calls to Mass
—but there will be a mass soon
on the weighted branches

       —their smiles vanish
at the age of four. Later they
sob and throw their arms about my
waist, babies I have myself delivered
from their agonized mothers. They
sob and cling to me, their breasts heavy
with milk, pressing my coat and refuse
to let go until their sobs
quiet. Then they smile (at me) through
their tears. But it is only
for a moment— they soon become
women again   .

       The wind howled still at my
bedroom window but here, overlooking the
garden, I no longer hear its howls
nor see it moving   .

       My thoughts
are like the distant smile of a child
who will (never) be a beautiful woman

       like
the distant smile of a woman who
will say:
       —only to keep you a moment
longer. Oh I know I'm a stinker—

       but

only to keep you, it's only
to keep you   .   a few moments

       Let me have a cigarette.

The little flowers
got the names we might bestow now
upon drugs for headaches and obesity.
It is periwinkle time now.

How can you, my countrymen
                              (what bathos
hangs about that title, unwarranted
in good measure but there: a fault
of art)
            how can you permit yourselves
to be so cheated—your incomes
taken away and you, chromium
in your guts (rat poison)
                              until you are swollen
beyond all recognition   .

It is not in a return to the ideals
preserved for us
by primitive peoples that our society
will heal itself of its maladies

We read, after breakfast, Flossie,
our son and I—or rather I read to
them from a friendly poet's translations,
*Plato's Inscription for a Statue
of Pan* (I know no Greek)   He said:

Be still O green cliffs of the Dryads
Still O springs bubbling from the rocks
                              and be still
Many voiced crying of the ewes:
                                    It is Pan
Pan with his sweet pipe:
                              the clever lips run
Over the withed reeds
                              while all about him
Rise from the ground to dance
                              with joyous tread
The nymphs of the water

                              nymphs of the oaken forest
—forgot   .   (baby)
                    but it seems less
out of place than the present, all the
present for all that it is present
                              (baby)

The two or three young fruit trees,
even the old and battered watering can
of characteristic shape
                    (made to pour from the bottom)
are looking up at us   .   I
say "us" but I mean, alas, only me.

                    II

                    E L E N A

          You lean the head forward
          and wave the hand,
          with a smile,
          twinkling the fingers
                    I say to myself
                    Now it is spring
                    Elena is dying

          What snows, what snow
          enchained her—
          she of the tropics
          is melted
                    now she is dying

          The mango, the guava
          long forgot for
          apple and cherry
          wave good-bye
          now it is spring
          Elena is dying
                    Good-bye

You think she's going to die?
said the old boy.
She's not going to die—not now.
In two days she'll be
all right again. When she dies
she'll   .

      If only she wouldn't
exhaust herself, broke in
the sturdy woman, his wife. She
fights so. You can't quieten her.

When she dies she'll go out
like a light. She's done it now
two or three times when
the wife's had her up, absolutely
out. But so far she's always
come out of it.
      Why just an hour ago
she sat up straight on that bed, as
straight as ever I saw her
in the last ten years, straight
as a ram-rod. You wouldn't believe
that would you? She's not
going to die   .   she'll be
raising Cain, looking for her grub
as per usual in the next two
or three days, you wait and see

Listen, I said, I met a man
last night told me what he'd brought
home from the market:

      2 partridges
      2 Mallard ducks
      a Dungeness crab
      24 hours out
      of the Pacific

and 2 live-frozen
trout
from Denmark

What about that?

Elena is dying (I wonder)
willows and pear trees
whose encrusted branches
blossom all a mass
attend her on her way—

a guerdon
                (a garden)
                and cries of children
        indeterminate
Holy, holy, holy

                (no ritual
but fact . in fact)

        until
the end of time (which is now)

How can you weep for her? I
cannot, I her son—though
I could weep for her without
compromising the covenant

        She will go alone.

—or pat to the times: go wept
by a clay statuette
                (if there be miracles)
a broken head of a small
St. Anne who wept at a kiss
from a child:
        She was so lonely   .

And Magazine #1 sues Magazine
#2, no less guilty—for libel
or infringement or dereliction
or confinement   .

Elena is dying (but perhaps
not yet)

Pis-en-lit attend her (I see
the children have been here)

Said Jowles, from under the
Ionian sea: What do you think
about that miracle, Doc?—that
little girl kissing
the head of that statue and making
it cry?

                    I hadn't
seen it.
                    It's in the papers,
tears came out of the eyes.
I hope it doesn't turn
out to be something funny.

Let's see now: St. Anne
is the grandmother of Jesus. So
that makes St. Anne the mother
of the Virgin Mary   .

          M's a great letter, I confided.

What's that? So now it gets
to be Easter—you never know.

          Never. No, never.

The river, throwing off sparks
in a cold world

Is this a private foight
or kin I get into it?

This is a private fight.

Elena is dying.
In her delirium she said
a terrible thing:

Who are you? NOW!
I, I, I, I stammered. I
am your son.

Don't go. I am unhappy.

About what? I said

About what is what.

The woman (who was watching)
added:
She thinks I'm her father.

Swallow it now: she wants
to do it herself.

Let her spit.

At last! she said two days later
coming to herself and seeing me:

—but I've been here
every day, Mother.

Well why don't
they put you where I can see you
then?

She was crying this morning,
said the woman, I'm glad you came.

              Let me clean your
glasses.

              They put them on my nose!
They're trying to make a monkey
out of me.

              Were you thinking
of La Fontaine?

              Can't you give me
something to make me disappear
completely, said she sobbing—but
completely!

              No I can't do that
Sweetheart (You God damned belittling
fool, said I to myself)

There's a little Spanish wine,
pajarete
              p-a-j-a-r-e-t-e
But pure Spanish! I don't suppose
they have it any more.

(The woman started to move her)

But I have to see my child   .

Let me straighten you

I don't want the hand (my hand)
there (on her forehead)
—digging the nail of
her left thumb hard into my flesh,
the back of my own thumb
holding her hand   .   .   .

"If I had a dog ate meat
on Good Friday I'd kill him,"
said someone off to the left

Then after three days:
I'm glad to see you up and doing,
said she to me brightly.

I told you she wasn't going to
die, that was just a remission,
I think you call it, said
the 3 day beard in a soiled
undershirt

I'm afraid I'm not much use
to you, Mother, said I feebly.
I brought you a bottle of wine
—a little late for Easter

Did you? What kind of wine?
A light wine?

Sherry.

What?

Jeres. You know, *jerez.* Here
          (giving it to her)

So big! That will be my baby
now!
      (cuddling it in her arms)
Ave Maria Purissime! It is heavy!
I wonder if I could take
a little glass of it now?

                    Has
she eaten anything yet?

                    Has
she eaten anything yet!

Six oysters—she said
she wanted some fish and that's

all we had. A round
of bread and butter and a
banana   .

              My God!

—two cups of tea and some
ice-cream.

      Now she wants the wine.

Will it hurt her?

              No, I think
nothing will hurt her.

            She's
one of the wonders of the world
I think, said his wife.

            (To make the language
record it, facet to facet
not bored out—
            with an auger.

—to give also the unshaven,
            the rumblings of a
catastrophic past, a delicate
defeat—vivid simulations of
the mystery   .   )

We had leeks for supper, I said
What?

      Leeks! Hulda
gave them to me, they were going
to seed, the rabbits had
eaten everything else. I never

tasted better—from Pop's old
garden   .

     Pop's old what?

I'll have to clean out her ears.

So my year is ended. Tomorrow
it will be April, the glory gone
the hard-edged light elapsed. Were
it not for the March within me,
the intensity of the cold sun, I
could not endure the drag
of the hours opposed to that weight,
the profusion to come later, that
comes too late. I have already
swum among the bars, the angular
contours, I have already lived
the year through   .

     Elena is dying

The canary, I said, comes and sits
on our table in the morning
at breakfast, I mean walks about
on the table with us there
and pecks at the table-cloth

     He must
be a smart little bird

     Good-bye!

THE SALE

Why should I, who know the cost so well,
Denounce the sale if you contrive to sell?

And why, overriding my extreme objections
Should you, for that, be forfeit my affections?

You are yourself and shall remain so still
And I be I, come world end when it will.

ALL THAT IS PERFECT IN WOMAN

The symbol of war, a war
fast accomplished
flares in all our faces
an alcoholic flame—

Miami sunlight:
the pattern of waves
mottled with foam
against a blond day!

The fish scream
in soundless agony
trapped by its
sulphuric acid—

a blow-torch flame
at exorbitant cost
virginity
longing for snow and

a quiet life
that will (rightly)
blossom as
a mangled corpse:

Our own Joppolo Schmidt
the G.I. Joe
acted by himself,
a pathetic scene laid

upon thin slices
of sympathy, a snack

between halves
to rouse a smile.

And in our mouths!
a foot minus three toes—
In our embraces

a head partly scorched,
hairless and with
no nose! Between

the thighs a delicious
lung with entrails
and a tongue or gorget!

Blithe spirit! Monody
with feces—you
must sing of her and

behold the overpowering
fetor of her
girlish breasts and breath:

tumbled seas,
washing waves, the grave's
grandfather.

Let us praise! praise
the dreadful symbol of
carnivorous sex—

The gods live!
severally amongst us—
This is their familiar!

—whose blue eyes
and laughing mouth affirm
the habeas corpus
of our resignation:

Oh Lorca, Lorca—
shining singer if you
could have been
alive for this!

At five in the afternoon.

—fecund and jocund
are familiar to the sea
and what dangles, lacerant,
under the belly of
the Portuguese Man O'War is also
familiar to the sea, familiar
to the sea, the sea.

AN ETERNITY

Come back, Mother, come back from
the dead—not to "Syria," not there
but hither—to this place.

You are old, Mother, old
and almost cold, come back from
the dead—where I cannot yet join you.
Wait awhile, wait a little while.
Like Todhunter
let us give up rhyme. This
winter moonlight is a bitter thing,
I like it no better than you do.
Let us wait
for some darker moment of the moon.

At ninety the strangeness of death
is upon you. I have been to all
corners of the mind. What gift
can I bring you but luxury and that
you have taught me to despise. I
turn my face to the wall,

revert to my beginnings and turn
my face also to the wall.

And yet, Mother, that isn't true.
—the night, the night we face
is black but of no more weight than
the day—the day we faced and were
defeated and yet lived
to face the night in which
the fair moon shines—its continents
visible to the naked eye! Naked
is a good word in that context
—makes the night light! light as
a feather (in the night!)

The soul, my dear, is paramount,
the soul of things
that makes the dead moon shine.

Frankly, I do not love you.

All I can see (by the moon's flame)
whatever answer
there may be otherwise, *that* we know,
is abandoned

I remember how at eighty-five
you battled through the crisis and
                    survived!

I suppose, in fact I know,
you've never heard of Shapley—
an astronomer. Now there's a man—
the best   .   .

                    Not like Flammarion,
your old favorite, who wanted
to popularize astronomy, Shapley's
not like Flammarion

You preceded him.

It is the loveless soul, the soul
of things that has surpassed
our loves. In this—you live,
Mother, live in me   .
                                                always.

THE THREE GRACES

We have the picture of you in mind,
when you were young, posturing
(for a photographer) in scarves
(if you could have done it) but now,
for none of you is immortal, ninety-
three, the three, ninety and three,
Mary, Ellen and Emily, what
beauty is it clings still about you?
Undying? Magical? For there is still
no answer, why we live or why
you will not live longer than I
or that there should be an answer why
any should live and whatever other
should die. Yet you live. You live
and all that can be said is that
you live, time cannot alter it—
and as I write this Mary has died.

3 A.M.
THE GIRL WITH THE HONEY COLORED HAIR

Everyone looked and, passing, revealed
himself
by the light of her hair heavy
upon her shoulders

—the haggard drunk
holding onto the backs of the seats,

face tense of a fixed purpose
toward the toilet

—the savage-looking female wearing
a picture hat and
mascara, hard eyes. And the two
colored women:

an older in a small beret and a younger
in slicked glossy hair
sitting,
for protection and with side-

long looks, close to her friend—all
were affected as she
turned frightened to address
me, pitifully alone.

THE SELF

The poem
is a discipline
What you need
to sober you
is what you have

Your children

Let them
children
teach you

the peach flower
the grape
globular locks
curling pathetically about
the temples
their eyes
their rosy cheeks

the poem
laid crudely
delicately
before you.

MOON AND STARS

January! The beginning!
A moon
scoured by the wind
calls

from its cavern. A vacant
eye
stares. The wind
howls.

Among bones in rose flesh
singing
wake the stormy
stars.

THE GIRL

The wall, as I watched, came neck-high
to her walking difficultly
seaward of it over sand and stones. She

made the effort, mounted it while I
had my head turned, I merely
saw her on top at the finish rolling

over. She stood up dusted off her skirt
then there lifted her feet
unencumbered to skip dancing away

POEM

Looking up, of a sudden,
my old eyes saw
the new moon in the sky

But it was of my eyes,
a jigging star.
No moon was in the sky

AND WHO DO YOU THINK "THEY" ARE?

The day when the under-cover writings
of the Russians are in, that day
we'll have an anthology, all around,
to knock their heads off.

War will grow sick, puke its guts
and if, dog-like, it wants to lick up
that, let it (after we have
put poison in it) for good and all.

THE END OF THE ROPE

Paper by Maillol, no kiddin'
made by his own hand—for cash—
view by New Jersey (out of the studio window)
Sun—by God, no kiddin'.
The ladies coming. Hurry!

Whitman—not gone—
not at the end of his rope
—that's jewel weed out there not lamb's quarters

Let's say we've a little unraveled
the end of the rope
and go on from there.   Walt, Ben
See you again   Some day

THE GENTLE REJOINDER

These are the days I want to
give up my job and join
the old men I once saw
on the wharf at Villefranche
fishing for sea-snails,
with a split stick,
in the shallow water—

           I know
something else you could catch,
she said, in the spring
as easily, if you
wanted to. But you probably
don't want to, do you?

THE WOODPECKER

Innocence! Innocence is the condition of heaven.
Only in that which we do not yet know shall we
be fêted, fed. That is to say, with ceremony. The
unknown is our refuge toward which we hurtle. For
even tho', lacking parachute, we be flattened
upon the earth it will not be the same earth we left
to fly upward. To seek what? There is nothing
there. It is not even the unknown for us now. But
we never knew the earth so solidly as when we were
crushed upon it. From a height we fall, innocent,
to our deaths.

           I'd rather in the November
be a woodpecker of the woods. A cry, a movement,
red dabbled, among the bare branches. A light, a
destination where destinations are endless and
the beetle the end of flight. Fed and the ceremony
unwitnessed other than by the lichened rocks, the
dry leaves and the upright bodies of the trees.
It is innocence flings the black and white body

through the air, innocence guides him. Flight
means only desire and desire the end of flight,
stabbing there with a barbed tongue which *succeeds!*

BALLAD OF FAITH

No dignity without chromium
No truth but a glossy finish
If she purrs she's virtuous
If she hits ninety she's pure

ZZZZZZZZZ!
Step on the gas, brother
(the horn sounds hoarsely)

THE NON-ENTITY

The rusty-gold green trees
cone-shaped, animadvertent
cissiform, cramped

—a maple solitary
upon the wood's face. Behind
it an ocean roars, rocks

the mind, janistically
pours autumn, shaking nerves
of color over it

CHILDE HAROLD TO THE ROUND TOWER CAME

Obviously, in a plutocracy
the natural hero
is the man who robs a bank

Look at him, the direct eyes,
the forehead! Clearly
he is intelligent—but

with humor. Half suppressed
it leaps from his eyes
crinkling the skin under them.

His face has two sides,
brows that bespeak courage—
directed by research, that

purple word of the elite!
And love! bulbous (in
the lower lip) with desire

as in all full blooded
creatures at their best, affec-
tionate but alas, guarded to

survive. To survive is
the crown of virtue in this
world of finance. He will be

groined like a manager,
but more humane, the eyes
bluer, he will have

a more piercing look, greater
dash, be more freehanded
—the face deeper lined.

What *must* he be who is
their master? makes them shake,
steel themselves against

him at great cost, a whole
fleet of armored trucks, in
which, snails, oh what

poverty of means lies encased
there to insure
against his bounty . . .

IO BACCHO!

God created alcohol
and it wasn't privately for the Russians
    God created alcohol
and it wasn't for Dr. Goldsmith

    It was for Mrs. Reiter
who is bored with having children
        though she loves them.
God created alcohol to release
        and engulf us. Shall I
say it is the only evidence of God
        in this environment?

    Mrs. R. doesn't drink
but I drink and I told the angel,
        God created alcohol!
—if it weren't for that I'd say
        there wasn't Any—
thinking of Mrs. R. who is
        one eighth American Indian
and what with the pain in her guts
        stands like an Indian
        "If I had the strength"
Why should I bother to tell you?

    God created alcohol
Shall I swoon like Mr. Keats?
        and not from looking
at a Grecian urn. God created alcohol
        to allay us

JINGLE

There ought to be a wedding
a wedding, a wedding!
There ought to be a wedding
between Russia and the United States

There'd be some pretty children
some children, some children
There'd be some pretty children
to cheer the world along

The classes liquidated
liquidated, liquidated
the rich would be supplanted
by the meek enriched by love

And we'd vote the tyrant under
tyrant under, tyrant under
by a landslide, by a landslide
when we would. We would, we would!

EVERY DAY

Every day that I go out to my car
I walk through a garden
and wish often that Aristotle
had gone on
to a consideration of the dithyrambic
poem—or that his notes had survived

Coarse grass mars the fine lawn
as I look about right and left
tic toc—
And right and left the leaves
upon the yearling peach grow along
the slender stem

No rose is sure. Each is one rose
and this, unlike another,
opens flat, almost as a saucer without
a cup. But it is a rose, rose
pink. One can feel it turning slowly
upon its thorny stem

THE COMPLEXITY

Strange that their dog
should look like the woman:
the eyes close together
the jowls prominent. But
the man loves the dog too,
an area curious in its
resemblance to that other,
a pleasant change
from the woman. Volpe
the man's name is. Wolf he
calls himself, a kindly
fellow who sells Italian
goat cheese . . .

A NOTE

When the cataract dries up, my dear
all minds attend it.
There is nothing left. Neither sticks
nor stones can build it up again
nor old women with their rites of green twigs

Bending over the remains, a body
struck through the breast bone
with a sharp spear—they have borne him
to an ingle at the wood's edge
from which all maidenhood is shent

—though he roared
once the cataract is dried up and done.
What rites can do to keep alive
the memory of that flood they will do
then bury it, old women that they are,
secretly where all male flesh is buried.

DRUGSTORE LIBRARY

That's the kind of books
they read.
They love their filth.
Knee boots
and they want to hear
it suck
when they pull 'em out

THE R R BUMS

Their most prized possession—
their liberty—
          Hands behind a coat
shiny green. Tall, the eyes
downcast—
          Sunlight through a clutter of
wet clouds, lush weeds—
                 The oriole!
Hungry as an oriole.

INCOGNITO

I want to be where Fordie is
(Bury my face in the dirt
—like a Maori, those

who slash their faces
with knives, carving new lips,
a nose dismembered

the cheeks scar-coils,
the forehead seamed—to
live (for such a face is

incognito, the man gone)
like Fordie, no man now but
an art for Cherubim

and Seraphim to reface
with words, intaglio. There
Fordie sings to the harp, sighing.

TURKEY IN THE STRAW

I'll put this in my diary:

On my 65th birthday
I kissed her while she pissed

(Your thighs are apple trees
whose blossoms touch the sky!)

On my 65th birthday
I tussled her breasts.
She didn't even turn away
        but smiled!

It's your 65th birthday!

(I kissed her while she pissed)

THE LESSON

    The hydrangea
    pink cheeked nods its head
    a paper brain
    without a skull

    a brain intestined
    to the invisible root
    where
    beside the rose and acorn

    thought lies communal
    with
    the brooding worm
    True but the air

remains
the wanton the dancing
that
holding enfolds it

a flower
aloof
Flagrant as a flag
it shakes that seamy head

or
snaps it drily
from the anchored stem
and sets it rolling

TO CLOSE

Will you please rush down and see
ma baby. You know, the one I talked
to you about last night

What was that?

Is this the baby specialist?

Yes, but perhaps you mean my son,
can't you wait until   .   ?

I, I, I don't think it's brEAthin'

DEATH

So this is death that I
refuse to rouse and write
but prefer to lie here
half asleep with a mind

not aflame but merely
flickering lacking breath

to fan it—from
the comfortable dark womb

THE MARRIAGE OF SOULS

That heat!
That terrible heat
That coldness!
That terrible coldness

Alone!
At the flame's tip
Alone!
In the sparkling crystal

So they stay
Adjacent
Like to like
In terrible isolation

Like to like
In terrible intimacy
Unfused
And unfusing

HOW BAD IT IS TO SAY:

I cannot sing
I cannot sing of cash the king
But I would sing
of cash the king if I could sing
of anything

King cash is got by fear with child
innocence defiled irrational
unreconciled

CHRISTMAS 1950

The stores
guarded
by the lynx-eyed
dragon

money
humbly
offer their
flowers.

Kalenchios.
Spanish?
No
they originated

in Germany.
They
bloom so
long!

They're
very easy
to take care of
too

In spring
you
can put them
out

side
and they'll
thrive
there also.

JUNE 9

That profound cleft
at whose bottom
is the surface
          where we would hide

Clap! clap! claps
at us
not merrily
but as a catbird calls

—not of Athens
not out of Athens but
from a privet hedge
here!

drenched with that tone
of dread we feel
          (bred of the newspapers
          What bread!)
generally

How can we love
hearing that cry always
in our ears
          half drowned out by

roar of trucks
and motor cars? Our bottoms
          ache from the heat

STILL LIFE

Astride the boney jointed ridge
that lifts and falls
to which

in pain and ecstasy the hand
is lifted for assurance
ride

the tender pointed breasts
and there in women when
they are young

they ride twin fountains to
the whole dry world's gaping
misery

DECEMBER

White rose your sea shell
petals falling
fill the world of
death aflame

Burn aromatically!
singing bright eyed
silver bird
of fire. Phoenix!

it is you! Beat the air
of ice! Mend
the glass fallen
shattered to the ground.

FRAGMENT

My God, Bill, what have you done?

What do you think I've done? I've
opened up the world.

Where did you get them? Marvelous
beautiful!

Where does all snot come from? Under
the nose,

Yea-uh?

—the gutter, where everything comes
from, the manure heap.

MISTRUST OF THE BELOVED

At the height of love
a darkness intervenes:
I hated you the whole
first year.

It will reawaken.
Be patient. (Ah but what
of the need to be
patient?)

It will reawaken by
somersaults
and see-saws, your hatred
will reawaken.

PASSER DOMESTICUS

Shabby little bird
I suppose it's
the story every-
where, if you're

domestic you're drab.
Peep peep!
the nightingale
's your cousin but

these flagrant
amours get you no-

where. Dull
to the eye you have

crept in unmolested.

DESCENT

From disorder (a chaos)
order grows
—grows fruitful.
The chaos feeds it. Chaos
feeds the tree.

THE WRONG DOOR

Gi' me a reefer, Lawd
cause I wan' to think different
I wan' to think
all around this subject

I wan' to think
I wan' to think where I is
an' I wan' to think my way out
of where I is by a new door

PATERSON, BOOK V: THE RIVER OF HEAVEN

Of asphodel, that greeny flower, the least,
        that is a simple flower
                like a buttercup upon its
branching stem, save
        that it's green and wooden
              We've had a long life
and many things have happened in it.
        There are flowers also
              in hell. So today I've come
to talk to you about them, among

other things, of flowers
>that we both love, even
of this poor, colorless
>thing which no one living
>>prizes but the dead see
and ask among themselves,
>What do we remember that was shaped
>>as this thing
is shaped? while their eyes
>fill
>>with tears. By which
and by the weak wash of crimson
>colors it, the rose
>>is predicated

THE PROBLEM

How to fit
>an old brownstone church
>>among a group
of modern office buildings:
>The feat stands,
>>so that the argument
must be after the fact.
>We can learn from it
>>how—
if it is not too late—
>to conduct
>>our lives.
Unlike the Acropolis,
>on which there is
>>no destructive pressure
but time,
>this building
>>is threatened
from all sides.
>What is it
>>that has made
its fragile masonry,

four-square,
        simple in design,
so comparatively
        indestructible?
          It does not lodge,
per se,
        in the materials.
          Yet,
that is,
        precisely,
          the point. Where else,
if not in the materials,
        does it lodge?
          Strong forces,
not necessarily of evil,
        are involved.
          But this building
peacefully
        stands.
          Witness merely how
in the morning light
        it preserves itself,
          how confidently,
and without strain,
        it faces the world.
          As if,
and indeed it is so,
        should it be tumbled down,
          nothing
could replace it.

THE CLOCK OF THE YEARS

Every man
is his own clock
  Tic toc
he may rise
by the sun
and go to sleep

with the stars
    Tic toc
but if he
take stock
and come to knock
at fate's door
he may find
that he himself
has sprung the lock
against himself.
Useless
to knock
now, the door
will not open—
save only
at the shock
of love,
to deliver him
from that block,
unlock
his heart and
set it beating again:
    Tic toc
    Tic toc
    tic toc!

THE DESERT MUSIC
1954

THE DESERT MUSIC

AND OTHER POEMS BY

WILLIAM CARLOS WILLIAMS

RANDOM HOUSE · NEW YORK

THE DESCENT

The descent beckons
        as the ascent beckoned.
                Memory is a kind
of accomplishment,
        a sort of renewal
              even
an initiation, since the spaces it opens are new places
        inhabited by hordes
              heretofore unrealized,
of new kinds—
        since their movements
              are toward new objectives
(even though formerly they were abandoned).

No defeat is made up entirely of defeat—since
the world it opens is always a place
        formerly
              unsuspected. A
world lost,
        a world unsuspected,
              beckons to new places
and no whiteness (lost) is so white as the memory
of whiteness   .

With evening, love wakens
        though its shadows
              which are alive by reason
of the sun shining—
        grow sleepy now and drop away
              from desire   .

Love without shadows stirs now
        beginning to awaken

as night
advances.

The descent
      made up of despairs
          and without accomplishment
realizes a new awakening:
         which is a reversal
of despair.
       For what we cannot accomplish, what
is denied to love,
      what we have lost in the anticipation—
        a descent follows,
endless and indestructible   .

TO DAPHNE AND VIRGINIA

The smell of the heat is boxwood
     when rousing us
        a movement of the air
stirs our thoughts
     that had no life in them
        to a life, a life in which
two women agonize:
     to live and to breathe is no less.
       Two young women.
The box odor
     is the odor of that of which
       partaking separately,
each to herself
     I partake also
       .   .   separately.

Be patient that I address you in a poem,
     there is no other
       fit medium.
The mind
     lives there. It is uncertain,
       can trick us and leave us

agonized. But for resources
          what can equal it?
                   There is nothing. We
should be lost
          without its wings to
               fly off upon.

The mind is the cause of our distresses
          but of it we can build anew.
                   Oh something more than
it flies off to:
          a woman's world,
                   of crossed sticks, stopping
thought. A new world
          is only a new mind.
                   And the mind and the poem
are all apiece.
          Two young women
               to be snared,
odor of box,
          to bind and hold them
                   for the mind's labors.

All women are fated similarly
          facing men
                   and there is always
another, such as I,
          who loves them,
                   loves all women, but
finds himself, touching them,
          like other men,
                   often confused.

I have two sons,
          the husbands of these women,
               who live also
in a world of love,
          apart.
               Shall this odor of box in
               the heat

not also touch them
>   fronting a world of women
>>   from which they are
debarred
>   by the very scents which draw them on
>>   against easy access?

In our family we stammer unless,
>   half mad,
>>   we come to speech at last   .

And I am not
>   a young man.
>>   My love encumbers me.
It is a love
>   less than
>>   a young man's love but,
like this box odor
>   more penetrant, infinitely
>>   more penetrant,
in that sense not to be resisted.

There is, in the hard
>   give and take
>>   of a man's life with
>   a woman
a thing which is not the stress itself
>   but beyond
>>   and above
that,
>   something that wants to rise
>>   and shake itself
free. We are not chickadees
>   on a bare limb
>>   with a worm in the mouth.
The worm is in our brains
>   and concerns them
>>   and not food for our
offspring, wants to disrupt
>   our thought

and throw it
to the newspapers
or anywhere.
There is, in short,
a counter stress,
born of the sexual shock,
which survives it
consonant with the moon,
to keep its own mind.
There is, of course,
more.
Women
are not alone
in that. At least
while this healing odor is abroad
one can write a poem.

Staying here in the country
on an old farm
we eat our breakfasts
on a balcony under an elm.
The shrubs below us
are neglected. And
there, penned in,
or he would eat the garden,
lives a pet goose who
tilts his head
sidewise
and looks up at us,
a very quiet old fellow
who writes no poems.
Fine mornings we sit there
while birds
come and go.
A pair of robins
is building a nest   .
for the second time
this season. Men
against their reason
speak of love, sometimes,

when they are old. It is
all they can do   .
                or watch a heavy goose
                    who waddles, slopping
                    noisily in the mud of
                    his pool.

THE ORCHESTRA

The precise counterpart
        of a cacophony of bird calls
                lifting the sun almighty
into his sphere: wood-winds
        clarinet and violins
                sound a prolonged A!
Ah! the sun, the sun! is about to rise
        and shed his beams
                as he has always done
upon us all,
        drudges and those
                who live at ease,
women and men,
        upon the old,
                upon children and the sick
who are about to die and are indeed
        dead in their beds,
                to whom his light
is forever lost. The cello
        raises his bass note
                manfully in the treble din:
Ah, ah and ah!
        together, unattuned
                seeking a common tone.
Love is that common tone
        shall raise his fiery head
                and sound his note.

The purpose of an orchestra
        is to organize those sounds

and hold them
to an assembled order   .
            in spite of the
                    "wrong note." Well, shall we
think or listen? Is there a sound addressed
            not wholly to the ear?
                    We half close
our eyes. We do not
            hear it through our eyes.
                    It is not
a flute note either, it is the relation
            of a flute note
                    to a drum. I am wide
awake. The mind
            is listening. The ear
                    is alerted. But the ear
in a half-reluctant mood
            stretches
                    .   .   and yawns.

And so the banked violins
            in three tiers
                    enliven the scene,
pizzicato. For a short
            memory or to
                    make the listener listen
the theme is repeated
            stressing a variant:
                    it is a principle of music
to repeat the theme. Repeat
            and repeat again,
                    as the pace mounts. The
theme is difficult   .
            but no more difficult
                    than the facts to be
resolved. Repeat
            and repeat the theme
                    and all it develops to be
until thought is dissolved
            in tears.

Our dreams
have been assaulted
by a memory that will not
sleep. The
French horns
interpose
.   .   their voices:
I love you. My heart
is innocent. And this
the first day of the world!

Say to them:
"Man has survived hitherto because he was too ignorant
to know how to realize his wishes. Now that he can realize
them, he must either change them or perish."

Now is the time   .
in spite of the "wrong note"
I love you. My heart is
innocent.
And this the first
(and last) day of the world

The birds twitter now anew
but a design
surmounts their twittering.
It is a design of a man
that makes them twitter.
It is a design.

FOR ELEANOR AND BILL MONAHAN

Mother of God! Our Lady!
the heart
is an unruly Master:
Forgive us our sins
as we
forgive
those who have sinned against
us.

We submit ourselves
to Your rule
as the flowers in May
submit themselves to
Your Holy rule—against
that impossible springtime
when men
shall be the flowers
spread at your feet.

As far as spring is
from winter
so are we
from you now. We have not come
easily
to your environs
but painfully
across sands
that have scored our
feet. That which we have suffered
was for us
to suffer. Now,
in the winter of the year,
the birds who know how
to escape suffering
by flight
are gone. Man alone
is that creature who
cannot escape suffering
by flight   .

I do not come to you
save that I confess
to being
half man and half
woman. I have seen the ivy
cling
to a piece of crumbled
wall so that
you cannot tell

by which either
stands: this is to say
if she to whom I cling
is loosened both
of us go down.

Mother of God
I have seen you stoop
to a merest flower
and raise it
and press it to your cheek.
I could have called out
joyfully
but you were too far off.
You are a woman and
it was
a woman's gesture.

You have no lovers now
in the bare skies
to bring you flowers,
to whisper to you
under a hedge
howbeit
you are young
and fit to be loved
I declare it boldly
with my heart
in my teeth
and my knees knocking
together. Yet I declare
it, and by God's word
it is no lie. Make us
humble and obedient to His rule.

There are men
who as they live
fling caution to the
wind and women praise them
and love them for it.

                              Cruel as the claws of
a cat   .   .

The moon which
                they have vulgarized recently
                            is still
your planet
                as it was Dian's before
                            you. What
do they think they will attain
                by their ships
                            that death has not
already given
                them? Their ships
                            should be directed
inward upon   .   But I
                am an old man. I
                            have had enough.

The female principle of the world
                is my appeal
                            in the extremity
to which I have come.
                O clemens! O pia! O dolcis!
                            Maria!

TO A DOG INJURED IN THE STREET

It is myself,
                not the poor beast lying there
                            yelping with pain
that brings me to myself with a start—
                as at the explosion
                            of a bomb, a bomb that has laid
all the world waste.
                I can do nothing
                            but sing about it
and so I am assuaged
                from my pain.

A drowsy numbness drowns my sense
            as if of hemlock
                        I had drunk. I think
of the poetry
            of René Char
                        and all he must have seen
and suffered
            that has brought him
                        to speak only of
sedgy rivers,
            of daffodils and tulips
                        whose roots they water,
even to the free-flowing river
            that laves the rootlets
                        of those sweet-scented flowers
that people the
            milky

                  way   .

I remember Norma
            our English setter of my childhood
                        her silky ears
and expressive eyes.
            She had a litter
                        of pups one night
in our pantry and I kicked
            one of them
                        thinking, in my alarm,
that they
            were biting her breasts
                        to destroy her.

I remember also
            a dead rabbit
                        lying harmlessly
on the outspread palm
            of a hunter's hand.
                        As I stood by
watching
            he took a hunting knife

and with a laugh
thrust it
up into the animal's private parts.
I almost fainted.

Why should I think of that now?
The cries of a dying dog
are to be blotted out
as best I can.
René Char
you are a poet who believes
in the power of beauty
to right all wrongs.
I believe it also.
With invention and courage
we shall surpass
the pitiful dumb beasts,
let all men believe it,
as you have taught me also
to believe it.

THE YELLOW FLOWER

What shall I say, because talk I must?
That I have found a cure
for the sick?
I have found no cure
for the sick   .
but this crooked flower
which only to look upon
all men
are cured. This
is that flower
for which all men
sing secretly their hymns
of praise. This
is that sacred
flower!

Can this be so?
   A flower so crooked
     and obscure? It is
a mustard flower
   and not a mustard flower,
     a single spray
topping the deformed stem
   of fleshy leaves
     in this freezing weather
under glass.

An ungainly flower and
   an unnatural one,
     in this climate; what
can be the reason
   that it has picked me out
     to hold me, openmouthed,
rooted before this window
   in the cold,
     my will
drained from me
   so that I have only eyes
     for these yellow,
twisted petals . ?

That the sight,
   though strange to me,
     must be a common one,
is clear: there are such flowers
   with such leaves
     native to some climate
which they can call
   their own.

But why the torture
   and the escape through
     the flower? It is
as if Michelangelo
   had conceived the subject
     of his *Slaves* from this

—or might have done so.
        And did he not make
            the marble bloom? I
am sad
        as he was sad
            in his heroic mood.
But also
        I have eyes
            that are made to see and if
they see ruin for myself
        and all that I hold
            dear, they see
also
        through the eyes
            and through the lips
and tongue the power
        to free myself
            and speak of it, as
Michelangelo through his hands
        had the same, if greater,
            power.

Which leaves, to account for,
        the tortured bodies
            of
the slaves themselves
        and
            the tortured body of my flower
which is not a mustard flower at all
        but some unrecognized
            and unearthly flower
for me to naturalize
        and acclimate
            and choose it for my own.

THE HOST

According to their need,
        this tall Negro evangelist

(at a table separate from the
rest of his party);
these two young Irish nuns
(to be described subsequently);
and this white-haired Anglican
have come witlessly
to partake of the host
laid for them (and for me)
by the tired waitresses.

It is all
(since eat we must)
made sacred by our common need.
The evangelist's assistants
are most open in their praise
though covert
as would be seemly
in such a public
place. The nuns
are all black, a side view.
The cleric,
his head bowed to reveal
his unruly poll
dines alone.

My eyes are restless.
The evangelists eat well,
fried oysters and what not
at this railway restaurant. The Sisters
are soon satisfied. One
on leaving,
looking straight before her under steadfast brows,
reveals
blue eyes. I myself
have brown eyes
and a milder mouth.

There is nothing to eat,
seek it where you will,
but of the body of the Lord.

The blessed plants
      and the sea, yield it
            to the imagination
intact. And by that force
      it becomes real,
            bitterly
to the poor animals
      who suffer and die
            that we may live.

The well-fed evangels,
         the narrow-lipped and bright-eyed nuns,
            the tall,
white-haired Anglican,
      proclaim it by their appetites
            as do I also,
chomping with my worn-out teeth:
      the Lord is my shepherd
            I shall not want.

No matter how well they are fed,
      how daintily
            they put the food to their lips,
it is all
      according to the imagination!
Only the imagination
      is real! They have imagined it,
            therefore it is so:
of the evangels,
      with the long legs characteristic of the race—
            only the docile women
of the party smiled at me
      when, with my eyes
            I accosted them.
The nuns—but after all
      I saw only a face, a young face
            cut off at the brows.
It was a simple story.
      The cleric, plainly
            from a good school,

interested me more,
        a man with whom I might
                carry on a conversation.

No one was there
        save only for
                the food. Which I alone,
being a poet,
        could have given them.
                But I
had only my eyes
        with which to speak.

DEEP RELIGIOUS FAITH

Past death
        past rainy days
                or the distraction
of lady's-smocks all silver-white;
        beyond the remote borders
                of poetry itself
if it does not drive us,
        it is vain.
                Yet it is
that which made El Greco
        paint his green and distorted saints
                and live
lean.
        It is what in life drives us
                to praise music
and the old
        or sit by a friend
                in his last hours.

All that which makes the pear ripen
        or the poet's line
                come true!
Invention is the heart of it.

Without the quirks
      and oddnesses of invention
          the paralytic is confirmed
in his paralysis,
      it is from a northern
          and half-savage country
where the religion
      is hate.
          There
the citizens are imprisoned.
      The rose
          may not be worshipped
or the poet look to it
      for benefit.

In the night a
      storm of gale proportions came
      up.
          No one was there to envisage
a field of daisies!
      There were bellowings
          and roarings
from a child's book
      of fairy tales,
          the rumble
of a distant bombing
      —or of a bee!
          Shame on our poets,
they have caught the prevalent fever:
      impressed
          by the "laboratory,"
they have forgot
      the flower!
          which goes beyond all
laboratories!
      They have quit the job
          of invention. The
imagination has fallen asleep
      in a poppy-cup.

THE MENTAL HOSPITAL GARDEN

It is far to Assisi,
　　　　but not too far:
　　　　　　　Over this garden,
brooding over this garden,
　　　　there is a kindly spirit,
　　　　　　　brother to the poor
and who is poorer than he
　　　who is in love
　　　　　　when birds are nesting
in the spring of the year?
　　　They came
　　　　　　to eat from his hand
who had nothing,
　　　and yet
　　　　　　from his plenty
he fed them all.
　　　All mankind
　　　　　　grew to be his debtors,
a simple story.
　　　Love is in season.

At such a time,
　　　hyacinth time
　　　　　in
the hospital garden,
　　　the time
　　　　　　of the coral-flowered
and early salmon-pink
　　　clusters, it is
　　　　　　the time also of
abandoned birds' nests
　　　before
　　　　　　the sparrows start
　　　　　　to tear them apart
against the advent of that bounty
　　　from which
　　　　　　they will build anew.

All about them
          on the lawns
                    the young couples
embrace   .
          as in a tale
                    by Boccaccio.
They are careless
          under license of the disease
                    which has restricted them
to these grounds.
          St. Francis forgive them
                    and all lovers
whoever they may be.
          They have seen
                    a great light, it
springs from their own bawdy foreheads.
          The light
                    is sequestered there
by these enclosing walls.
          They are divided
                    from their fellows.
It is a bounty
          from a last year's bird's nest.
                    St. Francis,
who befriended the wild birds,
          be their aid,
                    those who
have nothing,
          and live
                    by the Holy light of love
that rules,
          blocking despair,
                    over this garden.

Time passes.
          The pace has slackened
                    But with the falling off
of the pace
          the scene has altered.

                         The lovers raise their heads,
          at that which has come over them.
                    It is summer now.
                         The broad sun
          shines!
                    Blinded by the light
                         they walk bewildered,
          seeking
                    between the leaves
                         for a vantage
          from which to view
                    the advancing season.
                         They are incredulous
          of their own cure
                    and half minded
                         to escape
          into the dark again.
                    The scene
                         indeed has changed.
          By St. Francis
                    the whole scene
                         has changed.
          They glimpse
                    a surrounding sky
                         and the whole countryside.
          Filled with terror
                    they seek
                         a familiar flower
          at which to warm themselves,
                    but the whole field
                         accosts them.
          They hide their eyes
                    ashamed
                         before that bounty,
          peering through their fingers
                    timidly.
                         The saint is watching,
          his eyes filled with pity.

The year is still young
>   but not so young
>   as they
who face the fears
>   with which
>   they are confronted.
Reawakened
>   after love's first folly
>   they resemble children
roused from a long sleep.
>   Summer is here,
>   right enough.
The saint
>   has tactfully withdrawn.
>   One
emboldened,
>   parting the leaves before her,
>   stands in the full sunlight,
alone
>   shading her eyes
>   as her heart
beats wildly
>   and her mind
>   drinks up
the full meaning
>   of it
>   all!

THE ARTIST

Mr. T.
>   bareheaded
>   in a soiled undershirt
his hair standing out
>   on all sides
>   stood on his toes
heels together
>   arms gracefully

for the moment
curled above his head.
Then he whirled about
bounded
into the air
and with an *entrechat*
perfectly achieved
completed the figure.
My mother
taken by surprise
where she sat
in her invalid's chair
was left speechless.
Bravo! she cried at last
and clapped her hands.
The man's wife
came from the kitchen:
What goes on here? she said.
But the show was over.

WORK IN PROGRESS
[ASPHODEL, THAT GREENY FLOWER: BOOK 1]

Included in *Journey to Love:* see p. 310.

THEOCRITUS: IDYL I
A Version from the Greek

THYRSIS

The whisper of the wind in
that pine tree,
goatherd,
is sweet as the murmur of live water;
likewise
your flute notes. After Pan
you shall bear away second prize.

And if he
          take the goat
with the horns,
          the she-goat
                    is yours: but if
he choose the she-goat,
          the kid will fall
                    to your lot.
And the flesh of the kid
          is dainty
                    before they begin milking them.

GOATHERD

Your song is sweeter,
          shepherd,
                    than the music
of the water as it plashes
          from the high face
                    of yonder rock!
If the Muses
          choose the young ewe
                    you shall receive
a stall-fed lamb
          as your reward,
                    but if
they prefer the lamb
          you
                    shall have the ewe for
                    second prize.

THYRSIS

Will you not, goatherd,
          in the Nymph's name
                    take your place on this
                    sloping knoll
among the tamarisks
          and pipe for me
                    while I tend my sheep.

GOATHERD

No, shepherd,
            nothing doing;
                        it's not for us
to be heard during the noon hush.
            We dread Pan,
                        who for a fact
is stretched out somewhere,
            dog tired from the chase;
                        his mood is bitter,
anger ready at his nostrils.
            But, Thyrsis,
                        since you are good at
singing of *The Afflictions of Daphnis,*
            and have most deeply
                        meditated the pastoral mode,
come here,
            let us sit down,
                        under this elm
facing Priapus and the fountain fairies,
            here where the shepherds come
                        to try themselves out
by the oak trees.
            Ah! may you sing
                        as you sang that day
facing Chromis out of Libya,
            I will let you milk, yes,
                        three times over,
a goat that is the mother of twins
            and even when
                        she has sucked her kids
her milk fills
            two pails. I will give besides,
                        new made, a two-eared bowl
of ivy-wood,
            rubbed with beeswax
                        that smacks still
of the knife of the carver.
            Round its upper edges

                    winds the ivy, ivy
flecked with yellow flowers
            and about it
                    is twisted
a tendril joyful with the saffron fruit.
            Within,
                    is limned a girl,
as fair a thing as the gods have made,
            dressed in a sweeping
                    gown.
Her hair
            is confined by a snood.
                    Beside her
two fair-haired youths
            with alternate speech
                    are contending
but her heart is
            untouched.
                    Now,
        she glances at one,
            smiling,
                    and now, lightly
she flings the other a thought,
            while their eyes,
                    by reason of love's
long vigils, are heavy
            but their labors
                    all in vain.
In addition
            there is fashioned there
                    an ancient fisherman
and a rock,
            a rugged rock,
                    on which
with might and main
            the old man poises a great net
                    for the cast
as one who puts his whole heart into it.
            One would say
                    that he was fishing

with the full strength of his limbs
    so big do his muscles stand out
        about the neck.
Gray-haired though he be,
    he has the strength
        of a young man.
Now, separated
    from the sea-broken old man
        by a narrow interval
is a vineyard,
    heavy
        with fire-red clusters,
and on a rude wall
    sits a small boy
        guarding them.
Round him
    two she-foxes are skulking.
        One
goes the length of the vine-rows
    to eat the grapes
        while the other
brings all her cunning to bear,
    by what has been set down,
        vowing
she will never quit the lad
    until
        she leaves him bare
and breakfastless.
    But the boy
        is plaiting a pretty
cage of locust stalks and asphodel,
    fitting in the reeds
        and cares less for his scrip
and the vines
    than he takes delight
        in his plaiting.
All about the cup
    is draped the mild acanthus
        a miracle of varied work,

a thing for you to marvel at.
         I paid
                  a Caledonian ferryman
a goat and a great white
        cream-cheese
                for the bowl.
It is still virgin to me,
        its lip has never touched mine.
                To gain my desire,
I would gladly
        give this cup
                if you, my friend,
will sing for me
        that delightful song.
                I hold nothing back.
Begin, my friend,
        for you cannot,
                you may be sure,
take your song,
        which drives all things out of mind,
                with you to the other world.

THE DESERT MUSIC

—the dance begins: to end about a form
propped motionless—on the bridge
between Juárez and El Paso—unrecognizable
in the semi-dark

                Wait!

The others waited while you inspected it,
on the very walk itself   .

                Is it alive?

                      —neither a head,
legs nor arms!

It isn't a sack of rags someone
has abandoned here   .   torpid against
the flange of the supporting girder   .   ?

                    an inhuman shapelessness,
knees hugged tight up into the belly

    Egg-shaped!

                    What a place to sleep!
on the International Boundary.   Where else,
interjurisdictional, not to be disturbed?

How shall we get said what must be said?

Only the poem.

Only the counted poem, to an exact measure:
to imitate, not to copy nature, not
to copy nature

NOT, prostrate, to copy nature
                    but a dance! to dance
two and two with him—
                    sequestered there asleep,
                            right end up!

    A music
supersedes his composure, hallooing to us
across a great distance   .   .

                        wakens the dance
who blows upon his benumbed fingers!

                    Only the poem
only the made poem, to get said what must
be said, not to copy nature, sticks
in our throats   .

The law?   The law gives us nothing
but a corpse, wrapped in a dirty mantle.

The law is based on murder and confinement,
long delayed,
but this, following the insensate music,
is based on the dance:

                    an agony of self-realization
bound into a whole
by that which surrounds us   .

                    I cannot escape

I cannot vomit it up

Only the poem!

Only the made poem, the verb calls it
                              into being.

                    —it looks too small for a man.
A woman.   Or a very shriveled old man.
Maybe dead.   They probably inspect the place
and will cart it away later   .

                    Heave it into the river.
A good thing.

Leaving California to return east, the fertile desert,
                    (were it to get water)
surrounded us, a music of survival, subdued, distant, half
                    heard; we were engulfed
by it as in the early evening, seeing the wind lift
                    and drive the sand, we
passed Yuma. All night long, heading for El Paso to
                    meet our friend,
we slept fitfully.   Thinking of Paris, I waked to the tick
                    of the rails.   The
jagged desert   .

                    —to tell
        what subsequently I saw and what heard

       —to place myself (in
my nature) beside nature

      —to imitate
nature (for to copy nature would be a
  shameful thing)

     I lay myself down:

The Old Market's a good place to begin:
Let's cut through here—
       tequila's only
a nickel a slug in these side streets.
Keep out though. Oh, it's all right at
this time of day but I saw H. terribly
beaten up in one of those joints. He
asked for it. I thought he was going to
be killed. I do
my drinking on the main drag .

     That's the bull ring
Oh, said Floss, after she got used to the
change of light .
      What color! Isn't it
wonderful!

   —paper flowers (*para los santos*)
baked red-clay utensils, daubed
with blue, silverware,
dried peppers, onions, print goods, children's
clothing . the place deserted all but
for a few Indians squatted in the
booths, unnoticing (don't you think it)
as though they slept there .

   There's a second tier. Do you
want to go up?

   What makes Texans so tall?
We saw a woman this morning in a mink cape
six feet if she was an inch. What a woman!

Probably a Broadway figure.

—tell you what else we saw: about a million
sparrows screaming their heads off
in the trees of that small park where
the buses stop, sanctuary,
I suppose,
from the wind driving the sand in that way
about the city   .

                        Texas rain they call it

—and those two alligators in the fountain   .

There were four

            I saw only two

                        They were looking
right at you all the time   .

Penny please!   Give me penny please, mister.

                  Don't give them anything.

                              .   instinctively
one has already drawn one's naked
wrist away from those obscene fingers
as in the mind a vague apprehension speaks
and the music rouses   .

                        Let's get in here.
                  a music!   cut off as
the bar door closes behind us.

                  We've got
another half hour.

                  —returned to the street,
the pressure moves from booth to booth along

the curb.   Opposite, no less insistent
the better stores are wide open.   Come in
and look around.   You don't have to buy: hats,
riding boots, blankets

            Look at the way,
slung from her neck with a shawl, that young
Indian woman carries her baby!

               —a stream of Spanish,
as she brushes by, intense, wide-
eyed in eager talk with her boy husband

—three half-grown girls, one of them eating a
pomegranate.   Laughing.

               and the serious tourist,
man and wife, middle-aged, middle-western,
their arms loaded with loot, whispering
together—still looking for bargains   .

               and the aniline
red and green candy at the little booth
tended by the old Indian woman.
      Do you suppose anyone actually
buys—and eats the stuff?

My feet are beginning to ache me.

             We still got a few minutes.
Let's try here.   They had the mayor
up last month for taking $3000 a week from
the whorehouses of the city.   Not much left
for the girls.   There's a show on.

             Only a few tables
occupied.   A conventional orchestra—this
place livens up later—playing the usual local
jing-a-jing—a boy and girl team, she
             confidential with someone
off stage.   Laughing: just finishing the act.

So we drink until the next turn—a strip tease.

Do you mean it?   Wow!   Look at her.

                              You'd have to be
pretty drunk to get any kick out of that.
She's no Mexican.   Some worn-out trouper from
the States.   Look at those breasts

                    There is a fascination
                    seeing her shake
                    the beaded sequins from
                    a string about her hips

                    She gyrates but it's
                    not what you think,
                    one does not laugh
                    to watch her belly.

                    One is moved but not
                    at the dull show.   The
                    guitarist yawns.   She
                    cannot even sing.   She

                    has about her painted
                    hardihood a screen
                    of pretty doves which
                    flutter their wings.

                    Her cold eyes perfunc-
                    torily moan but do not
                    smile.   Yet they bill
                    and coo by grace of
                    a certain candor.   She

                    is heavy on her feet.
                    That's good.   She
                    bends forward leaning
                    on the table of the
                    balding man sitting

upright, alone, so that
everything hangs for-
ward.
    What the hell
are you grinning
to yourself about?   Not
at *her?*
    The music!
I like her.   She fits

the music   .

Why don't these Indians get over this nauseating prattle
about their souls and their loves and sing us something
else for a change?

    This place is rank
with it.   She
at least knows she's
part of another tune,
knows her customers,
has the same
opinion of them as I
have.   That gives her
one up   .   one up
following the lying
music   .

There is another music.   The bright-colored candy
of her nakedness lifts her unexpectedly
to partake of its tune   .

                    Andromeda of those rocks,
the virgin of her mind   .   those unearthly
greens and reds
                  in her mockery of virtue
she becomes unaccountably virtuous   .
              though she in no
way pretends it   .

Let's get out of this.

<blockquote>In the street it hit</blockquote>
me in the face as we started to walk again.   Or
am I merely playing the poet?   Do I merely invent
it out of whole cloth?   I thought   .

> What in the form of an old whore in
> a cheap Mexican joint in Juárez, her bare
> can waggling crazily can be
> so refreshing to me, raise to my ear
> so sweet a tune, built of such slime?

> Here we are.   They'll be along any minute.
> The bar is at the right of the entrance,
> a few tables opposite which you have to pass
> to get to the dining room, beyond.

> A foursome, two oversize Americans, no
> longer young, got up as cowboys,
> hats and all, are drunk and carrying on
> with their gals, drunk also,

> especially one inciting her man, the
> biggest, *Yip ee*! to dance in
> the narrow space, oblivious to everything
> —she is insatiable and he is trying

> stumblingly to keep up with her.
> Give it the gun, pardner!   *Yip ee*!   We
> pushed by them to our table, seven
> of us.   Seated about the room

> were quiet family groups, some with
> children, eating.   Rather a better
> class than you notice
> on the streets.   So here we are.   You

> can see through into the kitchen
> where one of the cooks, his shirt sleeves

rolled up, an apron over
the well-pressed pants of a street

suit, black hair neatly parted,
a tall
good-looking man, is working
absorbed, before a chopping block

Old Fashioneds all around?

So this is William
Carlos Williams, the poet   .

Floss and I had half consumed
our quartered hearts of lettuce before
we noticed the others hadn't touched theirs   .
You seem quite normal.   Can you tell me?   Why
does one want to write a poem?

Because it's there to be written.

Oh.   A matter of inspiration then?

Of necessity.

Oh.   But what sets it off?

I am that he whose brains
are scattered
aimlessly

—and so,
the hour done, the quail eaten, we were on
our way back to El Paso.

Good night.   Good
night and thank you   .   No.   Thank you.   We're
going to walk   .

—and so, on the naked wrist, we feel again
those insistent fingers   .

                              Penny please, mister.
Penny please.   Give me penny.

                              Here! now go away.

—but the music, the music has reawakened
as we leave the busier parts of the street
and come again to the bridge in the semi-dark,
pay our fee and begin again to cross   .
seeing the lights along the mountain back of El
Paso and pause to watch the boys calling out
to us to throw more coins to them standing
in the shallow water   .   so that's
where the incentive lay, with the annoyance
of those surprising fingers.

                       So you're a poet?
a good thing to be got rid of—half drunk,
a free dinner under your belt, even though you
get typhoid—and to have met people you
can at least talk to   .

                  relief from that changeless, endless
inescapable and insistent music   .   .

                  What else, Latins, do you yourselves
seek but relief!
with the expressionless ding dong you dish up
to us of your souls and your loves, which
we swallow. Spaniards! (though these are mostly
Indians who chase the white bastards
through the streets on their Independence Day
and try to kill them)   .

                              What's that?

Oh, come on.

            But what's THAT?

                        the music! the

music! as when Casals struck
and held a deep cello tone
and I am speechless   .

                              There it sat
in the projecting angle of the bridge flange
as I stood aghast and looked at it—
in the half-light: shapeless or rather returned
to its original shape, armless, legless,
headless, packed like the pit of a fruit into
that obscure corner—or
a fish to swim against the stream—or
a child in the womb prepared to imitate life,
warding its life against
a birth of awful promise.   The music
guards it, a mucus, a film that surrounds it,
a benumbing ink that stains the
sea of our minds—to hold us off—shed
of a shape close as it can get to no shape,
a music! a protecting music   .

                          I *am* a poet! I
am.   I am.   I am a poet, I reaffirmed, ashamed

Now the music volleys through as in
a lonely moment I hear it.   Now it is all
about me.   The dance!   The verb detaches itself
seeking to become articulate   .

            And I could not help thinking
            of the wonders of the brain that
            hears that music and of our
            skill sometimes to record it.

JOURNEY TO LOVE
1955

JOURNEY TO LOVE

BY

WILLIAM CARLOS WILLIAMS

RANDOM HOUSE · NEW YORK

A NEGRO WOMAN

carrying a bunch of marigolds
       wrapped
              in an old newspaper:
She carries them upright,
       bareheaded,
              the bulk
of her thighs
       causing her to waddle
              as she walks
looking into
       the store window which she passes
              on her way.
What is she
       but an ambassador
              from another world
a world of pretty marigolds
       of two shades
              which she announces
not knowing what she does
       other
              than walk the streets
holding the flowers upright
       as a torch
              so early in the morning.

THE IVY CROWN

The whole process is a lie,
       unless,
              crowned by excess,
it break forcefully,
       one way or another,
              from its confinement—

or find a deeper well.
        Antony and Cleopatra
                were right;
they have shown
        the way. I love you
                or I do not live
at all.

Daffodil time
        is past. This is
                summer, summer!
the heart says,
        and not even the full of it.
                No doubts
are permitted—
        though they will come
                and may
before our time
        overwhelm us.
                We are only mortal
but being mortal
        can defy our fate.
                We may
by an outside chance
        even win! We do not
                look to see
jonquils and violets
        come again
                but there are,
still,
        the roses!

Romance has no part in it.
        The business of love is
                cruelty *which,*
by our wills,
        we transform
                to live together.
It has its seasons,
        for and against,

              whatever the heart
fumbles in the dark
      to assert
              toward the end of May.
Just as the nature of briars
        is to tear flesh,
              I have proceeded
through them.
        Keep
              the briars out,
they say.
        You cannot live
              and keep free of
briars.

Children pick flowers.
        Let them.
              Though having them
in hand
        they have no further use for them
              but leave them crumpled
at the curb's edge.

At our age the imagination
        across the sorry facts
              lifts us
to make roses
        stand before thorns.
              Sure
love is cruel
        and selfish
              and totally obtuse—
at least, blinded by the light,
        young love is.
              But we are older,
I to love
        and you to be loved,
              we have,
no matter how,
        by our wills survived

                              to keep
          the jeweled prize
                    always
                              at our finger tips.
          We will it so
                    and so it is
                              past all accident.

VIEW BY COLOR PHOTOGRAPHY
ON A COMMERCIAL CALENDAR

The church of Vico-Morcote
          in the Canton Ticino
                    with its apple blossoms
is beautiful
          as anything I have ever seen
                    in or out of
Switzerland.
          The beauty of holiness
                    the beauty of a man's anger
reflecting his sex
          or a woman's either,
                    mountainous,
or a little stone church
          from a height
                    or
close to the camera
          the apple tree in blossom
                    or the far lake
below
          in the distance—
                    are equal
as they are unsurpassed.
          Peace
                    after the event
comes from their contemplation,
          a great peace.
                    The sky is cut off,
there is no horizon

just the mountainside
　　　　bordered by water
on which tiny waves
　　　　without passion
　　　　　　unconcerned
cover the invisible fish.
　　　　And who but we are concerned
　　　　　　with the beauty of apple blossoms
and a small church
　　　　on a promontory,
　　　　　　an ancient church—
by the look of its masonry—
　　　　abandoned
　　　　　　by a calm lake
in the mountains
　　　　where the sun shines
　　　　　　of a springtime
afternoon. Something
　　　　has come to an end here,
　　　　　　it has been accomplished.

THE SPARROW

(To My Father)

This sparrow
　　　　who comes to sit at my window
　　　　　　is a poetic truth
more than a natural one.
　　　　His voice,
　　　　　　his movements,
his habits—
　　　　how he loves to
　　　　　　flutter his wings
in the dust—
　　　　all attest it;
　　　　　　granted, he does it
to rid himself of lice
　　　　but the relief he feels

                    makes him
cry out lustily—
            which is a trait
                    more related to music
than otherwise.
            Wherever he finds himself
                    in early spring,
on back streets
            or beside palaces,
                    he carries on
unaffectedly
            his amours.
                    It begins in the egg,
his sex genders it:
            What is more pretentiously
                    useless
or about which
            we more pride ourselves?
                    It leads as often as not
to our undoing.
            The cockerel, the crow
                    with their challenging voices
cannot surpass
            the insistence
                    of his cheep!
Once
            at El Paso
                    toward evening,
I saw—and heard!—
            ten thousand sparrows
                    who had come in from
the desert
            to roost. They filled the trees
                    of a small park. Men fled
(with ears ringing!)
            from their droppings,
                    leaving the premises
to the alligators
            who inhabit
                    the fountain. His image

is familiar
                as that of the aristocratic
                        unicorn, a pity
there are not more oats eaten
                nowadays
                        to make living easier
for him.
                At that,
                        his small size,
keen eyes,
                serviceable beak
                        and general truculence
assure his survival—
                to say nothing
                        of his innumerable
brood.
                Even the Japanese
                        know him
and have painted him
                sympathetically,
                        with profound insight
into his minor
                characteristics.
                        Nothing even remotely
subtle
                about his lovemaking.
                        He crouches
before the female,
                drags his wings,
                        waltzing,
throws back his head
                and simply—
                        yells! The din
is terrific.
                The way he swipes his bill
                        across a plank
to clean it,
                is decisive.
                        So with everything
he does. His coppery

eyebrows
        give him the air
of being always
     a winner—and yet
        I saw once,
the female of his species
     clinging determinedly
        to the edge of
a water pipe,
     catch him
        by his crown-feathers
to hold him
     silent,
        subdued,
hanging above the city streets
     until
        she was through with him.
What was the use
     of that?
        She hung there
herself,
     puzzled at her success.
        I laughed heartily.
Practical to the end,
     it is the poem
        of his existence
that triumphed
     finally;
        a wisp of feathers
flattened to the pavement,
     wings spread symmetrically
        as if in flight,
the head gone,
     the black escutcheon of the breast
        undecipherable,
an effigy of a sparrow,
     a dried wafer only,
        left to say
and it says it

without offense,
                    beautifully;
This was I,
        a sparrow.
                  I did my best;
farewell.

THE KING!

Nell Gwyn,
        it says in the dictionary,
                actress
and mistress of Charles the Second:
        what a lot
                of pious rot there is
surrounding
        that
                simple statement.
She waked in the morning,
        bathed in
                the King's bountiful
water
        which enveloped her
                completely and,
magically,
        with the grit, took away
                all her sins.
It was the King's body
        which was served;
                the King's boards which
in the evening
        she capably trod;
                she fed
the King's poor
        and when she died,
                left them some slight moneys
under certain
        conditions.

Happy the woman
    whose husband makes her
        the "King's whore."
All this you will find
    in the dictionary
        where it has been
preserved forever—
    since it is beautiful
        and true.

TRIBUTE TO THE PAINTERS

Satyrs dance!
    all the deformities take wing
        centaurs
leading to the rout of the vocables
    in the writings
of Gertrude
    Stein—but
        you cannot be
an artist
    by mere ineptitude
The dream
    is in pursuit!

The neat figures of
    Paul Klee
        fill the canvas
but that
    is not the work
        of a child
The cure began, perhaps,
    with the abstractions
        of Arabic art
Dürer
    with his *Melancholy*
        was ware of it—
the shattered masonry. Leonardo
    saw it,

the obsession,
and ridiculed it
in *La Gioconda.*
Bosch's
congeries of tortured souls and devils
who prey on them
fish
swallowing
their own entrails
Freud
Picasso
Juan Gris.
The letter from a friend
saying:
For the last
three nights
I have slept like a baby
without
liquor or dope of any sort!
We know
that a stasis
from a chrysalis
has stretched its wings—
like a bull
or the Minotaur
or Beethoven
in the scherzo
of his 5th Symphony
stomped
his heavy feet
I saw love
mounted naked on a horse
on a swan
the back of a fish
the bloodthirsty conger eel
and laughed
recalling the Jew
in the pit
among his fellows
when the indifferent chap

with the machine gun
was spraying the heap.
He
had not yet been hit
but smiled
comforting his companions.

Dreams possess me
and the dance
of my thoughts
involving animals
the blameless beasts
and there came to me
just now
the knowledge of
the tyranny of the image
and how
men
in their designs
have learned
to shatter it
whatever it may be,
that the trouble
in their minds
shall be quieted,
put to bed
again.

TO A MAN DYING ON HIS FEET

—not that we are not all
"dying on our feet"
but the look you give me
and to which I bow,
is more immediate.
It is keenly alert,
suspicious of me—
as of all that are living—and
apologetic.

Your jaw
   wears the stubble
     of a haggard beard,
a dirty beard,
   which resembles
     the snow through which
your long legs
   are conducting you.
     Whither? Where are you going?
This would be a fine day
   to go on a journey.
     Say to Florida
where at this season
   all go
     nowadays.
There grows the hibiscus,
   the star jasmine
     and more than I can tell
but the odors
   from what I know
     must be alluring.
Come with me there!
   you look like a good guy,
     come this evening.
The plane leaves at 6:30
   or have you another
     appointment?

THE PINK LOCUST

I'm persistent as the pink locust,
   once admitted
     to the garden,
you will not easily get rid of it.
   Tear it from the ground,
     if one hair-thin rootlet
remain
   it will come again.
     It is

flattering to think of myself
  so. It is also
    laughable.
A modest flower,
  resembling a pink sweet-pea,
    you cannot help
but admire it
  until its habits
    become known.
Are we not most of us
  like that? It would be
    too much
if the public
  pried among the minutiae
    of our private affairs.
Not
  that we have anything to hide
    but could *they*
stand it? Of course
  the world would be gratified
    to find out
what fools we have made of ourselves.
  The question is,
    would they
be generous with us—
  as we have been
    with others? It is,
as I say,
  a flower
    incredibly resilient
under attack!
  Neglect it
    and it will grow into a tree.
I wish I could *so* think of myself
  and of what
    is to become of me.
The poet himself,
  what does he think of himself
    facing his world?
It will not do to say,

as he is inclined to say:
                   Not much. The poem
would be in *that* betrayed.
                   He might as well answer—
                           "a rose is a rose
is a rose" and let it go at that.
                   A rose *is* a rose
                           and the poem equals it
if it be well made.
                   The poet
                           cannot slight himself
without slighting
                   his poem—
                           which would be
ridiculous.
                   Life offers
                           no greater reward.
And so,
                   like this flower,
                           I persist—
for what there may be in it.
                   I am not,
                           I know,
in the galaxy of poets
                   a rose
                           but *who*, among the rest,
will deny me
                   my place.

CLASSIC PICTURE

It is a classic picture,
                   women have always fussed with their hair
                           (having no sisters
I never watched the process
                   so intimately
                           as this time); the reason for it
is not clear—
                   tho' I acknowledge,

                              an unkempt head of hair,
          while not as repulsive as a nest of snakes,
                    is repulsive enough
                              in a woman.
          Therefore
                    she fusses with her hair
                    for
          a woman does not want to seem repulsive,
                    unless   .
                              to gain for herself   .
          she be hungry,
                    hungry!
                              as would be a man
          and all hunger is repulsive
                    and puts on
                              an ugly face.
          Their heads are not made as a man's,
                    an ornament
                              in itself. They have
          other charms—
                    needless
                              to enumerate. Under
          their ornate coiffures
                    lurks a specter,
                              coiling snakes
          doubling for tresses   .

          A woman's brains
                    which can be keen
                              are condemned,
          like a poet's,
                    to what deceptions she can muster
                              to lead men
          to their ruin.
                    But look more deeply
                              into her maneuvers,
          and puzzle as we will about them   ·
                    they may mean
                              anything   .

THE LADY SPEAKS

A storm raged among the live oaks
　　　　while my husband and I
　　　　　　　　sat in the semi-dark
listening!
　　　　We watched from the windows,
　　　　　　　　the lights off,
saw the moss
　　　　whipped upright
　　　　　　　　by the wind's force.
Two candles we had lit
　　　　side by side
　　　　　　　　before us
so solidly had our house been built
　　　　kept their tall flames
　　　　　　　　unmoved.
May it be so
　　　　when a storm sends the moss
　　　　　　　　whipping
back and forth
　　　　upright
　　　　　　　　above my head
like flames in the final
　　　　fury.

ADDRESS:

To a look in my son's eyes—
　　　　I hope he did not see
　　　　　　　　that I was looking—
that I have seen
　　　　often enough
　　　　　　　　in the mirror,
a male look
　　　　approaching despair—
　　　　　　　　there is a female look
to match it

no need to speak of that:
Perhaps
it was only a dreamy look
not an unhappy one
but absent
from the world—
such as plagued the eyes
of Bobby Burns
in his youth and threw him
into the arms
of women—
in which he could
forget himself,
not defiantly,
but with full acceptance
of his lot
as a man   .   .
His Jean forgave him
and took him to her heart
time after time
when he would be
too drunk
with Scotch
or the love of other women
to notice
what he was doing.
What was he intent upon
but to drown out
that look? What
does it portend?
A war
will not erase it
nor a bank account,
estlin,
amounting to 9 figures.
Flow gently sweet Afton
among thy green braes—
no matter
that he wrote the song

to another woman
                    it was never for sale.

THE DRUNK AND THE SAILOR

The petty fury
                    that disrupts my life—
                              at the striking of a wrong key
as if it had been
                    a woman lost
or a fortune   .   .
                    The man was obviously drunk,
                              Christopher Marlowe
could have been no drunker
                    when he got himself
                              stuck through the eye
with a poniard.
                    The bus station was crowded.
The man
          heavy-set
                    about my own age
seventy
          was talking privately
                    with a sailor.
He had an ugly jaw on him.
          Suddenly
                    sitting there on the bench
too drunk to stand
          he began menacingly
                    his screaming.
The young sailor
          who could have flattened him
                    at one blow
kept merely looking at him.
                    The nerve-tingling screeches
                              that sprang
sforzando
          from that stubble beard

                    would have distinguished
an operatic tenor.
          But me—
                    the shock of it—
my heart leaped in my chest
          so that I saw red
                    wanted
to strangle the guy   .
          The fury of love
                    is no less.

A SMILING DANE

The Danish native
          before the Christian era
                    whose body
features intact
          with a rope
                    also intact
round the neck
          found recently
                    in a peat bog
is dead.
          Are you surprised?
                    You should be.
The diggers
          who discovered him
                    expected more.
Frightened
          they quit the place
                    thinking
his ghost might walk.

The cast of his features
          shows him
                    to be
a man of intelligence.
          It did him no good.
                    What his eyes saw

cannot be more
             than the male
                        and female
of it—
          if as much.
                      His stomach
its contents examined
             shows him
                        before he died
to have had
          a meal
                      consisting of local grains
swallowed whole
             which he probably enjoyed
                        though he did not
much as we do
          chew them.
                      And what if
the image of his frightened executioners
             is not recorded?
                        Do we not know
their features
          as if
                      it had occurred
today?
          We can still see in his smile
                        their grimaces.

COME ON!

A different kind of thought
             blander
                        and more desperate
like that of
          Sergeant So-and-So
                        at the road
in Belleau Wood:
          Come on!
                      Do you want to live

forever?—
　　　　That
　　　　　　　　is the essence
of poetry.
　　　　But it does not
　　　　　　　always
take the same form.
　　　　For the most part
　　　　　　　it consists
in listening
　　　　to the nightingale
　　　　　　　or fools.

SHADOWS

I

Shadows cast by the street light
　　　　under the stars,
　　　　　　　the head is tilted back,
the long shadow of the legs
　　　　presumes a world
　　　　　　　taken for granted
on which the cricket trills.
　　　　The hollows of the eyes
　　　　　　　are unpeopled.
Right and left
　　　　climb the ladders of night
　　　　　　　as dawn races
to put out the stars.
　　　　That
　　　　　　　is the poetic figure
but we know
　　　　better: what is not now
　　　　　　　will never
be. Sleep secure,
　　　　the little dog in the snapshot
　　　　　　　keeps his shrewd eyes
pared. Memory

is liver than sight.
                A man
looking out,
              seeing the shadows—
                      it is himself
that can be painlessly amputated
              by a mere shifting
                      of the stars.
A comfort so easily not to be
              and to be at once one
                      with every man.
The night blossoms
              with a thousand shadows
                  so long
as there are stars,
              street lights
                    or a moon and
who shall say
              by their shadows
which is different
              from the other
                    fat or lean.

11

Ripped from the concept of our lives
              and from all concept
                    somehow, and plainly,
the sun will come up
              each morning
                    and sink again.
So that we experience
              violently
                    every day
two worlds
              one of which we share with the
              rose in bloom
                  and one,
by far the greater,
              with the past,

the world of memory,
the silly world of history,
the world
of the imagination.
Which leaves only the beasts and trees,
crystals
with their refractive
surfaces
and rotting things
to stir our wonder.
Save for the little
central hole
of the eye itself
into which
we dare not stare too hard
or we are lost.
The instant
trivial as it is
is all we have
unless—unless
things the imagination feeds upon,
the scent of the rose,
startle us anew.

ASPHODEL, THAT GREENY FLOWER

BOOK I

Of asphodel, that greeny flower,
like a buttercup
upon its branching stem—
save that it's green and wooden—
I come, my sweet,
to sing to you.
We lived long together
a life filled,
if you will,
with flowers. So that
I was cheered

when I came first to know
that there were flowers also
in hell.
Today
I'm filled with the fading memory of those flowers
that we both loved,
even to this poor
colorless thing—
I saw it
when I was a child—
little prized among the living
but the dead see,
asking among themselves:
What do I remember
that was shaped
as this thing is shaped?
while our eyes fill
with tears.
Of love, abiding love
it will be telling
though too weak a wash of crimson
colors it
to make it wholly credible.
There is something
something urgent
I have to say to you
and you alone
but it must wait
while I drink in
the joy of your approach,
perhaps for the last time.
And so
with fear in my heart
I drag it out
and keep on talking
for I dare not stop.
Listen while I talk on
against time.
It will not be
for long.

I have forgot   .
          and yet I see clearly enough
                    something
central to the sky
          which ranges round it.
                    An odor
springs from it!
          A sweetest odor!
                    Honeysuckle! And now
there comes the buzzing of a bee!
          and a whole flood
                    of sister memories!
Only give me time,
          time to recall them
                    before I shall speak out.
Give me time,
          time.
When I was a boy
          I kept a book
                    to which, from time
to time,
          I added pressed flowers
                    until, after a time,
I had a good collection.
          The asphodel,
                    forebodingly,
among them.
          I bring you,
                    reawakened,
a memory of those flowers.
          They were sweet
                    when I pressed them
and retained
          something of their sweetness
                    a long time.
It is a curious odor,
          a moral odor,
                    that brings me
near to you.
          The color

was the first to go.
There had come to me
     a challenge,
         your dear self,
mortal as I was,
     the lily's throat
         to the hummingbird!
Endless wealth,
     I thought,
         held out its arms to me.
A thousand tropics
     in an apple blossom.
         The generous earth itself
gave us lief.
     The whole world
         became my garden!
But the sea
     which no one tends
         is also a garden
when the sun strikes it
     and the waves
         are wakened.
I have seen it
     and so have you
         when it puts all flowers
to shame.
     Too, there are the starfish
         stiffened by the sun
and other sea wrack
     and weeds. We knew that
         along with the rest of it
for we were born by the sea,
     knew its rose hedges
         to the very water's brink.
There the pink mallow grows
     and in their season
         strawberries
and there, later,
     we went to gather
         the wild plum.

I cannot say
        that I have gone to hell
                for your love
but often
        found myself there
                in your pursuit.
I do not like it
        and wanted to be
                in heaven. Hear me out.
Do not turn away.
I have learned much in my life
        from books
                and out of them
about love.
        Death
                is not the end of it.
There is a hierarchy
        which can be attained,
                I think,
in its service.
        Its guerdon
                is a fairy flower;
a cat of twenty lives.
        If no one came to try it
                the world
would be the loser.
        It has been
                for you and me
as one who watches a storm
        come in over the water.
                We have stood
from year to year
        before the spectacle of our lives
                with joined hands.
The storm unfolds.
        Lightning
                plays about the edges of the clouds.
The sky to the north
        is placid,
                blue in the afterglow

as the storm piles up.
        It is a flower
                that will soon reach
the apex of its bloom.
        We danced,
                in our minds,
and read a book together.
        You remember?
                It was a serious book.
And so books
        entered our lives.
The sea! The sea!
        Always
                when I think of the sea
there comes to mind
        the *Iliad*
                and Helen's public fault
that bred it.
        Were it not for that
                there would have been
no poem but the world
        if we had remembered,
                those crimson petals
spilled among the stones,
        would have called it simply
                murder.
The sexual orchid that bloomed then
        sending so many
                disinterested
men to their graves
        has left its memory
                to a race of fools
or heroes
        if silence is a virtue.
                The sea alone
with its multiplicity
        holds any hope.
                The storm
has proven abortive
        but we remain

after the thoughts it roused
to
re-cement our lives.
It is the mind
the mind
that must be cured
short of death's
intervention,
and the will becomes again
a garden. The poem
is complex and the place made
in our lives
for the poem.
Silence can be complex too,
but you do not get far
with silence.
Begin again.
It is like Homer's
catalogue of ships:
it fills up the time.
I speak in figures,
well enough, the dresses
you wear are figures also,
we could not meet
otherwise. When I speak
of flowers
it is to recall
that at one time
we were young.
All women are not Helen,
I know that,
but have Helen in their hearts.
My sweet,
you have it also, therefore
I love you
and could not love you otherwise.
Imagine you saw
a field made up of women
all silver-white.
What should you do

but love them?
             The storm bursts
                          or fades! it is not
the end of the world.
             Love is something else,
                          or so I thought it,
a garden which expands,
             though I knew you as a woman
                          and never thought otherwise,
until the whole sea
             has been taken up
                          and all its gardens.
It was the love of love,
             the love that swallows up all else,
                          a grateful love,
a love of nature, of people,
             animals,
                          a love engendering
gentleness and goodness
             that moved me
                          and *that* I saw in you.
I should have known,
             though I did not,
                          that the lily-of-the-valley
is a flower makes many ill
             who whiff it.
                          We had our children,
rivals in the general onslaught.
             I put them aside
                          though I cared for them
as well as any man
             could care for his children
                          according to my lights.
You understand
             I had to meet you
                          after the event
and have still to meet you.
             Love
                          to which you too shall bow
along with me—

a flower
a weakest flower
shall be our trust
and not because
we are too feeble
to do otherwise
but because
at the height of my power
I risked what I had to do,
therefore to prove
that we love each other
while my very bones sweated
that I could not cry to you
in the act.
Of asphodel, that greeny flower,
I come, my sweet,
to sing to you!
My heart rouses
thinking to bring you news
of something
that concerns you
and concerns many men. Look at
what passes for the new.
You will not find it there but in
despised poems.
It is difficult
to get the news from poems
yet men die miserably every day
for lack
of what is found there.
Hear me out
for I too am concerned
and every man
who wants to die at peace in his bed
besides.

BOOK II

Approaching death,
as we think, the death of love,

no distinction
any more suffices to differentiate
the particulars
of place and condition
with which we have been long
familiar.
All appears
as if seen
wavering through water.
We start awake with a cry
of recognition
but soon the outlines
become again vague.
If we are to understand our time,
we must find the key to it,
not in the eighteenth
and nineteenth centuries,
but in earlier, wilder
and darker epochs   .   .
So to know, what I have to know
about my own death,
if it be real,
I have to take it apart.
What does your generation think
of Cézanne?
I asked a young artist.
The abstractions of Hindu painting,
he replied,
is all at the moment which interests me.
He liked my poem
about the parts
of a broken bottle,
lying green in the cinders
of a hospital courtyard.
There was also, to his mind,
the one on gay wallpaper
which he had heard about
but not read.
I was grateful to him
for his interest.

Do you remember
        how at Interlaken
                we were waiting, four days,
to see the Jungfrau
        but rain had fallen steadily.
            Then
just before train time
        on a tip from one of the waitresses
                we rushed
to the Gipfel Platz
        and there it was!
                in the distance
covered with new-fallen snow.
        When I was at Granada,
           I remember,
in the overpowering heat
        climbing a treeless hill
                overlooking the Alhambra.
At my appearance at the summit
        two small boys
                who had been playing
there
        made themselves scarce.
                Starting to come down
by a new path
        I at once found myself surrounded
                by gypsy women
who came up to me,
        I could speak little Spanish,
                and directed me,
guided by a young girl,
        on my way.
                These were the pinnacles.
The deaths I suffered
        began in the heads
                about me, my eyes
were too keen
        not to see through
                the world's niggardliness.
I accepted it

as my fate.
>   The wealthy
I defied
>   or not so much they,
>   for they have their uses,
as they who take their cues from them.
>   I lived
>   to breathe above the stench
not knowing how I in my own person
>   would be overcome
>   finally. I was lost
failing the poem.
>   But if I have come from the sea
>   it is not to be
wholly
>   fascinated by the glint of waves.
>   The free interchange
of light over their surface
>   which I have compared
>   to a garden
should not deceive us
>   or prove
>   too difficult a figure.
The poem
>   if it reflects the sea
>   reflects only
its dance
>   upon that profound depth
>   where
it seems to triumph.
>   The bomb puts an end
>   to all that.
I am reminded
>   that the bomb
>   also
is a flower
>   dedicated
>   howbeit
to our destruction.
>   The mere picture

of the exploding bomb
fascinates us
so that we cannot wait
to prostrate ourselves
before it. We do not believe
that love
can so wreck our lives.
The end
will come
in its time.
Meanwhile
we are sick to death
of the bomb
and its childlike
insistence.
Death is no answer,
no answer—
to a blind old man
whose bones
have the movement
of the sea,
a sexless old man
for whom it is a sea
of which his verses
are made up.
There is no power
so great as love
which is a sea,
which is a garden—
as enduring
as the verses
of that blind old man
destined
to live forever.
Few men believe that
nor in the games of children.
They believe rather
in the bomb
and shall die by
the bomb.

Compare Darwin's voyage of the *Beagle*,
   a voyage of discovery if there ever was one,
     to the death
incommunicado
   in the electric chair
     of the Rosenbergs.
It is the mark of the times
   that though we condemn
     what they stood for
we admire their fortitude.
   But Darwin
     opened our eyes
to the gardens of the world,
   as *they* closed them.
     Or take that other voyage
which promised so much
   but due to the world's avarice
     breeding hatred
through fear,
   ended so disastrously;
     a voyage
with which I myself am so deeply concerned,
   that of the *Pinta*,
     the *Niña*
and the *Santa María*.
   How the world opened its eyes!
     It was a flower
upon which April
   had descended from the skies!
     How bitter
a disappointment!
   In all,
     this led mainly
to the deaths I have suffered.
   For there had been kindled
     more minds
than that of the discoverers
   and set dancing
     to a measure,
a new measure!

Soon lost.
                    The measure itself
has been lost
                    and we suffer for it.
                            We come to our deaths
in silence.
                    The bomb speaks.
                            All suppressions,
from the witchcraft trials at Salem
                    to the latest
                            book burnings
are confessions
                    that the bomb
                            has entered our lives
to destroy us.
                    Every drill
                            driven into the earth
for oil enters my side
                    also.
                            Waste, waste!
dominates the world.
                    It is the bomb's work.
                            What else was the fire
at the Jockey Club in Buenos Aires
                    (*malos aires,* we should say)
                            when with Perón's connivance
the hoodlums destroyed,
                    along with the books
                            the priceless Goyas
that hung there?
                    You know how we treasured
                            the few paintings
we still cling to
                    especially the one
                            by the dead
Charlie Demuth.
                    With your smiles
                            and other trivia of the sort
my secret life
                    has been made up,

some baby's life
which had been lost
            had I not intervened.
                        But the words
made solely of air
            or less,
                        that came to me
out of the air
            and insisted
                        on being written down,
I regret most—
            that there has come an end
                        to them.
For in spite of it all,
            all that I have brought on myself,
                        grew that single image
that I adore
            equally with you
                        and so
it brought us together.

B O O K   I I I

What power has love but forgiveness?
            In other words
                        by its intervention
what has been done
            can be undone.
                        What good is it otherwise?
Because of this
            I have invoked the flower
                        in that
frail as it is
            after winter's harshness
                        it comes again
to delect us.
            Asphodel, the ancients believed,
                        in hell's despite
was such a flower.
            With daisies pied

and violets blue,
we say, the spring of the year
comes in!
So may it be
with the spring of love's year
also
if we can but find
the secret word
to transform it.
It is ridiculous
what airs we put on
to seem profound
while our hearts
gasp dying
for want of love.
Having your love
I was rich.
Thinking to have lost it
I am tortured
and cannot rest.
I do not come to you
abjectly
with confessions of my faults,
I have confessed,
all of them.
In the name of love
I come proudly
as to an equal
to be forgiven.
Let me, for I know
you take it hard,
with good reason,
give the steps
if it may be
by which you shall mount,
again to think well
of me.
The statue
of Colleoni's horse
with the thickset little man

on top
    in armor
        presenting a naked sword
comes persistently
    to my mind.
        And with him
the horse rampant
    roused by the mare in
        the Venus and Adonis.
These are pictures
    of crude force.
        Once at night
waiting at a station
    with a friend
        a fast freight
thundered through
    kicking up the dust.
        My friend,
a distinguished artist,
    turned with me
        to protect his eyes:
That's what we'd all like to be, Bill,
    he said. I smiled
        knowing how deeply
he meant it. I saw another man
    yesterday
        in the subway.
I was on my way uptown
    to a meeting.
        He kept looking at me
and I at him:
    He had a worn knobbed stick
        between his knees
suitable
    to keep off dogs,
        a man of perhaps forty.
He wore a beard
    parted in the middle,
        a black beard,
and a hat,

                    a brown felt hat
                              lighter than
his skin. His eyes,
              which were intelligent,
                              were wide open
but evasive, mild.
                    I was frankly curious
                              and looked at him
closely. He was slight of build
              but robust enough
                              had on
a double-breasted black coat
              and a vest
                              which showed at the neck
the edge of a heavy and very dirty
              undershirt.
                              His trousers
were striped
              and a lively
                              reddish brown. His shoes
which were good
              if somewhat worn
                              had been recently polished.
His brown socks
              were about his ankles.
                              In his breast pocket
he carried
              a gold fountain pen
                              and a mechanical
pencil. For some reason
              which I could not fathom
                              I was unable
to keep my eyes off him.
              A worn leather zipper case
                              bulging with its contents
lay between his ankles
              on the floor.
                              Then I remembered:
When my father was a young man—
              it came to me

from an old photograph—
he wore such a beard.
        This man
                reminds me of my father.
I am looking
        into my father's
                face! Some surface
of some advertising sign
        is acting
                as a reflector. It is
my own.
        But at once
                the car grinds to a halt.
Speak to him,
        I cried. He
                will know the secret.
He was gone
        and I did nothing about it.
                With him
went all men
        and all women too
                were in his loins.
Fanciful or not
        it seemed to me
                a flower
whose savor had been lost.
        It was a flower
                some exotic orchid
that Herman Melville had admired
        in the
                Hawaiian jungle.
Or the lilacs
        of men who left their marks,
                by torchlight,
rituals of the hunt,
        on the walls
                of prehistoric
caves in the Pyrenees—
        what draftsmen they were—
                bison and deer.

Their women
  had big buttocks.
    But what
draftsmen they were!
  By my father's beard,
    what draftsmen.
And so, by chance,
  how should it be otherwise?
    from what came to me
in a subway train
  I build a picture
    of all men.
It is winter
  and there
    waiting for you to care for them
are your plants.
  Poor things! you say
    as you compassionately
pour at their roots
  the reviving water.
    Lean-cheeked
I say to myself
  kindness moves her
    shall she not be kind
also to me? At this
  courage possessed me finally
    to go on.
Sweet, creep into my arms!
  I spoke hurriedly
    in the spell
of some wry impulse
  when I boasted
    that there was
any pride left in me.
  Do not believe it.
    Unless
in a special way,
  a way I shrink to speak of
    I am proud. After that manner

I call on you
          as I do on myself the same
                    to forgive all women
who have offended you.
          It is the artist's failing
                    to seek and to yield
such forgiveness.
          It will cure us both.
                    Let us
keep it to ourselves but trust it.
          These heads
                    that stick up all around me
are, I take it,
          also proud.
                    But the flowers
know at least this much,
          that it is not spring
                    and will be proud only
in the proper season.
          A trance holds men.
                    They are dazed
and their faces in the public print
          show it. We follow them
                    as children followed
the Pied Piper
          of Hamelin—but he
                    was primarily
interested only in rats.
          I say to you
                    privately
that the heads of most men I see
          at meetings
                    or when I come up against them
elsewhere
          are full of cupidity.
                    Let us breed
from those others.
          They are the flowers of the race.
                    The asphodel

poor as it is
   is among them.
      But in their pride
there come to my mind
   the daisy,
       not the shy flower
of England but the brilliance
   that mantled
      with white
the fields
   which we knew
      as children.
Do you remember
   their spicy-sweet
      odor? What abundance!
There are many other flowers
   I could recall
      for your pleasure:
the small yellow sweet-scented violet
   that grew
      in marshy places!
You were like those
   though I quickly
      correct myself
for you were a woman
   and no flower
      and had to face
the problems which confront a woman.
   But you were for all that
      flowerlike
and I say this to you now
   and it is the thing
      which compounded
my torment
   that I never
      forgot it.
You have forgiven me
   making me new again.
      So that here

in the place
        dedicated in the imagination
                to memory
of the dead
        I bring you
                a last flower. Don't think
that because I say this
        in a poem
                it can be treated lightly
or that the facts will not uphold it.
        Are facts not flowers
                and flowers facts
or poems flowers
        or all works of the imagination,
                interchangeable?
Which proves
        that love
                rules them all, for then
you will be my queen,
        my queen of love
                forever more.

CODA

Inseparable from the fire
        its light
                takes precedence over it.
Then follows
        what we have dreaded—
                but it can never
overcome what has gone before.
        In the huge gap
                between the flash
and the thunderstroke
        spring has come in
                or a deep snow fallen.
Call it old age.
        In that stretch
                we have lived to see

a colt kick up his heels.
       Do not hasten
             laugh and play
in an eternity
          the heat will not overtake the light.
             That's sure.
That gelds the bomb,
       permitting
             that the mind contain it.
This is that interval,
       that sweetest interval,
             when love will blossom,
come early, come late
       and give itself to the lover.
Only the imagination is real!
       I have declared it
             time without end.
If a man die
       it is because death
             has first
possessed his imagination.
       But if he refuse death—
             no greater evil
can befall him
       unless it be the death of love
             meet him
in full career.
       Then indeed
             for him
the light has gone out.
But love and the imagination
       are of a piece,
             swift as the light
to avoid destruction.
       So we come to watch time's flight
             as we might watch
summer lightning
       or fireflies, secure,
             by grace of the imagination,

safe in its care.
      For if
           the light itself
has escaped,
      the whole edifice opposed to it
          goes down.
Light, the imagination
      and love,
          in our age,
by natural law,
      which we worship,
          maintain
all of a piece
      their dominance.
So let us love
      confident as is the light
          in its struggle with darkness
that there is as much to say
      and more
          for the one side
and that not the darker
      which John Donne
          for instance
among many men
      presents to us.
          In the controversy
touching the younger
      and the older Tolstoy,
          Villon, St. Anthony, Kung,
Rimbaud, Buddha
      and Abraham Lincoln
          the palm goes
always to the light;
      who most shall advance the light—
          call it what you may!
The light
      for all time shall outspeed
          the thunder crack.
Medieval pageantry

is human and we enjoy
          the rumor of it
as in our world we enjoy
          the reading of Chaucer,
                    likewise
a priest's raiment
          (or that of a savage chieftain).
                    It is all
a celebration of the light.
          All the pomp and ceremony
                    of weddings,
"Sweet Thames, run softly
          till I end
                    my song,"—
are of an equal sort.
For our wedding, too,
          the light was wakened
                    and shone. The light!
the light stood before us
          waiting!
                    I thought the world
stood still.
          At the altar
                    so intent was I
before my vows,
          so moved by your presence
                    a girl so pale
and ready to faint
          that I pitied
                    and wanted to protect you.
As I think of it now,
          after a lifetime,
                    it is as if
a sweet-scented flower
          were poised
                    and for me did open.
Asphodel
          has no odor
                    save to the imagination

but it too
celebrates the light.
It is late
but an odor
as from our wedding
has revived for me
and begun again to penetrate
into all crevices
of my world.

POEMS

1955-1962

ON ST. VALENTINE'S DAY

On St. Valentine's Day
        I went to seek my love,
                up one street
and down another.
        My heart was heavy
                because I had nothing to
                give her.
What should I say?
        The streets were empty
                so I met no one.

Yet I knew she could not be far
        for the sun was shining
                merrily!

Old though you find me
        and penniless,
                I said to the silence of
                the garden,
I shall take courage
        for a snow-drop is about to blossom,
                smiling at me
from my own yard,
        smiling, smiling up at me
                from my own yard.

I love you, I love you!
        I said to the flower
                knowing my love shall not be
                lost
knowing that I am not mistaken.

HYMN AMONG THE RUINS
OCTAVIO PAZ

Where foams the Sicilian sea . . .
                                        Góngora

Self crowned the day displays its plumage.
A shout tall and yellow,
impartial and beneficent,
a hot geyser into the middle sky!
Appearances are beautiful in this their momentary truth.
The sea mounts the coast,
clings between the rocks, a dazzling spider;
the livid wound on the mountain glistens;
a handful of goats becomes a flock of stones;
the sun lays its gold egg upon the sea.
All is god.
A broken statue,
columns gnawed by the light,
ruins alive in a world of death in life!

Night falls on Teotihuacán.
On top of the pyramid the boys are smoking marijuana,
harsh guitars sound.
What weed, what living waters will give life to us,
where shall we unearth the word,
the relations that govern hymn and speech,
the dance, the city and the measuring scales?
The song of Mexico explodes in a curse,
a colored star that is extinguished,
a stone that blocks our doors of contact.
Earth tastes of rotten earth.

Eyes see, hands touch.
Here a few things suffice:
prickly pear, coral and thorny planet,
the hooded figs,
grapes that taste of the resurrection,
clams, stubborn maidenheads,
salt, cheese, wine, the sun's bread.

An island girl looks on me from the height of her duskiness,
a slim cathedral clothed in light.
A tower of salt, against the green pines of the shore,
the white sails of the boats arise.
Light builds temples on the sea.

New York, London, Moscow.
Shadow covers the plain with its phantom ivy,
with its swaying and feverish vegetation,
its mousy fur, its rats swarm.
Now and then an anemic sun shivers.
Propping himself on mounts that yesterday were cities,
    Polyphemus yawns.
Below, among the pits, a herd of men dragging along.
Until lately people considered them unclean animals.

To see, to touch each day's lovely forms.
The light throbs, all darties and wings.
The wine-stain on the tablecloth smells of blood.
As the coral thrusts branches into the water
I stretch my senses to this living hour:
the moment fulfills itself in a yellow harmony.
Midday, ear of wheat heavy with minutes,
eternity's brimming cup.

My thoughts are split, meander, grow entangled,
start again,
and finally lose headway, endless rivers,
delta of blood beneath an unwinking sun.
And must everything end in this spatter of stagnant water?

Day, round day,
shining orange with four-and-twenty bars,
all one single yellow sweetness!
Mind embodies in forms,
the two hostile become one,
the conscience-mirror liquifies,
once more a fountain of legends:
man, tree of images,
words which are flowers become fruits which are deeds.

TO FRIEND-TREE OF COUNTED DAYS
RENÉ CHAR

Brief harp of the larches
On mossy spur of stone crop
—Façade of the forest,
Against which mists are shattered—
Counterpoint of the void in which
    I believe.

REVERIE AND INVOCATION

Whether the rain comes down
or there be sunny days
the sleets of January or the haze
of autumn afternoons, when
we dream of our youth our gaze
grows mellow, wise man or fool,
we were young, the future
beckoned us.

Now we grow old and grey
and all we knew is forgotten
there comes alive in
the ash of today, memory! a god
who revives us! the apple trees
we climbed as a boy
the caress on our necks of
a summer breeze.

Come back and give us
those days when passion drove us
to break every rule.
We weren't bad, but good!
May our preachers find us
the courage still to sin so
and win so! and win so!
a life everlasting.

BALLAD

To a man and his wife
and four children,
he's a musician and
teaches school.

He might be a Campion,
no matter,
his wife is lean from
her calling. But the man,

the man,
has his music and
teaching, he has also
his wife!

She looks forward
and back
and is worried
it shows in her face.

But give them
their music, like Mozart,
they're happy
and thrill to a tune.

Hymen!
god of married lovers
has blessed them and
their house.

THE BIRTH

A 40 odd year old Para 10
        Navarra
                or Navatta she didn't know
uncomplaining

in a small room where we had been working
    all night long.

Dozing off by 10 or 15 minute intervals
    I watched
            her pendulous belly
marked
        by contraction rings under
            the skin.
No progress.

It was restfully quiet on Guinea Hill
        approaching dawn in
                those days.
Wha's a ma', Doc.
        It no wanna come?

That finally roused me.
        I got me a strong sheet
            wrapped it
tight around her belly.
        When the pains came again
                the direction
was changed
    not
                against her own backbone
but downward
        toward the exit.
            It began to move—stupid
not to have thought of that earlier.

Finally
        without a cry out of her more than
            a low animal grunting
the head emerged
    up to the neck.

It took its own time
        rotating.
                I thought
of a lewd joke
        about a child

                    suspended thus
upside down
            by the neck
as we are most of us
            at that moment
                        of our careers.
After a time
            I was able
                        to extract the shoulders
one at a time
            a tight fit.
                        Madonna!
13½ pounds!
            Not a man among us at least
                        can have equaled
that.

THIS IS PIONEER WEATHER

        Me, go to Florida!
        Ha ha!
        At Northfield when
        we were girls

        we used to take
        the trays
        we
        had in the kitchen

        and sit on them
        Wow!
        what a thrill!
        in the field

        back of the
        school!
        down hill screaming
        our heads off!

SAPPHO

That man is peer of the gods, who
face to face sits listening
to your sweet speech and lovely
      laughter.

It is this that rouses a tumult
in my breast. At mere sight of you
my voice falters, my tongue
      is broken.

Straightway, a delicate fire runs in
my limbs; my eyes
are blinded and my ears
      thunder.

Sweat pours out: a trembling hunts
me down. I grow
paler than grass and lack little
      of dying.

THE LOVING DEXTERITY
[First Version]

The flower
      fallen
a pink petal
      intact on the ground

Deftly
      she raised it
and placed it
      on its stem again

AT THE BRINK OF WINTER

At the brink of winter
planting the bulbs

Sh!
she said to the garden,
They are going to sleep!

Five Translated Poems

GREEN EYES
ALÍ CHUMACERO

Solemnity of a bemused tiger, there in his eyes
temptation goes wandering and a shipwrecked man
sleeps on a hoary pillow of jade
the unwaited day of marvels
in ages which herds of horses have trampled.

A furious face, violence
is a river tumbled upon quietness in the valley,
awe where time abandons itself
to a motionless current, bathed
in rest repeating
the same phrase over and over from the first syllable.

Only a sound beneath the water insists
with loud clamor, and tardy precincts
of the hurricane, its exile
leaving a world fatigued and remote.

If perchance we understand, the epilogue
would be the thought of a world music,
languors broken by a chord
as the grape in a vertiginous shower
casts shadows confusing the eye.

With decorum let us proceed to the inn
where the smoke of our cigars has preceded us,
let us go to the brothel while waiting:
for at last beauty awaits us.

NAKED
ALVARO FIGUEREDO

The azure yielder
of the skylark's way or the foam
ceaselessly re-created
made into ultimate marble
there where the mediterranean
navel imposes
its majesty and casts
precious strokes of gold upon cheeks
advanced by Sirius between
two breasts that give
hard commands to the wind
asleep in the blue shepherding
slowness between her thighs
now that I part them a siesta to see her
strictly disciplined horizontals
crowds forges vineyard country
instant shadows glaciers
blueblue cocks
of weather vanes when
their noble bellies isolate
the flow of the ocean as
the young huntress sleeps
and a birch tree quickens upon her knees.

PIANO SOLO
NICANOR PARRA

Since man's life is nothing but a bit of action at a distance,
A bit of foam shining inside a glass;
Since trees are nothing but moving trees;
Nothing but chairs and tables in perpetual motion;
Since we ourselves are nothing but beings
(As the godhead itself is nothing but God);
Now that we do not speak solely to be heard
But so that others may speak

And the echo precede the voice that produces it;
Since we do not even have the consolation of a chaos
In the garden that yawns and fills with air,
A puzzle that we must solve before our death
So that we may nonchalantly resuscitate later on
When we have led woman to excess;
Since there is also a heaven in hell,
Permit me to propose a few things:

I wish to make a noise with my feet
I want my soul to find its proper body.

THE INFINITE HORSES
SILVINA OCAMPO

I have seen them asleep on the grass,
mirroring themselves in the fields;
seen them furious, on their knees,
like haughty gods, all white,
dressed in ribbons, savage
with manes flying like the loose hair
of legended sirens on the shores.
Vile vipers have dreamt of them,
reeds and bedded mothers
keep them closed in the palms.
Trembling they foretell battles,
like the beat of their trotting hoofs,
like applause thundering in a vast theater.
They have seen wounds bleeding into the clay,
died among flowers, in the mire,
intimates of birds and vermin.
They draw near bearing armed men,
approach on their backs vile tyrants,
dressed in blood and purple.
I shall remember implacable horses:
Russian trappings; the Przewalski;
the names of the hundred and twenty
Roman horses, chiseled in marble;

at the Olympus of Dionus of Argus,
with a hard penumbra aphrodisiac on
their bronze flanks, the horse
most favored by the others
was that of Altis; he who was so loved
by Semiramis, the queen of Asia;
those who tasted with blessed transports—
long before the Chinese tasted them—
green tea from those inspired leaves;
that horse created by Virgil
whose benign and virtuous shadow was gifted
with the power to heal all horses.
I shall remember in an orange sky,
horses so left in shadow,
concernedly bringing lovers together
in peaceful grottoes from a distance.

ODE TO LAZINESS
PABLO NERUDA

Yesterday I felt this ode
would not get off the floor.
It was time, I ought
at least
show a green leaf.
I scratch the earth: "Arise,
sister ode
—said to her—
I have promised you,
do not be afraid of me,
I am not going to crush you,
four-leaf ode,
four-hand ode,
you shall have tea with me.
Arise,
I am going to crown you among the odes,
we shall go out together along the shores
of the sea, on a bicycle."
It was no use.

Then,
on the pine peaks,
laziness
appeared in the nude,
she led me dazzled
and sleepy,
she showed me upon the sand
small broken bits
of ocean substance,
wood, algae, pebbles,
feathers of sea birds.
I looked for but did not find
yellow agates.
The sea
filled all spaces
crumbling towers,
invading
the shores of my country,
advancing
successive catastrophes of the foam.
Alone on the sand
spread wide
its corolla.
I saw the silvery petrels crossing
and like black creases
the cormorants
nailed to the rocks.
I released a bee
that was agonizing in a spider's net.
I put a little pebble
in my pocket,
it was smooth, very smooth
as the breast of a bird,
meanwhile on the shore,
all afternoon
sun struggled with mist.
At times
the mist was steeped
in thought,
topaz-like,

at others fell
a ray from the moist sun
distilling yellow drops.

At night,
thinking of the duties of my fugitive ode,
I pull off my shoes
near the fire;
sand slid out of them
and soon I began to fall
asleep.

AN OLD-FASHIONED
GERMAN CHRISTMAS CARD

Armed with
a bass-violin
horn

clarinet and
fiddle
go four

poor musicians
trudging
the snow

between
villages in
the cold

Alí Chumacero: Two Poems

WIDOWER'S MONOLOGUE

I open the door, return to the familiar mercy
of my own house where a vague
sense protects me the son who never was
smacking of shipwreck, waves or a passionate cloak
whose acid summers
cloud the fading face. Archaic refuge
of dead gods fills the region,
and below, the wind breathes, a conscious
gust which fanned my forehead yesterday
still sought in the perturbed present.

I could not speak of sheets, candles, smoke
nor humility and compassion, calm
at the afternoon's edges, I could not
say "her hands," "her sadness," "our country"
because everything in her name
is lighted by her wounds. Like a signal sprung
of foam, an epitaph, curtains, a bed, rugs
and destruction moving toward disdain
while the lime triumphs denying her nakedness
the color of emptiness.

Now time begins, the bitter smile
of the guest who in sleeplessness sings,
waking his anger, within the vile city
the calcined music with curled lip
from indecision
that flows without cease. Star or dolphin, yonder
beneath the wave his foot vanishes,
tunics turned to emblems
sink their burning shows and with ashes
score my own forehead.

THE WANDERINGS OF THE TRIBE

Autumn surrounds the valley, iniquity
overflows, and the hill sacred to splendor
responds in the form of a revenge. The dust measures
and misfortune knows who gallops
where all gallop with the same fury:
constrained attendance on the broken circle
by the son who startles his father gazing
from a window buried in the sand.

Blood of man's victim
besieges doors, cries out: "Here no one lives,"
but the mansion is inhabited by the barbarian who seeks
dignity, yoke of the fatherland
broken, abhorred by memory.
as the husband looks at his wife face to face
and close to the threshold, the intruder
hastens the trembling that precedes misfortune.

Iron and greed, a decisive leprosy
of hatreds that were fed by rapine and deceits
wets the seeds. Brother against brother
comes to the challenge without pity
brings to a pause its stigma against the kingdom of pity:
arrogance goads the leap into the void
that as the wind dies the eagles abandon
their quest like tumbled statues.

Emptied upon the mockery of the crowd
the afternoon defends itself, redoubles its hide
against stones that have lost their foundations.
Her offense is compassion when we pass
from the gilded alcove to the somber one
with the fixety of glowing coals: hardly
a moment, peaceful light as upon
a drunken soldier awaiting his degradation.

We can smile later at our childish furies
giving way to rancor and sometimes envy

before the ruffian who without a word taking leave
descends from the beast
in search of surcease. The play is his:
mask quitting the scene, catastrophy
overtaking love with its delirium and with delight
looses the last remnant of its fury.

Came doubt and the lust for wine,
bodies like daggers, that transform
youth to tyranny: pleasures
and the crew of sin.
A bursting rain of dishonor
a heavy tumult and the nearnesses
were disregarded drums and cries and sobs
to those whom no one calls by the name of "brother."

At last I thought the day calmed
its own profanities. The clouds, contempt,
the site made thunderbolts by love's phrases,
tableware, oil, sweet odors, was all
a cunning propitiation of the enemy,
and I discovered later floating over
the drowned tribes, links of foam tumbling
blindly against the sides of a ship.

TRIBUTE TO NERUDA THE POET COLLECTOR OF SEASHELLS

Now that I am all but blind,
however it came about,
though I can see as well
as anyone—the imagination

has turned inward as happened
to my mother when she
became old: dreams took the
place of sight. Her native

tongue was Spanish which,
of course, she
never forgot. It was the
language also of Neruda the

Chilean poet—who collected
seashells on his
native beaches, until he
had by reputation, the second

largest collection in the
world. Be patient with
him, darling mother, the
changeless beauty of

seashells, like the
sea itself, gave
his lines the variable pitch
which modern verse requires.

MIDWINTER

laughing with ice
the stubblefield
has paced

its measured tread
across the crowded
amphi-

theater of oaks
and one posturing
elm to

a jeweled chorus'
thunderous if silent
applause

The Cassia Tree

A collection of translations and adaptations
from the Chinese in collaboration with David Rafael Wang

(For Mark Linenthal, Jr.)

POPULAR T'ANG AND SUNG POEMS

I
MENG HAO-JAN, *689–740*

In spring you sleep and never know when the morn comes,
   Everywhere you hear the songs of the birds,
But at night the sound of the wind mingles with the rain's,
   And you wonder how many flowers have fallen.

II
LI PO, *701–762*

Spotting the moonlight at my bedside,
I wonder if it is frost on the ground.
After raising my head to look at the bright moon,
I lower it to think of my old country.

III
LIU CHUNG-YUAN, *773–819*

The birds have flown away from the mountains,
The sign of men has gone from all the paths,
But under a lone sail stoops an old fisherman,
Angling in the down-pouring snow.

IV
HO CHIH-CHANG, *659–744*

Returning after I left my home in childhood,
I have kept my native accent but not the color of my hair.

Facing the smiling children who shyly approach me,
I am asked from where I come.

V
MENG HAO-JAN

Steering my little boat towards a misty islet,
I watch the sun descend while my sorrows grow:
In the vast night the sky hangs lower than the treetops,
But in the blue lake the moon is coming close.

VI
WANG WEI, *699–759*

Alighting from my horse to drink with you,
I asked, "Where are you going?"
You said, "Retreating to lie in the southern mountains."
Silent,
I watch the white clouds endless in the distance.

VII
LI YU, *the last king of the Southern T'ang Dynasty, 937–978*

Silently I ascend the western pavilion.
The moon hangs like a hairpin.
In the deep autumn garden
    The wu-t'ung stands alone.
Involute,
Entangled,
The feeling of departure
    Clings like a wet leaf to my heart.

THE MAID
ANCIENT FOLK POEM

Drives sheep through ravine,
With the white goat in front.
The ole gal unmarried,
Her sigh reaches heaven.

Aihe! Aihe!
Endless dream of the shepherd.
"Hold man's left arm,
Turn and toss with him."

"Stroke man's whiskers,
watch changin' expression."
The shepherd unmindful
Can she force him?

LAMENT OF A GRAYING WOMAN
CHO WEN-CHUN, *Han poetess, 2nd century B.C.*

White as the snow on mountaintop,
Bright as the moon piercing the clouds,
Knowing that you have a divided heart,
I come to you before you are gone.

We have lived long together in this town.
What need is there for a feast of wine?
But a feast we must have today,
For tomorrow we'll be by the stream
And I'll lag behind you at the fork,
Watching the waters flow east or west.

Tears and still more tears.
Why should we lament?
If only there is a constant man
Till white-hair shall we never part!

SOCIETY OF POETS

I TO LI PO
TU FU, *712–770*

The floating cloud follows the sun.
The traveler has not yet returned.
For three nights I dreamt of you, my friend,
So clearly that I almost touched you.

You left me in a hurry.
Your passage is fraught with trouble:
The wind blows fiercely over lakes and rivers.
Be watchful lest you fall from your boat!
You scratched your white head when leaving the door,
And I knew the journey was against your wishes.

Silk-hatted gentlemen have swamped the capital,
While you, the poet, are lean and haggard.
If the net of heaven is not narrow,
Why should you be banished when you are old?
Ten thousand ages will remember your warmth;
When you are gone the world is silent and cold.

II TO MENG HAO-JAN
LI PO

I love Meng-fu-tsu.
His name is known throughout China.
While rosy-cheeked he gave up his office;
Now with white hair he lies in the pine clouds.
Drunk with the moon he is a hermit-saint;
Lost in flowers he will not serve any kings.
Can I reach him who is like a high mountain?
I am contented if I only breathe in his fragrance.

III TO WANG WEI
MENG HAO-JAN

Quietly, quietly, why have I been waiting?
Emptily, emptily, I return every day alone.
I have been in search of fragrant grass
And miss the friend who can accompany me.

Who will let me roam his private park?
Understanding ones in the world are rare.
I shall walk back home all by myself
And fasten the latch on the gate of my garden.

AFTER THE PARTY
MENG HAO-JAN

The guest, still drunk, sprawls in my bed
How am I going to get him awake?
The chicken congee is boiling on the stove
And the new wine is heated to start our day.

LATE SPRING
MENG HAO-JAN

In April the lake water is clear
Everywhere the birds are singing
The ground just swept, the petals fall again
The grass, though stepped on, remains green
My drinking companions gather to compare fortunes
Open the keg to get over the bout of drinking
With cups held high in our hands
We hear the voices of sing-song girls
                                    ringing.

CE-LIA THE IMMORTAL BEAUTY
WANG WEI

The beauty of a maiden is coveted by the world.
So how could a girl like Ce-Lia be slighted for long?
In the morning she was just another lass in the village,
But in the evening she has become the king's concubine.

Was she different from the rest in her days of poverty?
Now that she is favored, all begin to realize her beauty is rare.
She can command her maids to powder and perfume her face,
And is no longer obliged to don her own clothing.
The adoration of her Emperor has brought pride to her being,
And the king's "Yes" and "No" vary in accordance with her caprice.

The companions who washed at the brookside along with her
Are not entitled any more to ride back home in the same carriage.

Why should we bother to sympathize with these rustic girls,
Since they'll never have Beauty to accompany them,
　　even if they should master the art of coquetry?

THE PEERLESS LADY
WANG WEI

Look, there goes the young lady across the street
She looks about fifteen, doesn't she?
Her husband is riding the piebald horse
Her maids are scraping chopped fish from a gold plate.

Her picture gallery and red pavilion stand face to face
The willow and the peach trees shadow her eaves
Look, she's coming thru the gauze curtains to get into her chaise:
Her attendants have started winnowing the fans.

Her husband got rich early in his life
A more arrogant man you never find around!
She keeps busy by teaching her maids to dance
She never regrets giving jewels away.

There goes the light by her window screen
The green smoke's rising like petals on wave
The day is done and what does she do?
Her hair tied up, she watches the incense fade.

None but the bigwigs visit her house
Only the Chaos and the Lees get by her guards
But do you realize this pretty girl
Used to beat her clothes at the river's head?

A LETTER
LI PO

My love,
　　　When you were here there was
　　　a hall of flowers.

When you are gone there is
    an empty bed.
Under the embroidered coverlet
    I toss and turn.
After three years I
    smell your fragrance.
Your fragrance never leaves,
But you never return.
I think of you, the yellow leaves are ended
And the white dew dampens the green moss.

SPRING SONG
LI PO

A young lass
Plucks mulberry leaves by the river

Her white hand
Reaches among the green

Her flushed cheeks
Shine under the sun

The hungry silkworms
Are waiting

Oh, young horseman
Why do you tarry. Get going.

SUMMER SONG
LI PO

The Mirror Lake
    (Three hundred miles),

Where lotus buds
    Burst into flowers.

The slippery shore
Is jammed with admirers,

While the village beauty
Picks the blossoms.

Before the sails
Breast the rising moon,

She's shipped away
To the king's harem.

IN THE WINESHOP OF CHINLING
LI PO

The wind scatters the fragrance of the willows over the shop
The sing-song girls pour the rice wine heated for the guests
My friends have gathered to say goodbye
Drinking cup after cup, I wonder why I should start
"Say, can you tell me about the east-flowing river—
Does it stretch as long as this feeling of departure?"

SOLO
LI PO

The pavilion pierces the green sky
Below is the white jade chamber
The bright moon is ready to set
Casting its glance behind the screen window

Solitary she stands
Her thin silk skirt ruffled by autumn frost
She fingers softly the séchin
Composing the Mulberry Song.

The sound reverberates
And the wind circles the crossbeams
Outside the pedestrians are turning away
And the birds are gone to their nests.

The weight of feeling
Cannot be carried away by song and
She longs for someone
To soar with her like a mandarin drake.

THE YOUTH ON HORSEBACK
LI PO

The youth from the capital rides by the east of the city.
His white horse and silver saddle sail through the spring breeze.
Having trampled all the flowers where else could he go?
Smiling, he enters the barroom of the white prostitute.

THE KNIGHT
LI PO

In March the dust of Tartary has swept over the capital.
Inside the city wall the people sigh and complain.
Under the bridge the water trickles with warm blood
And bales of white bones lean against one another.

I departed east for the Kingdom of Wu.
Clouds block the four fortresses and the roads are long.
Only the crows announce the rise of the sun.
Someone opens the city gate to sweep away the flowers.

Wu-t'ungs and willows hover above the well.
Drunk, I come to the knight-errant's home.
The knights-errant of Fu Fêng are rare in this world:
With arms around their friends they'll heave mountains.
The posture of the generals means little to them
And, drinking, they ignore the orders of the cabinet.

With fancy food on carved plates they entertain their guests.
With songs and dance their sing-song girls unwind a fragrant wind.
The fabulous dukes of the six kingdoms
Were known for their entertainment:
In the dining hall of each three thousands were fed.

But who knew which one would remember to repay?
They stroke their long swords, arching their eyebrows;
By the clear water and white rock they decline to separate.

Doffing my hat I turn to you smiling.
Drinking your wine I recite only for you.

I have not yet met my master of strategy—
The bridgeside hermit may read my heart.

DRINKING TOGETHER
LI PO

We drink in the mountain while the flowers bloom,
A pitcher, a pitcher, and one more pitcher.
As my head spins you get up.
So be back any time with your guitar.

THE MARCH
LI PO

The bay horse is fitted with a white jade saddle.
The moon shivers over the battlefield.
The sound of iron drums still shakes the city walls
And in the case the gold sword oozes blood.

LONG BANISTER LANE
LI PO

When my hair was first trimmed across my forehead,
I played in front of my door, picking flowers.
You came riding a bamboo stilt for a horse,
Circling around my yard, playing with green plums.
Living as neighbors at Long Banister Lane,
We had an affection for each other that none were suspicious of.

At fourteen I became your wife,
With lingering shyness, I never laughed.

Lowering my head towards a dark wall,
I never turned, though called a thousand times.

At fifteen I began to show my happiness,
I desired to have my dust mingled with yours.
With a devotion ever unchanging,
Why should I look out when I had you?

At sixteen you left home
For a faraway land of steep pathways and eddies,
Which in May were impossible to traverse,
And where the monkeys whined sorrowfully towards the sky.

The footprints you made when you left the door
Have been covered by green moss,
New moss too deep to be swept away.
The autumn wind came early and the leaves started falling.
The butterflies, yellow with age in August,
Fluttered in pairs towards the western garden.
Looking at the scene, I felt a pang in my heart,
And I sat lamenting my fading youth.

Every day and night I wait for your return,
Expecting to receive your letter in advance,
So that I will come traveling to greet you
As far as Windy Sand.

THE VISITOR
Adaptation of LI PO

See that horseman from the distant land,
Greeneyed and wearing a tigerskin hat.
Smiling, he lifts two arrows from his case,
And ten thousand people shy away.

He bends his bow like a circling moon
And from the clouds white geese spin down in pairs.
Shaking his whip high in the air,
He starts out hunting with his pack.

Once out of his dooryard what does he care?
What matters if he dies *pro patria*?

Prouder he is than five sultans
And has the wolf's love for seeking out a herd.
He drives the cattle further north
And with a tiger's appetite tastes the freshly killed.

But he camps at the Swallow Mountain,
Far from the arctic snow.
From his horse a woman smiles at him,
Her face a vermilion vessel of jade.

As his flying darts haunt birds and beasts,
Flowers and the moon land drunk in his saddle.
The light of the alien star flashes and spreads
While war gathers head like the swarming of wasps.

From the edge of his white sword blood drips and drips.
It covers the floating sand.

Are there any more reckless generals left?—
The soldiers are too tired to complain.

PROFILE OF A LADY
TU FU

A pretty, pretty girl
Lives in the empty mountain
Came from a celebrated family
Now alone with her fagots.

In the civil war
All her brothers were killed.
Why talk of pedigree,
When she couldn't collect their bones?

World feeling rises against the decline,
Then follows the rotating candle.

Husband has a new interest:
A beauty subtle as jade.

The acacia knows its hour
The mandarin duck never lies alone.
Husband listens to the laughter of new girl
deaf to the tears of the old.

Spring in the mountains is clear,
Mud underfoot.
She sends the maid to sell jewels
Picks wisteria to mend the roof

Wears no fresh flower
Bears cypress boughs in her hands.
Leans cold against the bamboo
Her green sleeves flutter.

VISIT
TU FU

In life we could seldom meet
Separate as the stars.
What a special occasion tonight
That we gather under the candle-lamp!

How long can youth last?
Our hair is peppered with white.
Half of our friends are ghosts
It's so good to see you alive.

How strange after twenty years
To revisit your house!
When I left you were single
Your children are grown up now.
They treat me with great respect,
Ask where I came from.

Before I can answer
You send your son for the wine.

In the rain you cut scallions
And start the oven to cook rice.

"It's so hard to get together
Let's finish up these ten goblets."
After ten goblets we are still sober
The feeling of reunion is long.

Tomorrow I have to cross the mountain
Back to the mist of the world.

CHANT OF THE FRONTIERSMAN
WANG CH'ANG-LING, 698–756

I

The cicadas are singing in the mulberry forest:
It is August at the fortress.
We pass the frontiers to enter more frontiers.
Everywhere the rushes are yellow.

The sodbusters from the provinces
Have disappeared with the dust they kicked up.
Why should we bother to be knights-errant?
Let us discuss the merits of bayards.

II

I lead the horse to drink in the autumn river.
The river is icy and the wind cuts like knives.
In the desert the sun has not yet gone down;
In the shade I see my distant home.

When the war first spread to the Great Wall,
We were filled with patriotic fervor.
The yellow sand has covered the past glories;
The bleached bones are scattered over the nettles.

THE NEWLYWED'S CUISINE
WANG CHIEN, *751–c. 830*

The third night after wedding
    I get near the stove.

Rolling up my sleeves
    I make a fancy broth.

Not knowing the taste
    of my mother-in-law,

I try it first upon her
    youngest girl.

BELLA DONNA IU
LI YU

Spring flowers, autumn moon—when will you end?
How much of the past do you recall?
At the pavilion last night the east wind sobbed.
I can hardly turn my head homeward
               in this moonlight.

The carved pillars and the jade steps are still here.
But the color of your cheeks is gone.
When asked: "How much sorrow do you still have?"
"Just like the flood of spring water
               rushing eastward."

IN DREAM'S WAKE
LI TS'UN-HSU, *Emperor Chuang*
of the later T'ang Dynasty,
10th century

We dine in a glade concealed in peach petals.
We dance like linnets and sing like phoenixes.
Then we part.

Like a dream,
Like a dream,
A mist envelops the pale moon and fallen blossoms.

From PHOENIX UNDYING
KUO MO-JO, *1892–1978*

Ah!
Our floating and inconstant life
Is like a delirious dream in a dark night.
Before us is sleep,
Behind us is sleep;
It comes like the fluttering wind,
It comes like the trailing smoke;
Enters like wind,
Departs like smoke.
Behind us: sleep,
Before us: sleep.
In the midst of our sleep we appear
Like the momentary wind and smoke.

SPRING IN THE SNOW-DRENCHED GARDEN
MAO TSE-TUNG, *1893–1976*

The northern countryside of China
Is bound by miles and miles of ice.
Snow flies over the border,
And outside of the Great Wall
Waste land stretches as though endless.
The great Hwang Ho rushes in torrents
Up and down the skyline.
The mountains thrash like silvery snakes,
Their contours soar like waxen elephants
Vying with the gods in height.
On a fine day,
The landscape unveils like a maiden
Dressing up in her boudoir.
Such enchanting mountains and rivers

Have led countless heroes to rival in homage.
Pity that the founders of Ch'in and Han
    Were unversed in the classics;
Pity that the great kings of T'ang and Sung
    Were deficient in poetry;
Pity that the magnificent, the pride of heaven,
    Genghis Khan
    Could only shoot with bows and arrows.
All these were of the past!
For the greatest man yet—only
My dynasty, my era will show.

THE OLD MAN AND THE CHILD
PING HSIN, 1900–

The old man to the child:
"Weep,
    Sigh,
        How dreary the world is!"

The child, laughing:
"Excuse me,
        mister!
I can't imagine what I haven't experienced."

The child to the old man:
"Smile,
    Jump,
        How interesting the world is!"

The old man, sighing:
"Forgive me,
        child!
I can't bear recalling what I have experienced."

THREE GENERATIONS
TSANG K'O-CHIA, *1905–*

The child
Is bathing in the mud.

The father
Is sweating in the mud.

The grandfather
Is buried in the mud.

CONSTRUCTION

on the sidewalk
in front of the funeral
home

where the high
school kids gather
at night

there was a used
condom squashed
flat

CÉZANNE

No pretense no more than the
French painters of
the early years of the nineteenth century

to scant the truth
of the light itself as
it was reflected from

a ballerina's thigh this Ginsberg
of *Kaddish* falls apart
violently to a peal of laughter or to

wrenched imprecation from a
man's head nothing can
stop the truth of it art is all we

can say to reverse
the chain of events and make a pileup
of passion to match the stars

No choice but between
a certain variation
hard to perceive in a shade of blue

BIRD SONG

It is May on every hand
when the Towhee sings
to his silent mate

at the bottom of
the garden
flaunting his startling

colors moving restlessly
from one
leafless magnolia twig

to another—
announcing spring is
here spring is here

THE ART

In spring looking at a
piece
of abstract art

call it anything
a
crocus clump

a new laid breast just
hatched
by Modigliani

GREETING FOR OLD AGE

Advance and take your place:
how do you do?
I salute you along with your half-blind

sister whom I know intimately
related by your cryptic smile.

I saw you approaching from
across the street
welcoming me making me feel my age

older than we would care to acknowledge
or you should admit
the sophistry of it.

STILL LIFES

All poems can be represented by
still lifes not to say
water-colors, the violence of
the Iliad lends itself to an arrangement
of narcissi in a jar.
The slaughter of Hector by Achilles
can well be shown by them
casually assembled yellow upon white
radiantly making a circle
sword strokes violently given
in more or less haphazard disarray

TRALA TRALA TRALA LA-LE-LA

When the time has arrived
for your birthday
which I celebrate not with dancing
but a measured tread

we must join hands
what else can we do?
create a measure ignoring
what we had to do

when we were young at
a celebration—let's
eat our cake and have
it too dancingly

as we may flinging
our feet upward and out
to the end of time trala
trala trala la-le-la

THE MORAL

Just junk
is what it amounts to
now-a-days

the sleeve
doesn't hold on the shaft
but slips

so that
nothing holds
firm any more

THE ORCHARD

This is the time
for which we have been
waiting

cherry blossom time
when lilacs are in bloom
we propose

to ourselves
im wunderschoensten Monat Mai
before

it is too late
the celebrated Revolution
is accomplished

but back of that
there is the memory of a
much loved

Cherry Orchard.
Lightheartedly enjoy the fruit
as you

may at the
time not forgetting to
spit out

the pit.

STORMY

what name could
better
explode from

a sleeping pup
but this
leaping

to his feet
Stormy!
Stormy! Stormy!

PICTURES FROM BRUEGHEL

BRUEGHEL

1962

Pictures from Brueghel
and other poems by
William Carlos Williams

including
The Desert Music & Journey to Love

A New Directions Paperbook

PICTURES FROM BRUEGHEL

I SELF-PORTRAIT

In a red winter hat blue
eyes smiling
just the head and shoulders

crowded on the canvas
arms folded one
big ear the right showing

the face slightly tilted
a heavy wool coat
with broad buttons

gathered at the neck reveals
a bulbous nose
but the eyes red-rimmed

from overuse he must have
driven them hard
but the delicate wrists

show him to have been a
man unused to
manual labor unshaved his

blond beard half trimmed
no time for any-
thing but his painting

II LANDSCAPE WITH THE FALL OF ICARUS

According to Brueghel
when Icarus fell
it was spring

a farmer was ploughing
his field
the whole pageantry

of the year was
awake tingling
near

the edge of the sea
concerned
with itself

sweating in the sun
that melted
the wings' wax

unsignificantly
off the coast
there was

a splash quite unnoticed
this was
Icarus drowning

III   THE HUNTERS IN THE SNOW

The over-all picture is winter
icy mountains
in the background the return

from the hunt it is toward evening
from the left
sturdy hunters lead in

their pack the inn-sign
hanging from a
broken hinge is a stag a crucifix

between his antlers the cold
inn yard is
deserted but for a huge bonfire

that flares wind-driven tended by
women who cluster
about it to the right beyond

the hill is a pattern of skaters
Brueghel the painter
concerned with it all has chosen

a winter-struck bush for his
foreground to
complete the picture   .   .

IV   THE ADORATION OF THE KINGS

From the Nativity
which I have already celebrated
the Babe in its Mother's arms

the Wise Men in their stolen
splendor
and Joseph and the soldiery

attendant
with their incredulous faces
make a scene copied we'll say

from the Italian masters
but with a difference
the mastery

of the painting
and the mind the resourceful mind
that governed the whole

the alert mind dissatisfied with
what it is asked to
and cannot do

accepted the story and painted
it in the brilliant
colors of the chronicler

the downcast eyes of the Virgin
as a work of art
for profound worship

V   PEASANT WEDDING

Pour the wine bridegroom
where before you the
bride is enthroned her hair

loose at her temples a head
of ripe wheat is on
the wall beside her the

guests seated at long tables
the bagpipers are ready
there is a hound under

the table the bearded Mayor
is present women in their
starched headgear are

gabbing all but the bride
hands folded in her
lap is awkwardly silent simple

dishes are being served
clabber and what not
from a trestle made of an

unhinged barn door by two
helpers one in a red
coat a spoon in his hatband

VI   HAYMAKING

The living quality of
the man's mind
stands out

and its covert assertions
for art, art, art!
painting

that the Renaissance
tried to absorb
but

it remained a wheat field
over which the
wind played

men with scythes tumbling
the wheat in
rows

the gleaners already busy
it was his own—
magpies

the patient horses no one
could take that
from him

VII THE CORN HARVEST

Summer!
the painting is organized
about a young

reaper enjoying his
noonday rest
completely

relaxed
from his morning labors
sprawled

in fact sleeping
unbuttoned
on his back

the women
have brought him his lunch
perhaps

a spot of wine
they gather gossiping
under a tree

whose shade
carelessly
he does not share the

resting
center of
their workaday world

VIII   THE WEDDING DANCE IN THE OPEN AIR

Disciplined by the artist
to go round
& round

in holiday gear
a riotously gay rabble of
peasants and their

ample-bottomed doxies
fills
the market square

featured by the women in
their starched
white headgear

they prance or go openly
toward the wood's
edges

round and around in
rough shoes and
farm breeches

mouths agape
Oya!
kicking up their heels

IX   THE PARABLE OF THE BLIND

This horrible but superb painting
the parable of the blind
without a red

in the composition shows a group
of beggars leading
each other diagonally downward

across the canvas
from one side
to stumble finally into a bog

where the picture
and the composition ends back
of which no seeing man

is represented the unshaven
features of the des-
titute with their few

pitiful possessions a basin
to wash in a peasant
cottage is seen and a church spire

the faces are raised
as toward the light
there is no detail extraneous

to the composition one
follows the others stick in
hand triumphant to disaster

X CHILDREN'S GAMES

I

This is a schoolyard
crowded
with children

of all ages near a village
on a small stream
meandering by

where some boys
are swimming
bare-ass

or climbing a tree in leaf
everything
is motion

elder women are looking
after the small
fry

a play wedding a
christening
nearby one leans

hollering
into
an empty hogshead

II

Little girls
whirling their skirts about
until they stand out flat

tops pinwheels
to run in the wind with
or a toy in 3 tiers to spin

with a piece
of twine to make it go
blindman's-buff follow the

leader stilts
high and low tipcat jacks
bowls hanging by the knees

standing on your head
run the gauntlet
a dozen on their backs

feet together kicking
through which a boy must pass
roll the hoop or a

construction
made of bricks
some mason has abandoned

III

The desperate toys
of children
their

imagination equilibrium
and rocks
which are to be

found
everywhere
and games to drag

the other down
blindfold
to make use of

a swinging
weight
with which

at random
to bash in the
heads about

them
Brueghel saw it all
and with his grim

humor faithfully
recorded
it

EXERCISE

Maybe it's his wife
the car is an official car
belonging

to a petty police officer
I think
but her get-up

was far from official
for that time
of day

SONG

beauty is a shell
from the sea
where she rules triumphant
till love has had its way with her

scallops and
lion's paws
sculptured to the
tune of retreating waves

undying accents
repeated till
the ear and the eye lie
down together in the same bed

THE WOODTHRUSH

fortunate man it is not too late
the woodthrush
flies into my garden

before the snow
he looks at me silent without
moving

his dappled breast reflecting
tragic winter
thoughts my love my own

THE POLAR BEAR

his coat resembles the snow
deep snow
the male snow
which attacks and kills

silently as it falls muffling
the world
to sleep that
the interrupted quiet return

to lie down with us
its arms
about our necks
murderously a little while

THE LOVING DEXTERITY

The flower
　　fallen
she saw it

　　where
it lay
　　a pink petal

intact
　　deftly
placed it

　　on
its stem
　　again

THE CHRYSANTHEMUM

how shall we tell
the bright petals
from the sun in the
sky concentrically

crowding the branch
save that it yields
in its modesty
to that splendor?

3 STANCES

I ELAINE

poised for the leap she
is not yet ready for
—save in her eyes

her bare toes
starting over the clipt
lawn where she may

not go emphasize summer
and the curl
of her blond hair

the tentative smile
for the adult plans laid
to trap her

calves beginning to flex
wrists
set for the getaway

II ERICA

the melody line is
everything
in this composition

when I first witnessed
your head
and held it

admiringly between
my fingers
I bowed

my approval
at the Scandinavian
name they'd

given you Erica after
your father's
forebears

the rest remains a
mystery
your snub nose spinning

on the bridge of it
points the way
inward

III   EMILY

your long legs
built
to carry high

the small head
your
grandfather

knows
if he knows
anything

gives
the dance as
your genius

the cleft in
your
chin's curl

permitting
may it
carry you far

SUZY

I

women your age have decided
wars and the beat
of poems your grandfather

is a poet and loves you
pay attention
to your lessons an inkling

of what beauty means to
a girl your age
may dawn soon upon you

II

life is a flower when it
opens you will
look trembling into it unsure

of what the traditional
mirror may reveal
between hope and despair while

a timorous old man
doubtfully half
turns away his foolish head

III

a bunch of violets clutched
in your idle
hand gives him a place

beside you which he cherishes
his back turned
from you casually appearing

not to look he yearns after
you protectively
hopelessly wanting nothing

PAUL

I

when you shall arrive
as deep
as you will need go

to catch the blackfish
the hook
has been featly baited

by the art you have
and
you do catch them

II

with what thoroughness
you know
seize that glistening

body translated
to
that language you

will understand gut
clean
roast garnish and

III

serve to yourself who
better
eat and enjoy

however you
divide
and share

that blackfish heft
and shine
is your own

FRAGMENT

as for him who
finds fault
may silliness

and sorrow
overtake him
when you wrote

you did not
know
the power of

your words

TO A WOODPECKER

December bird in the bare tree
your harsh cry sounds
reminding me

of death we celebrated by lamen-
tations crying out
in the old

days wails of anguish shrieking
wakes curses that the
gods

had been so niggardly sweet
nightingale of the
winter

woods hang out the snow as if
it were gay
curtains

SONG

I'd rather read an account
of a hidden
Carolina swamp where

the white heron breeds
protected from
the hunters reached only across

half-sunken logs a place
difficult of access the females
building their nests

in the stifling heat the males
in their mating splendor
than to witness

her broad pelvis
making her awkward at the
getaway . . .

but I have forgot beauty
that is no more than a sop
when our time

is spent and infirmities
bring us to
eat out of the same bowl!

THE CHILDREN

Once in a while
we'd find a patch
of yellow violets

not many
but blue big blue
ones in

the cemetery woods
we'd pick
bunches of them

there was a family
named Foltette
a big family

with lots of
children's graves
so we'd take

bunches of violets
and place one
on each headstone

THE PAINTING

Starting from black or
finishing
with it

her defeat stands
a delicate
lock

of blond hair dictated
by the
Sorbonne

this was her last
clear
act

a portrait of a
child
to which

she was indifferent
beautifully
drawn

then she married and
moved to
another country

THE STONE CROCK

In my hand I hold
a postcard
addressed to me
        by a lady

Stoneware crock
salt-glazed
a dandelion embossed
        dark blue

She selected it
for me to
admire casually
        in passing

she was a Jewess
intimate of
a man I
        admired

We often met in
her studio
and talked
        of him

he loved the early
art of this
country
            blue stoneware

stamped on the
bulge of it
Albany reminding me
            of him

Now he is dead how
gentle he
was and
            persistent

HE HAS BEATEN ABOUT THE BUSH LONG ENOUGH

What a team
Flossie, Mary, a chemistry prof
and I

make to confront
the
slowly hardening

brain
of an academician
The most

that can be said
for it
is

that it has the crystal-
line pattern
of

new ice on
a country
pool

IRIS

a burst of iris so that
come down for
breakfast

we searched through the
rooms for
that

sweetest odor and at
first could not
find its

source then a blue as
of the sea
struck

startling us from among
those trumpeting
petals

SONG

you are forever April
to me
the eternally unready

forsythia a blond
straight-
legged girl

whom I myself
ignorant
as I was taught

to read the poems
my arms
about your neck

we clung together
peril-
ously

more than a young
girl
should know

a burst of frost
nipped
yellow flowers

in the spring
of
the year

THE DANCE

When the snow falls the flakes
spin upon the long axis
that concerns them most intimately
two and two to make a dance

the mind dances with itself,
taking you by the hand,
your lover follows
there are always two,

yourself and the other,
the point of your shoe setting the pace,
if you break away and run
the dance is over

Breathlessly you will take
another partner
better or worse who will keep
at your side, at your stops

whirls and glides until he too
leaves off
on his way down as if
there were another direction

gayer, more carefree
spinning face to face but always down
with each other secure
only in each other's arms

But only the dance is sure!
make it your own.
Who can tell
what is to come of it?

in the woods of your
own nature whatever
twig interposes, and bare twigs
have an actuality of their own

this flurry of the storm
that holds us,
plays with us and discards us
dancing, dancing as may be credible.

JERSEY LYRIC

view of winter trees
before
one tree

in the foreground
where
by fresh-fallen

snow
lie 6 woodchunks ready
for the fire

TO THE GHOST OF MARJORIE KINNAN RAWLINGS

To celebrate your brief life
as you lived it grimly
under attack as it happens
to any common soldier
black or white
surrounded by the heavy scent
of orange blossoms solitary
in your low-lying farm among the young trees

Wise and gentle-voiced
old colored women
attended you among the reeds
and polonia
with its blobs of purple
flowers your pup smelling of
skunk beside your grove-men
lovesick maids and
one friend of the same sex
who knew how to handle a boat in a swamp

Your quick trips to your
New York publisher
beating your brains out
over the composition
under the trees to the tune
of a bull got loose
gathering the fruit and
preparing new fields to be put under the plough

You lived nerves drawn
tense beside dogtooth violets
bougainvillaea swaying
rushes and yellow jasmine
that smells so sweet
young and desperate
as you were taking chances
sometimes that you should be
thrown from the saddle

and get your neck broke
as it must have happened and it did in the end

TO BE RECITED TO FLOSSIE ON HER BIRTHDAY

Let him who may
among the continuing lines
seek out

that tortured constancy
affirms
where I persist

let me say
across cross purposes
that the flower bloomed

struggling to assert itself
simply under
the conflicting lights

you will believe me
a rose
to the end of time

METRIC FIGURE

gotta hold your nose
with the appropriate gesture
smiling

back of
the garbage truck
as the complex

city passes
to the confession
or psychiatric couch or booth

THE INTELLIGENT SHEEPMAN AND THE NEW CARS

I'd like to
pull
the back out

and use
one of them
to take

my "girls"
to
the fairs in

THE ITALIAN GARDEN

When she married years ago
her romantic ideas dominated
the builders

nightingale and hermit thrush
then the garden
fell into disuse.

Now her son has taken up her
old ideas formally
shut out

by high walls from the sheep run.
It is a scene from Comus
transported

to upper New York State. I remember
it already ruined
in

early May the trees crowded
with orioles chickadees
robins

brown-thrashers cardinals
in their scarlet
coats

vocal at dawn among pools
reft of their
lilies

and rarer plants flowers
given instead to
mallows

pampas-grass and cattails by
drought and winter
winds

where now hummingbirds touch
without touching.
Moss-covered

benches fallen apart among
sunken gardens
where

The Faerie Queene was read to
strains from
Campion

and the scent of wild strawberries
mingled with that
of eglantine

and verbena. Courtesy has revived
with visitors who
have

begun to stroll the paths
as in the quattrocento
covertly.

Maybe it will drive them to
be more civil
love

more jocosely (a good word) as
we presume they did
in that famous

garden where Boccaccio and
his friends hid
themselves

from the plague and rude manners
in the woods
of that garden

as we would similarly today
to escape the plague
of

our cars which cannot
penetrate
hers.

POEM

The rose fades
and is renewed again
by its seed, naturally
but where

save in the poem
shall it go
to suffer no diminution
of its splendor

A FORMAL DESIGN

This fleur-de-lis
at a fence rail
where a unicorn is

confined it is a tapestry
deftly woven
a millefleurs

design the fleur-de-lis
with its yellow
petals edges

a fruiting tree formally
enough in
this climate

a pomegranate to which
a princely
collar round his

arching neck the beast
is lightly
tethered

BIRD

Bird with outstretched
wings poised
inviolate unreaching

yet reaching
your image this November
planes

to a stop
miraculously fixed in my
arresting eyes

THE GOSSIPS

Blocking the sidewalk so
we had to go round
3 carefully coiffured
and perfumed old men
fresh from the barbers
a cartoon by Daumier
reflecting the times were
discussing with a foreign
accent one cupping his
ears not to miss a
syllable the news from
Russia on a view of
the reverse surface of
the moon   .   .

EXERCISE NO. 2

The metal smokestack
of my neighbor's chimney
greets me among the new leaves

it is a small house
adjacent to my bigger one
I have come in 3 years

to know much of her
an old lady as I am an old man
we greet each other

across the hedge
my wife gives her flowers
we have never visited each other

THE WORLD CONTRACTED TO A RECOGNIZABLE IMAGE

at the small end of an illness
there was a picture

probably Japanese
which filled my eye

an idiotic picture
except it was all I recognized
the wall lived for me in that picture
I clung to it as a fly

THE FRUIT

Waking
I was eating pears!
she said

I sat beside her on the bed
thinking
of Picasso

a portrait of
a sensitive young boy
gathered

into himself
Waking
I was eating pears!

she said
when separate jointly
we embraced

SHORT POEM

You slapped my face
oh but so gently
I smiled
at the caress

POEM

on getting a card
long delayed
from a poet whom I love
but

with whom I differ
touching
the modern poetic
technique

I was much moved
to hear
from him if
as yet he does not

concede the point
nor is he
indeed conscious of it
no matter

his style
has other outstanding
virtues
which delight me

TO FLOSSIE

who showed me
        a bunch of garden roses
she was keeping
        on ice

against an appointment
        with friends
for supper
        day after tomorrow

aren't they beautiful
>> you can't
smell them
>> because they're so cold

but aren't they
>> in wax
paper for the
>> moment beautiful

PORTRAIT OF A WOMAN AT HER BATH

it is a satisfaction
a joy
to have one of those
in the house

when she takes a bath
she unclothes
herself she is no
Venus

I laugh at her
an Inca
shivering at the well
the sun is

glad of a fellow to
marvel at
the birds and the flowers
look in

SOME SIMPLE MEASURES IN THE
AMERICAN IDIOM AND THE VARIABLE FOOT

I EXERCISE IN TIMING

Oh
the sumac died

it's
the first time
I
noticed it

II HISTOLOGY

There is
the
microscopic
anatomy

of
the whale
this is
reassuring

III PERPETUUM MOBILE

To all the girls
of all ages
who walk up and down on

the streets of this town
silent or gabbing
putting

their feet down
one before the other
one two

one two they
pause sometimes before
a store window and

reform the line
from here
to China everywhere

back and
forth and back and forth
and back and forth

IV   THE   BLUE   JAY

It crouched
just before the take-off

caught
in the cinematograph-

ic motion
of the mind wings

just set to spread a
flash a

blue curse
a memory of you

my friend
shrieked at me

—serving art
as usual

V   THE   EXISTENTIALIST'S   WIFE

I used to follow
the seasons
in this semi-northern

climate
and the warblers
that come

in May knew
the parula from
the myrtle

when I found it
dead on
the lawn there is

no season but
the one
for me now

VI   A   SALAD   FOR   THE   SOUL

My peasant soul
we may not be destined to
survive our guts
let's celebrate

what we eject
sometimes
with greatest fervor
I hear it

also from the ladies' room
what ho!
the source
of all delicious salads

VII   CHLOE

The calves of
the young girls legs
when they are well-made

knees
lithely built
in their summer clothes

show them
predisposed toward flight
or the dance

the magenta flower
of the
moth-mullen balanced

idly
tilting her weight
from one foot

to the other
shifting
to avoid looking at me

on my way to
mail a letter
smiling to a friend

VIII   THE COCKTAIL PARTY

A young woman
on whose belly I have never
slept though others

have
met today
at a cocktail party

not drunk
but by love
ignoring the others

we looked in
each other's eyes
ears alert to

what we were saying
eyes blinded
breathless by that alone

IX   THE STOLEN PEONIES

What I got out of women
was difficult
to assess Flossie

not you
you lived with me
many years you remember

that year
we had the magnificent
stand of peonies

how happy we were
with them
but one night

they were stolen
we shared the
loss together thinking

of nothing else for
a whole day
nothing could have

brought us closer
we had been
married ten years

THE HIGH BRIDGE ABOVE THE
TAGUS RIVER AT TOLEDO

A young man, alone, on the high bridge over the Tagus which
    was too narrow to allow the sheep driven by the lean,
    enormous dogs whose hind legs worked slowly on cogs
to pass easily . . .
    (he didn't speak the language)

Pressed against the parapet either side by the crowding sheep,
    the relentless pressure of the dogs communicated
    itself to him also
above the waters in the gorge below.

They were hounds to him rather than sheep dogs because of their
    size and savage appearance, dog tired from the day's work.
The stiff jerking movement of the hind legs, the hanging
    heads at the shepherd's heels, slowly followed the excited
    and crowding sheep.

The whole flock, the shepherd and the dogs, were covered with dust
    as if they had been all day long on the road. The pace of the
    sheep, slow in the mass,
governed the man and the dogs. They were approaching the city
    at nightfall, the long journey completed.

In old age they walk in the old man's dreams and still walk
    in his dreams, peacefully continuing in his verse
    forever.

15 YEARS LATER

on seeing my own play
Many Loves
on the stage for the first time

I recall
many a passage
of the original con-

versations with my
patients, especially the
women, myself

the interlocutor
laying myself bare for them
all there

in the play but who will
take the trouble
to evaluate

the serious aspects of
the case? One
of the actors by

dint of learning the lines
by heart
has come to me

his face aglow openmouthed
a light in his eyes
Nothing more

THE TITLE

—as in Gauguin's *The Loss of Virginity*—
how inessential it is to the composition:

the nude body, unattended save by a watchful
hound, forepaw against the naked breast,

there she lies on her back in an open field,
limbs quietly assembled—yet how by its

very unrelatedness it enhances the impact
and emotional dignity of the whole . . .

MOUNTED AS AN AMAZON

She rides her hips as
it were a horse
such women

tickle me a pat answer
to philosophy
or high heels would

put them on their
cans if fol-
lowed up most women

are more pliant
come of
a far different race

THE SNOW BEGINS

A rain of bombs, well placed,
is no less lovely
but this comes gently over all

all crevices are covered
the stalks of
fallen flowers vanish before

this benefice all the garden's
wounds are healed
white, white, white as death

fallen which dignifies it as
no violence ever can
gently and silently in the night.

CALYPSOS

I

Well God is
love
so love me

God
is love so
love me God

is
love so love
me well

II

Love the sun
comes
up in

the morning
and
in

the evening
zippy zappy
it goes

III

We watched
a red rooster
with

two hens
back
of the museum

at
St. Croix
flap his

wings
zippy zappy
and crow

AN EXERCISE

Sick as I am
confused in the head
I mean I have

endured this April
so far
visiting friends

returning home
late at night
I saw

a huge Negro
a dirty collar
about his

enormous neck
appeared to be
choking

him
I did not know
whether or not

he saw me though
he was sitting
directly

before me how
shall we
escape this modern

age
and learn
to breathe again

THREE NAHUATL POEMS

One by one I proclaim your songs:
    I bind them on, gold crabs, as if they were anklets:
    like emeralds I gather them.
Clothe yourself in them: they are your riches.
    Bathe in feathers of the quetzal,

your treasury of birds' plumes, black and yellow,
the red feathers of the macaw
beat your drums about the world:
deck yourself out in them: they are your riches.

Where am I to go, whither?
  The road's there, the road to Two-Gods.
  Well, who checks men here,
here where all lack a body,
at the bottom of the sky?
Or, maybe, it is only on Earth
that we lose the body?
  Cleaned out, rid of it completely,
His House: there remains none on this earth!
Who is it that said:
Where find them? our friends no longer exist!

Will he return will Prince Cuautli ever return?
Will Ayocuan, the one who drove an arrow into the sky?
Shall these two yet gladden you?
  Events don't recur: we vanish once only.
Hence the cause of my weeping:
Prince Ayocuan, warrior chief
governed us harshly.
His pride waxed more, he grew haughty
here among men.
  But his time is finished . . .
he can no longer come to bow down before Father and Mother. . . .
This is the reason for my weeping:
He has fled to the place where all lack a body.

SONNET IN SEARCH OF AN AUTHOR

Nude bodies like peeled logs
sometimes give off a sweetest
odor, man and woman

under the trees in full excess
matching the cushion of

aromatic pine-drift fallen
threaded with trailing woodbine
a sonnet might be made of it

Might be made of it! odor of excess
odor of pine needles, odor of
peeled logs, odor of no odor
other than trailing woodbine that

has no odor, odor of a nude woman
sometimes, odor of a man.

THE GIFT

As the wise men of old brought gifts
        guided by a star
                to the humble birthplace

of the god of love,
        the devils
                as an old print shows
retreated in confusion.

        What could a baby know
                of gold ornaments
        or frankincense and myrrh,
                of priestly robes
                        and devout genuflections?

But the imagination
        knows all stories
                before they are told
and knows the truth of this one
        past all defection

The rich gifts
        so unsuitable for a child
                though devoutly proffered,
stood for all that love can bring.

The men were old
　　　how could they know
of a mother's needs
　　or a child's
　　　　appetite?

But as they kneeled
　　　the child was fed.

　　　　They saw it
and
　　　gave praise!

　　　A miracle
had taken place,
　　　hard gold to love,
a mother's milk!
　　　before
　　　　their wondering eyes.

The ass brayed
　　　the cattle lowed.
　　　　　It was their nature.

All men by their nature give praise.
　　It is all
　　　　they can do.

The very devils
　　　by their flight give praise.
　　　　What is death,
beside this?

　　　Nothing. The wise men
　　　　came with gifts
and bowed down
　　　to worship
　　　　this perfection.

THE TURTLE

(For My Grandson)

Not because of his eyes,
            the eyes of a bird,
                        but because he is beaked,
birdlike, to do an injury,
            has the turtle attracted you.
                        He is your only pet.
When we are together
            you talk of nothing else
                        ascribing all sorts
of murderous motives
            to his least action.
                        You ask me
to write a poem,
            should I have poems to write,
                        about a turtle.

The turtle lives in the mud
            but is not mud-like,
                        you can tell it by his eyes
which are clear.
            When he shall escape
                        his present confinement
he will stride about the world
            destroying all
                        with his sharp beak.
Whatever opposes him
            in the streets of the city
                        shall go down.
Cars will be overturned.
            And upon his back
                        shall ride,
to his conquests,
            my Lord,
                        you!

You shall be master!
          In the beginning
                    there was a great tortoise
who supported the world.
          Upon him
                    all ultimately
rests.
          Without him
                    nothing will stand.
He is all wise
          and can outrun the hare.
                    In the night
his eyes carry him
          to unknown places.
                    He is your friend.

SAPPHO, BE COMFORTED

There is only one love
let it be a sparrow
to hold between the breasts
          greets us daily with its small cries

what does it matter?
I, we'll say, love a woman
but truth to tell
          I love myself more. Sappho loves

the music of her own
songs which men seldom
mean to her, a lovely girl
          of whom she is desperately fond:

This is myself though
my hateful mirror
shows every day my big nose.
          Men are indifferent to me, my sweet

but I would not trade
my skill in composition for
all, a second choice, you
     present for my passionate caresses.

TO MY FRIEND EZRA POUND

or he were a Jew or a
Welshman
I hope they do give you the Nobel Prize
it would serve you right
     —in perpetuity
with such a name

If I were a dog
I'd sit down on a cold pavement
in the rain
to wait for a friend (and so would you)
if it so pleased me
even if it were January or Zukofsky

Your English
is not specific enough
As a writer of poems
you show yourself to be inept not to say
usurious

TAPIOLA

He is no more dead than Finland herself is dead
under the blows of the mass-man who threatened
to destroy her until she felled her forests
about his head, ensnaring him. But, children, you
underestimated the power in your own song, *Finlandia!*
It holds you up but no more so than has he I celebrate
who had heard the icy wind in his ears and defied
it lovingly with a smile. The power of music,
of composition, the placing of sounds together,

edge against edge, Moussorgsky the half-mad Russian
had it and Dostoyevsky who knew the soul. In such
style whistled the winds grateful to be tamed,
we say, by a man. Whee-wow! You stayed up half
the night in your attic room under the eaves, composing
secretly, setting it down, period after period,
as the wind whistled. Lightning flashed! The roof
creaked about your ears threatening to give
way! But you had a composition to finish that could
not wait. The storm entered your mind where all
good things are secured, written down, for love's
sake and to defy the devil of emptiness. The
children are decked out in ribbons, bunting and
with flags in their hands to celebrate your birthday!
They parade to music! a joyous occasion. Sibelius
has been born and continues to live in all our
minds, all of us, forever. . . .

POEM

The plastic surgeon who has
concerned himself
with the repair of the mole

on my ear could not be
more pointedly
employed

let all men confess it
Gauguin or Van Gogh
were intimates

who fell out finally
and parted going
to the ends of the earth

to be apart, wild men
one of them cut
his ear off with a pair of shears

which made him none the less
a surpassing genius
this happened

yesterday forgive him
he was mad
and who among us has retained

his sanity or balance
in the course the
events have taken since those days

HEEL & TOE TO THE END

Gagarin says, in ecstasy,
he could have
gone on forever

he floated
ate and sang
and when he emerged from that

one hundred eight minutes off
the surface of
the earth he was smiling

Then he returned
to take his place
among the rest of us

from all that division and
subtraction a measure
toe and heel

heel and toe he felt
as if he had
been dancing

THE REWAKING

Sooner or later
we must come to the end
of striving

to re-establish
the image the image of
the rose

but not yet
you say extending the
time indefinitely

by
your love until a whole
spring

rekindle
the violet to the very
lady's-slipper

and so by
your love the very sun
itself is revived

Appendix A: A Note on the Text

In arranging the poems for this edition I have continued the practice of Volume I in retaining the integrity of Williams' original volumes with the exception of the collected volumes of 1934, 1938, 1950 and 1951. Poems that appear only in these collections, and all uncollected poems, are arranged by date of first publication. The only exceptions to this procedure (apart from posthumously published poems) are poems first published many years after they were written, and these are listed below.

I have also not reproduced in full the contents of the 1941 pamphlet *The Broken Span*. The pamphlet gathered together a number of poems from earlier years (these are printed in Volume I) as well as a fifteen poem sequence titled "For the Poem *Paterson*," and five other poems from 1939-1941 (two of which were reprinted in *The Wedge* in 1944). I have, however, reproduced the fifteen poem sequence in its chronological place and in the order in which it appeared in the pamphlet since these poems emerged from the *Detail & Parody for the poem Paterson* arrangement that Williams had been working on for much of the second half of the 1930s and that proved to be an abortive early approach to the thematic and formal problems of *Paterson*. Williams' instructions to the printer for the pamphlet distinguished between the fifteen poem sequence, which was to be printed "consecutively," and the rest of the poems, which could be one to a page. Of the other five late poems in the pamphlet, "Illegitimate Things" and "A Portrait of the Times" had been first published in 1939 and 1940, and I print them in their chronological place. "The Predicter of Famine" first appeared in *The Broken Span*, and thus appears among the poems for 1941. Williams collected "The Last Turn" and "Against the Sky" in *The Wedge* and I print them in their place in that volume. In the case of "The Last Turn," however, which was first printed in *The Broken Span*, the 1941 version differs to such a degree from the version in *The Wedge* that I print the earlier version in its chronological place beside "The Predicter of Famine" as a "First Version." I list the full table of contents of *The Broken Span* in Appendix C, along with the contents of *The Collected Later Poems* and the 1949 *Selected Poems*.

Most of the poems that I order by date of composition rather than of publication are from the years 1939-1941, and they are primarily poems published by John Thirlwall in *New Directions 16* in 1957 as "The Lost Poems of William Carlos Williams or The Past Recaptured." Although Thirlwall ascribed dates in the early 1930s to some of these poems, most of them clearly reflect Williams' concerns in the late 1930s and early 1940s, and almost all of the poems appear in the *Detail & Parody for the poem Paterson* typescript or in one or more of the various arrangements for *The Broken Span*. In the case of "The Genius" and "The Approaching Hour" I accept Thirlwall's dating of c. 1939. "A Love Poem," "Comfort," "Flattery," "Pigheaded Poet," "Details for Paterson," and "River Rhyme II," either appear in the *Detail & Parody for the poem*

Paterson typescript or are associated with it stylistically. It seemed to me most useful to print these poems following the sequence in *The Broken Span*. Thirlwall's dating of 1941 for a further three poems from the 1957 printing, "The United Front," "To a Chinese Woman," and "The Fight" appears accurate, and the poems are printed with that year under the general title "Three Poems for Horace Gregory." Other poems published in Williams' lifetime that I have ordered by date of composition rather than of publication are "The End of the Rope," "The Birth," and the translation "To regain the day again." I have also gathered together the 1941, 1944 and 1958 printings of Williams' translations from Yvan Goll's *Jean Sans Terre*, and the various printings of translations from the poetry of Nicolas Calas and published both as groups by probable date of composition.

The Chinese translations upon which Williams, late in his career, collaborated with David Wang, present a special problem. A few of these poems appeared separately in Williams' lifetime, although the majority received first publication in the 1966 printing of the entire sequence as "The Cassia Tree." The last individual translation to be published in Williams' lifetime, "Profile of a Lady," appeared in 1960, the year in which Williams began to lose interest in reworking Wang's versions, and so I have printed the entire sequence under that year.

I have used the texts of *Collected Earlier Poems*, *Collected Later Poems*, and *Pictures from Brueghel* for the poems included in those volumes (*Pictures from Brueghel* reprinted the contents of the earlier *The Desert Music* and *Journey to Love* and I have used this reprinting as the copy text for those volumes). Based upon a collation of all known printings of the poems, and an examination of all available typescripts, galleys, and page-proofs connected with the volumes, I have corrected a number of verbal, spacing and lineation errors in the texts of the collections.

On the whole, fewer errors crept into *The Collected Later Poems* text than into that of *Collected Earlier Poems*—in large part because preparations for the *Collected Later Poems* avoided the necessity of typing the script twice (see Volume I, pp. 467–70 for an account of the preparation of *Collected Earlier Poems*). As is clear from the reproduction of some house-styling, the poems were typed (not by Williams himself) from the original volumes—*The Wedge*, *The Clouds*, and *The Pink Church*. The typescript does contain a few corrections and changes from the volume printings. The printing errors in *The Pink Church* are not reproduced, for example. The uncollected poems are apparently typed from periodical printings. The top copy of the complete typescript is at the Houghton Library, Harvard, in the "Accessions File," while the carbon copy is deposited in the Beinecke Library, Yale, designated Williams Za47.

Williams' checking of the typescript—and of the subsequent galleys—was hampered by the same accumulation of commitments that marred his proofreading of the materials for *The Collected Earlier Poems* the following year. Between 1949 and 1951 Williams published, in addition to a large number of poems and essays in periodicals, two volumes of collected poems, his *Selected Poems*, *Paterson III* and *Paterson IV*, two collections of short stories, and his *Autobiography*. The arrival of the galleys for *Collected Later Poems* coincided with the beginning of a reading and teaching tour. As he confessed to Richard Emerson on 31 Jan. 1951: "The proofs of the poems had to be gone over at lightning speed at the very last moment before my leaving" (University of Maryland).

The Harvard typescript betrays Williams' hurried reading (as does the Harvard top copy of Yale Za50—the carbon of the typescript for *Collected Earlier Poems*—which is also in the Houghton "Accessions File"). Although Williams marks a couple of changes, he catches few of the typing errors in the script. Some of these errors are simply of spelling, occasionally a word or two is omitted, and sometimes spaces between lines or stanzas are incorrectly reproduced. A small number of these errors find their way into *The Collected Later Poems*. In addition, since the typescript mirrors the lineation of its source volumes, it reproduces runovers sometimes imposed merely by the design or physical space limitations of those volumes. Consequently, a number of the runovers reappear in *Collected Later Poems* as if part of Williams' design for his poem (e.g. the first line of "Russia" and the final line of "The Testament of Perpetual Change"). The format of *The Clouds* contributed to another kind of error in the typescript. In the 1948 volume the printers included a square bracketed catchword at the bottom of the page keyed to the top of the next page, and in two instances ("Philomena Andronico" and "Russia") these devices were typed as if part of the poem, and found their way into the text of *Collected Later Poems*.

Fortunately, Williams was able to rectify a further—and potentially most damaging—error. The typist misplaced and failed to return to him a group of poems intended for the volume, a group roughly corresponding to those chosen for the 1949 *Selected Poems*. Williams had failed to notice the omission, but it was drawn to his attention by Babette Deutsch upon receipt of a review copy, and the missing poems were hastily printed and bound and added to the book as a supplement. These poems do not appear in either the Harvard typescript or the Yale Za47 carbon.

The 1950s volumes *The Desert Music* and *Journey to Love* were published by Random House, to whom Williams moved in the early 1950s—following the move of his editor at New Directions, David McDowell. Yale's Beinecke Library holds double and sometimes triple sets of galleys for these volumes, as well as page proofs for both, but almost all the editing is marked by an in-house hand, not by Williams. In fact, McDowell failed to send Williams page proofs of either volume, with the result that although both books accurately reproduce Williams' submitted typescripts, both lack a number of changes the poet had intended to make. The text of *The Desert Music*, in particular, suffered from the oversight, and Williams sent McDowell a page full of changes and corrections to be incorporated into subsequent printings. (The letter is pasted into a copy of the volume now at the Harry Ransom Research Center, University of Texas.) Some of the changes were made in a Readers Subscription Club edition of *The Desert Music* that appeared the following year, but in a presentation copy of that text to his wife now at the University of Pennsylvania Williams marks a number of continuing problems. The reprinting of *The Desert Music* and *Journey to Love* in *Pictures from Brueghel* in 1962 was prepared from a script using pages cut from the 1950s volumes. This script, now deposited at Fairleigh Dickinson University, incorporates most—but not all—of the changes and corrections in the Readers Subscription Club edition, but few of the editorial markings are in Williams' by then very shaky hand.

The new poems collected in *Pictures from Brueghel* are represented in the Fairleigh Dickinson printer's text by typescript, although the various typed drafts of the poems that went into the volume are collected at Yale as Za192. The typescripts were prepared at a time when a number of strokes had seriously impaired Williams' vision and his typing ability. Williams gratefully accepted help from various quarters for the typing and re-typing of the scripts, with his grand-daughter Suzanne and Mrs. Thirlwall helping out at one point.

As preparations for publication continued, Williams became increasingly frustrated with his physical handicaps, at one point tearing up and tossing a copy of the poems into the garbage. Eventually, Mrs. Williams read him the galleys one morning, and told James Laughlin that she had herself corrected such obvious errors as she could find, but that she had to leave the rest of the proofreading to the publisher. The galleys at Yale contain very few markings, and a further set at the University of Delaware is completely unmarked. (None of these sets includes the poems from the two reprinted volumes.)

Despite these circumstances, *Pictures from Brueghel* emerged a fairly accurate text. Most of such errors as do creep in result from errors in the preparation of the typescript. While most of the poems are accurately typed, as one would expect from a script prepared by various hands, some poems, for example "Some Simple Measures in the American Idiom and the Variable Foot," contain errors. Sometimes an error in the Fairleigh Dickinson typescript is compounded by an editor who apparently had no access to the original poem. Thus lines 4-5 of "The Blue Jay," which read "in the cinematograph- / ic motion" in *Poetry* and the source typescripts, was typed with a dash instead of a hyphen. An editor assumed the error lay with "ic" rather than the punctuation, and 'corrected' to "in"—the reading which subsequently appeared in *Pictures from Brueghel*. "The World Contracted to a Recognizable Image" suffered from a similar guesswork correction. Changes in the text of the volume did not end with its first appearance in print. My collation of various printings revealed that some of the punctuation of the first printing disappeared in various subsequent printings. The usual victims of this process were the periods Williams began to use in the 1940s to distinguish pauses that were marked by neither commas nor by conventional period usage (see e.g. "The Orchestra" and "The Desert Music"). In such cases I have restored the punctuation of the first printing—which reflected the original printer's script.

In my collation of the various printings of the poems and my examination of the available typescripts and galleys, I have tried to confirm authorial sanction for all changes between periodical and book publication, and any subsequent changes. For uncollected poems I have examined typescripts, where possible, to ensure the accuracy of periodical publication. Although in many cases the source of a change is quite clear, in the case of some changes in the text of *Collected Later Poems* this is not so. As noted above, the typist prepared the

Harvard/Yale Za47 typescript from a corrected text of the individual printed volumes. There is no marked-up cut-and-paste source arrangement by which to confirm the changes, as with *The Collected Earlier Poems*. There is no printer's typescript at all for the ten poems in the section mislaid by the typist. Furthermore, Williams clearly introduced a small number of additional changes in the galleys (and one larger change: restoring lines to "To Ford Madox Ford in Heaven"), but if these galleys still exist they have yet to turn up. My policy, consequently, has been to accept all changes in *The Collected Later Poems* text that do not radically change the meaning of a line or poem, and that appear consistent with Williams' practice. The Annotations record the instances where I have preferred the reading of a previous printing.

The textual authority for restoring Williams' original lineation is strong for most of the poems in *Collected Earlier Poems* and *Collected Later Poems*. As noted above, page and design constraints sometimes produced runovers, and these were perpetuated through subsequent printings even though typescript evidence and, sometimes, earlier printings reveal that the runovers are not a part of Williams' intended lineation. The three-step line poems, however, most of which appeared in *The Desert Music* and *Journey to Love*, present a special case when it comes to runovers. In these poems, the additional fourth and sometimes fifth line in the otherwise consistent triadic arrangement (see e.g. lines 3-4 of "The Host") appear in Williams' own typescripts of the poems and in almost all of the periodical printings. Most, but not all, of the examples are 'third' lines i.e. to the furthest right of the page. But in only one instance, that of lines 56 and 67 of "Shadows," did I come across a direction to the printer to print the line alongside that above it, and this was on a photostat of the poem in the Fairleigh Dickinson arrangement that was erroneously included in the new poems to be printed in *Pictures from Brueghel* (the poem had been collected in *Journey to Love* and Mrs. Williams subsequently wrote to James Laughlin warning him of the duplication, which went as far as the galleys). The command is not in Williams' hand. In the Fairleigh Dickinson arrangement of the poems from *The Desert Music* and *Journey to Love* almost all of the lines that violate the three step arrangement are queried in pencil, but appear in *Pictures from Brueghel* as in the earlier volumes. A 1954 set of galleys for *The Desert Music* (Yale Za62) printed these runover lines as one line and the lines, in every case, are marked (but not by Williams) to be divided and printed as on the setting typescript.

A further consideration involves the appearance of the poem on the page. Even if the lines are technically runovers, to print the double lines as one line would radically alter the appearance of the poem on the page, distracting from the predominant triadic pattern with a number of lines that stretch across the page to the extreme right. Restoring Williams' original lineation in other instances usually has the effect of restoring a visual and organizational regularity to the poem's arrangement, but in this case the opposite effect would occur. In addition, sometimes the design and space limitations of this edition itself would require introducing a runover at a new, arbitrary, break point.

My discussion of these additional lines with Williams' scholars produced many shades of opinion. Some scholars felt that the lines were all runovers and should be printed with the lines above, others that some were runovers and some additional lines and that individual decisions should be made, while others argued that the·lines represent a deliberate introduction of variety into the triadic format. I have decided to leave the additional lines exactly as they appeared in *The Desert Music* or *Journey to Love*—and subsequently in *Pictures from Brueghel*—on the strength of the visual considerations outlined above, the evidence that the matter was probably discussed with Williams, and the fact that the format originated with his typescripts. It seems to me that the most useful way to consider such lines is in terms of Williams' own concept of the "variable foot." The poem as printed emphasizes the variation and/or extension of the lines in question, and whether one reads them as runovers, as additional lines, or as an idiosyncratic fusion of both depends upon one's own interpretation of Williams' metrical theory and practice. (The uncollected triadic poem "On St. Valentine's Day" is thus also reprinted exactly as in the typescript and the periodical publication.)

The textual notes in Appendix B record lineation changes of major interest as well as all verbal variants between printings (with the exception of the categories listed below). However, limitations of space and the complexity of recording multiple variants in lineation and format have made it impossible to record all changes between printings or all corrections to the text. In keeping with the principles governing the annotations to Volume I, I have not noted the following kinds of variants and corrections unless they seem to have important critical significance:

1) changes in punctuation.
2) changes in lineation or runovers.
3) changes of spacing within stanzas.
4) changes in the positioning of a line.
5) verbal variants in anthology printings with which Williams had no apparent connection.
6) spelling variants, or house-styling variants.
7) changes in hyphenation (I have usually retained the hyphenation of the final printing).
8) obvious typographical, printing, and transcription errors.

Because of the irregular line structures in some of WCW's poems, it can be difficult to tell whether the end of a page marks the close of a stanza or verse paragraph. In this volume the following pages end with a break:

3	5	9	10	13	17	18	19	20	22	25	28	34	35
37	40	43	45	57	63	64	66	67	68	71	76	77	78
89	93	100	101	102	103	108	109	110	114	125	128	131	132
135	137	139	141	144	147	153	155	161	167	169	170	171	172
173	177	178	179	181	183	193	195	202	204	205	207	209	210
211	212	215	217	219	221	225	227	230	231	235	236	255	257
262	266	269	273	275	276	278	280	282	295	352	357	360	361
365	366	369	376	377	380	385	386	387	388	389	390	392	393
394	396	397	398	400	401	402	403	404	406	407	411	412	417
420	421	422	423	424	425	427	429	430	432	433	435		

Appendix B. Annotations

These annotations follow the principles laid out in Volume I. The entries record significant verbal changes in the published versions of the poems and provide a number of explanatory notes drawn from published and unpublished sources. The annotations are not intended to be "complete," and I have excluded matters of general cultural knowledge that can be found in standard dictionaries or the *Encyclopaedia Britannica*. All quotations from letters are by Williams unless otherwise noted.

I have not repeated bibliographical information concerning first and subsequent printings that can be found in Emily Wallace's *A Bibliography of William Carlos Williams*, and I have kept the bibliographic citations as concise as possible. However, I have provided full citations for printings not listed in Wallace and have indicated the source of the text for all poems not included in *The Collected Earlier Poems, The Collected Later Poems*, or *Pictures from Brueghel* (these poems are marked by an asterisk). All page references to *Paterson* in the annotations are to the 1963 New Directions printing.

Since it is sometimes difficult to identify a poetic "line" in Williams' work, I have counted each printed line in giving references by line numbers.

The following abbreviations are used in the annotations:

A   *The Autobiography of William Carlos Williams* (1951)

ARI   *A Recognizable Image: William Carlos Williams on Art and Artists*, ed. Bram Dijkstra (1978)

BUFFALO   Neil Baldwin and Steven L. Meyers, *The Manuscripts and Letters of William Carlos Williams in the Poetry Collection of the Lockwood Memorial Library, State University of New York at Buffalo: A Descriptive Catalogue* (1978)

CEP   *The Collected Earlier Poems* (1951)

CLP   *The Collected Later Poems* (1950)

CPI   *The Collected Poems of William Carlos Williams, Volume I: 1909-1939* (1986)

FW   Florence Williams, WCW's wife

IWWP   *I Wanted to Write a Poem: The Autobiography of the Works of a Poet*, ed. Edith Heal (1958)

MARIANI   Paul Mariani, *William Carlos Williams: A New World Naked* (1981)

ND16   John C. Thirlwall, "The Lost Poems of William Carlos Williams," *New Directions 16* (1957)

PB   *Pictures from Brueghel* (1962)

SE   *Selected Essays of William Carlos Williams* (1954)

SL   *Selected Letters of William Carlos Williams*, ed. John C. Thirlwall (1957)

SP   *Selected Poems* (1949)

WALLACE   Emily Mitchell Wallace, *A Bibliography of William Carlos Williams* (1968)

WCWR   *William Carlos Williams Review* (before 1980 the *William Carlos Williams Newsletter*)

YALE   The Williams archive at the Beinecke Rare Book and Manuscript Library, Yale University

POEMS 1939-1944

THE DECEPTRICES   First published in *The New Yorker*, 12 August 1939, p. 20.

ILLEGITIMATE THINGS
8   cannon! / cannons!   (*Poetry*, Sept. 1939)

*THE POET AND HIS POEMS   *Poetry* (Sept. 1939). WCW published part of this poem as "The Poem" in *The Wedge* (see p. 74).

*DEFIANCE TO CUPID   *Poetry* (Sept. 1939).

*TAILPIECE   *The University Review* (Oct. 1939). Placed as the final poem of the typescript sequence *Detail & Parody for the poem Paterson* (see note p. 448), and titled there "What Time Is It?" Most of the poems WCW published in periodicals at this time came out of his work on this sequence.

*THE ROCKING WOMAN   First published in *The New Yorker*, 11 November 1939, p. 21.

*THE GENIUS   ND16, where the poem is dated c. 1939. The poem is part of the early typescript arrangements of both *The Broken Span* and *The Wedge*.

*THE APPROACHING HOUR   ND16, where the poem is dated c. 1939. The poem is part of an early typescript arrangement for *The Broken Span*.

A PORTRAIT OF THE TIMES
13   while / whereas   (*The Broken Span*)

*CHERRY BLOSSOMS AT EVENING   Sent with a letter to Kenneth Burke on 10 May 1940, and first published as part of an essay appreciation of WCW by Burke in *The New York Review of Books*, 20 May 1963.

*THE RITUALISTS   First published in *The New Yorker*, 18 May 1940, p. 80.

*THE SLEEPING BRUTE   *Diogenes* (Oct.-Nov. 1940).

*FROM A WINDOW   *Poetry* (Nov. 1940), reprinted in ND16 with the final six lines omitted.

*RIVER RHYME   *Poetry* (Nov. 1940).

*SKETCH FOR A PORTRAIT OF HENRY FORD, AN INFORMATIVE OBJECT, TO A WOMAN SEEN ONCE, THE NEW CLOUDS   *Matrix* (Nov.-Dec. 1940).

FOR THE POEM PATERSON   This numbered sequence of fifteen poems appeared as part of the pamphlet *The Broken Span,* which was published in January 1941. (For the full contents of *The Broken Span,* which contained a number of earlier poems, see Appendix C.) The sequence came out of the typescript arrangement *Detail & Parody for the poem Paterson,* an eighty-seven page version of which WCW gave to James Laughlin on 9 March 1939 (now at Houghton Library). *Detail & Parody* represents an early, soon abandoned, stage of WCW's thinking about the thematic, formal and organizational problems of his long poem *Paterson* (I-IV, 1946-1951, Book V, 1958). While working on the *Detail & Parody* typescript he told Mary Barnard: "I want to write more colloquially, more after the pattern of speech, maybe I want to discover singable patterns. I don't want to write pictures. . . . I don't want dilutions" (Mariani 416).

In addition to appearing in this sequence in *The Broken Span,* a number of the poems from the *Detail & Parody* typescript appeared in magazines between 1938 and 1943, some of these and some others appeared in *The Wedge* (1944), and still others remained unpublished, sometimes not being dropped until after being incorporated into the various typescript arrangements for *The Broken Span* and *The Wedge.* Another, slightly different typescript of *Detail & Parody* exists at Buffalo. For a full description and listing of the seventy-four poems and titles in this manuscript see Buffalo D4. Buffalo D5 represents three tentative arrangements of the material for *The Broken Span.* See also CPI 547-548, and the note on *The Wedge* p. 454.

A man like a city. . . . one man—like a city   "By 1941 the idea [for *Paterson*] was there, expressed in the three lines included in *The Broken Span,* lines that are used word for word, though spaced somewhat differently, in the first few pages of *Paterson 1*" (IWWP 72). The three lines were incorporated into *Paterson,* Book I (1946), p. 7.

SPARROWS AMONG DRY LEAVES   First printed in *The New Yorker,* 18 Nov. 1939, p. 59. This *Broken Span* version appeared in CEP with the title "Sparrow Among Dry Leaves" because of an error in the Yale typescript Za196. See the later version on p. 90.

SOMETIMES IT TURNS DRY AND THE LEAVES FALL BEFORE THEY ARE BEAUTIFUL
Title: "Love, the Tragedian," in *The Broken Span* and ND16, where in both printings the CLP title is printed as a subtitle.
6   do   Omitted in *The Broken Span,* ND16.
7   thistle-caps / of thistle caps   (*The Broken Span;* ND 16)

11   farther than— / longer—/than   (*The Broken Span*; ND16)
       longer than—   (*The Wedge*)

*RALEIGH WAS RIGHT   For the later version printed in *The Wedge* see p. 88.

DETAIL (HEY!)   Following this poem in the Buffalo D5 typescript arrangement for *The Broken Span* is the first of two prose notes that provide a sense of WCW's thinking about the function of the "Details" in these arrangements, and of their relationship to his developing sense of *Paterson:*

"The conception of a lyric (or tragic) drama demands lyrics! Studies in language should precede that, the spontaneous (not natural!) conformations of language as it is *heard*. Attempt to feel and then transcribe these lyrical language patterns. The drama, the lyric drama (Lope de Vega) should be one expanded metaphor. Poetry demands a different material than prose. It uses another facet of the same fact; the precise opposite of Shaw, for instance. Facts, but just before and just after the incident which prose (journalism) would select and, by that, miss the significance poetry catches aslant."

This note, but not the second, also appears in the earlier *Detail & Parody* typescript.

THE THOUGHTFUL LOVER
2   Have / Take   (*Poetry World*, July-Aug. 1939)
4   But it / It   (*Poetry World*)
10   However / But   (*Poetry World*)

THE END OF THE PARADE
6   strokes / notes   (*The Broken Span; The New Yorker*, 20 Nov. 1943)
9   cadenced melody / all honeyed sounds   (*The Broken Span; The New Yorker*)

DETAIL (DOC I BIN)   Following this "Detail" is the second prose note in the Buffalo D5 typescript arrangement of *The Broken Span:*

"This is the sort of thing, in its essential poetic nature, its rhythmic make up, (analysed) that the poetry I want to write is made. The reason I haven't gone on with Paterson is that I am not able to—as yet, if ever I shall be. It must be made up of such *speech* (analysed). V. C. Koch [Vivienne Koch, see the note to "The Visit" p. 470] is the first who has seen the trend of my mind—steadily where I *go* it—not always seeing or even bothering to look. Not enough, no doubt. That's why I have instinctively felt the rightness of her statement—her really valuable criticism in Voices [Winter 1939, pp. 47-49]. . . .

"Anyhow these small pieces, as Koch (thank God!—after some of the gut rot that has been distilled about my work) has seen are the developed (not yet developed) essence of it—to date."

*THE A B AND C OF IT   See p. 83 for the later version published in *The Wedge*.

*A LOVE POEM ND16. Of this and the following five poems, all but "Comfort" and one of the "Details" ("I keep those bests") are in the *Detail & Parody for the poem Paterson* typescript.

*COMFORT ND16. WCW submitted this poem to *The New Yorker* 24 July 1942 with the comment: "Here's this, I don't think it's too clinical. In fact I think what there is of clinical detail might amuse an alert reader, make him think he's really informed" (*New Yorker* files). The poem was not accepted.

*FLATTERY ND16.

*PIGHEADED POET ND16.

*DETAILS FOR PATERSON ND16.

*RIVER RHYME II ND16. See p. 12 for "River Rhyme," published in *Poetry* in November 1940.

*BRIEF LIEF, ELECTION DAY, CONVENTIONAL BALLAD, 10/14 These poems, together with "Reply," (see CPI 536), first appeared in *The Atlantic Monthly* (Nov. 1982). Of these poems only "10/14" appears in the various arrangements WCW was putting together between 1939 and 1944, although all four poems appear to date from this time. WCW gave dates as titles to a number of "Detail" poems in the Buffalo *Broken Span* typescript (as he had in the 1928 *The Descent of Winter*). However, "10/14" does not appear in any typescript of *The Broken Span*, and is titled "The Last Rose" in the *Detail & Parody* and *Wedge* arrangements.

THE PREDICTER OF FAMINE
7 low / low and slowly (*The Broken Span*) WCW marks the change in a dedication copy of *The Broken Span* to his wife, at the University of Pennsylvania.

*THE LAST TURN See p. 82 for the later version published in *The Wedge*.

*THREE POEMS FOR HORACE GREGORY ND16, dated c. 1941. Gregory had written of WCW's 1938 *Collected Poems* that they stemmed from "the very center of spoken language" (see Mariani 423).

*JEAN SANS TERRE These translations from Goll's autobiographical sequence *Jean Sans Terre* (1936-1943, 59 poems in all) appeared sporadically over seventeen years, although they almost certainly all date from spring 1940. The first translation appeared in *The Nation*, 4 Jan. 1941, and was not reprinted. The next three translations appeared in a 1944 edition of *Jean Sans Terre* published by the Grabhorn Press in San Francisco. A 1958 edition, put out by Thomas Yoseloff (from which the versions I print are taken), republished the 1944 printings and printed the final three translations. There were also periodical publications in *Decision* (Nov.-Dec. 1941) and *Accent* (Autumn 1955). The 1944 printing of "Jean Sans Terre at the Final Port" ("Landless John on a keelless boat") is designated a "First Version" in the 1958 printing, although the version printed in *The Nation* is probably earlier. Francis J. Carmody, in his critical edition of *Jean Sans Terre* (Berkeley, 1962), p. 147, suggests that on the basis of entries in Goll's diary, the 1941 translation corresponds to an early version of the *Jean Sans Terre* manuscript now lost. Goll wrote five further versions of this poem. For the purposes of this edition I have designated the 1944 printing a "second version." The other version of the poem ("John Landless sailing") is designated a "fifth version" in the 1958 volume, which also prints three versions translated by Galway Kinnell.

Aside from the version in *The Nation*, the only verbal differences between the various printings are: in "Jean Sans Terre Leads the Caravan" line 33 has "O" in *Decision* and Grabhorn for "I", and the Grabhorn printing has "lighthouse" for "beacon" in line 23 of "Jean Sans Terre at the Final Port" [second version]. In addition, the 1944 and 1955 printings substitute "Landless John" for "Jean Sans Terre," while the *Decision* printing has "John Landless."

Goll lived in New York from 1939 to 1946, and WCW met him at Alfred Stieglitz's gallery in March 1940. WCW sent Goll translations on 22 March 1940 and 2 June 1940, commenting in the June letter that they were "not very good, the difficulties were too great. Whereas your language is simple and direct the language of the translation is involved and awkward. I wish it might have been better. I tried to keep some semblance of rhyme, perhaps that was my mistake" (*Stony Brook*, 3/4 [1969]). However, Goll told WCW: "Votre traduction de ces quartre strophes qui sont aussi parmi mes preferées dans le petit livre, m'a surpris par sa spontanéité et par sa virtuosité" (quoted by Thirlwall in *The Massachusetts Review* [Winter 1962], 290. On the following page Thirlwall prints Goll's translation of WCW's "Metric Figure" [There is a bird in the poplars]).

The 1944 Grabhorn Press volume prints the French text on facing pages. The French text of the additional translations printed in the 1958 volume appeared in *Poésie 50* (Brochure 44, c. 1950).

*WRESTED FROM MIRRORS, THE AGONY AMONG THE CROWD, NARCISSUS IN THE DESERT   All three poems translated from Calas' French. The French originals were apparently never published, and are now unavailable. "Wrested From Mirrors" first appeared with an etching by Kurt Seligmann in a folio published by the Nierendorf Gallery, New York, in 1941. The other two translations appeared in *Decision*, 1, no. 2 (February 1941), 41. All three poems were discovered by Dickran Tashjian, and reprinted, with a commentary on the poems and WCW's relationship with Calas, in his "Translating Surrealism: Williams' 'Midas Touch,'" WCWN (Fall 1978), 1-8. Tashjian also reproduces the Seligmann etching, which WCW found "superbly appropriate. . . . Full of genius along an avenue I hadn't traveled" (WCW to Charles Henri Ford, 23 Feb. 1941, at Yale, cited by Tashjian). Writing to Calas of these translations, WCW told him: "You know, all this fits well into my scheme. I don't care how I say what I must say. If I do original work all well and good. But if I can say it (the matter of form I mean) by translating the work of others that also is valuable. What difference does it make?" (WCW to Calas, 4 December 1940, Lilly Library, Indiana, quoted by Tashjian).

WCW became interested in Calas' work largely through his admiration for Calas' book of art criticism *Foyers d'Incendie* (Paris, 1938). When *Books Abroad* polled "a number of writers and critics" in June 1939 for their opinions on a "Super-Nobel prize"—to determine "which is the most distinguished book or group of books from one writer that has appeared anywhere in the world . . . since November 1918," WCW's vote was for Calas. He commented: "Calas' book concerns the artist. The artist is the control board of the plane. What he does and says others in science, in philosophy, in government will be doing tomorrow." (WCW added a postscript that "Ezra Pound until his recent imbecilities would have been far ahead—but no more." The journal reported that Pound voted for himself.) *Books Abroad* (Spring 1940), p. 144 (WCW's letter, dated August 7, 1939, is in the World Literature Today Collection, Western History Collections, The University of Oklahoma).

See also the note on "The Phoenix and the Tortoise," p. 466.

*WRESTED FROM MIRRORS
13 lose I have followed the typescript at Lilly Library, designated a final version, rather than the printed version's "loose."

*TO REGAIN THE DAY AGAIN Quoted by John Thirlwall in his "Two Cities: Paris and Paterson," *The Massachusetts Review* (Winter 1962), 289. Thirlwall does not give a title for WCW's poem, but he reproduces Calas' original French text, which is titled "Voyager en dehors du passé."

*DEFENSE *The Providence Sunday Journal*, 4 May 1941.

THE PETUNIA First published in *The New Yorker*, 5 July 1941, p. 42.

*AN EXULTATION *Partisan Review* (July-Aug. 1941). The poem carried the following "Footnote":
"My English grandmother of whom I know very little, as I know very little of any of my forebears, herself told me at least this much: That she had been an orphan who was adopted by a 'rich' family of Godwins living in London. They brought her up. Something then happened, she always kept it a mystery, which caused her to leave them. Perhaps they threw her out. In any case she came to America with my father a five-year-old child, intending to go 'on the stage' but married instead, etc., etc. The point is she always carried a deep seated resentment against those who had treated her so badly in the country of her birth saying, that if she had had her rights things would have been very different. I have inherited her resentment against England, taking part with all those who have carried Empire on their shoulders and been given slums to live in for their pains. I have always hated the English ruling class and as a result feel that, in many ways, whatever England gets now is a just retribution. But, at heart, I am in great part proud of my English blood and so you have

the whole picture. Perhaps it should be added that my contempt for and distrust of T.S. Eliot and all he does and says comes from the feeling I have that he and others like him have allied themselves with that part of the English character which unless it is cleansed by an economic and therefore spiritual hurricane will destroy that which I, in a way very different from theirs, profoundly love. —W. C. Williams, June 1, 1941."

WCW's grandmother died in 1920, see CPI 548.

THE YELLOW SEASON   Kitty Hoagland, WCW's neighbor, and a close friend and writer who typed many of his manuscripts in the 1940s and early 1950s, added a note to the typescript of this poem at the University of Virginia: "Nov. 1 1940. A poem written upon my suggestion—I had seen the blackbirds rise against the vivid yellow trees of Ridge Rd." The postmark on the envelope in which WCW sent her the poem confirms the date.

13   crackle / cackle   (CEP) I have restored the reading in all of the typescripts and in the only previous printing, in *Calendar: An Anthology of 1941 Poetry* (1941).

*WAR, THE DESTROYER!   *Harper's Bazaar*, 1 March 1942. The poem was originally intended to accompany a photograph of Martha Graham by Barbara Morgan in a text on the Spanish Civil War, see Mariani 457. When the poem was reprinted in ND 16 in 1957, WCW asked James Laughlin to be sure that the dedication was included: "I'm proud to have my name associated with hers" (17 Jan. 1957, Yale).

*PASSAIC, N.J.   *The Harvard Advocate* (April 1942).

*FROM A PLAY   *The Harvard Advocate* (April 1942).

*PRELUDE IN BORICUA   *American Prefaces* (Winter 1942). WCW published a "note" with the poem: "This not-to-be-called translation of Matos' introductory poem from the collection *Tuntún de Pasa y Grifería* [Puerto Rico, 1937] is offered with profound apologies to the poet. It is no more than an approximate translation which makes no attempt to give the musical sense of the original. Some of the words cannot be rendered in English at all. . . . The mood is West Indian, as are the words which portray the mood. *Poemas Afroantillanos* is what Matos calls them." The "note" continues with biographical information on the poet.

Boricua is a corruption of the old native name for Puerto Rico.

*GOTHIC CANDOR   *American Prefaces* (Summer 1943).

*THE GENTLE NEGRESS (NO OTHER SUCH LUXURIANCE)   *Palisade* (Winter 1943). This poem is on the same subject as the poem with the same title in *The Wedge*, see p. 94.

TO THE DEAN   "I met a young man . . . who said that Durrell felt himself to be under the aegis of Henry Miller. Perhaps so but I'm awfully afraid the cart has been put before the horse in that case so far as sheer writing is concerned. Durrell is the better man—to my taste" (to James Laughlin, 26 Oct. 1942, Yale).

20-22   that Black Book with its / red sporran by the Englishman that does / you so much honor   Lawrence Durrell's *The Black Book: An Agon* (Paris, 1938).

WCW met Miller in 1935 (see Mariani 373).

*THE VIRTUOUS AGENT   *The University Review* (Spring 1944).

*THINKING BACK TOWARD CHRISTMAS: A STATEMENT FOR THE VIRGIN   *Experiment* (April 1944).

THE WEDGE (1944)

Dedication: "L.Z." [Louis Zukofsky]

WCW originally envisioned a more comprehensive arrangement than the published version of this book, to be titled at one stage "The (lang)WEDGE: A New Summary." His initial conception was to combine a number of forms, including improvisations from the 1920s, prose, and excerpts from his play *Many Loves*—as well as many poems from the *Detail & Parody for the poem Paterson* and *The Broken Span* arrangements. With the assistance of Louis Zukofsky, WCW revised and rearranged the poems, cut down the material, and finally eliminated the prose—although adding an introduction based upon a talk he gave at the New York Public Library on 26 October 1943 (Mariani 482). The various arrangements of the typescript are described in Buffalo D6.

Omitting the history of the manuscript revisions and the initial ambitious design, WCW told Ezra Pound in a 15 April 1949 letter that the book "was gathered together during the war under the incentive provided me by various GIs who wanted a book of my poems, so their letters said, that they could carry in their pockets. . . . So I gathered up what stray ends of poems I had and found enough to make a small book." The letter goes on to describe the various rejections by publishers on the grounds of literary quality or war shortages, the eventual handset printing by Harry Duncan and Wightman Williams at their Cummington Press, and the surreptitious binding—thanks to the wiles of a patient—on the premises and at the expense of one of the publishers who had originally rejected the book. The letter is printed in *Grand Street* (Winter 1984), 120-122.

In *The Wedge* WCW published many of the poems he had been writing since the late 1930s as part of what proved to be an abortive start on *Paterson*. "Paterson is coming along—this book is a personal finger-practicing to assist me in that: but that isn't all it is," WCW told James Laughlin, 24 Jan. 1943 (Yale). He could announce to Charles Abbott on 2 Feb. 1944 that he had finally arrived at a conception of his long poem that satisfied him: "I couldn't get the right lead and so have been stuck but now, at last, I see my way clear and time alone will stop me" (Buffalo F880).

AUTHOR'S INTRODUCTION   WCW reprinted this prose introduction in SE as well as in CLP. The text here is from SE, which follows *The Wedge* in matters of italicization and the seven minor verbal differences between the two later printings.

A SORT OF A SONG   "It's the idea that the poet and all that he stands for is absolutely insistent and *will* prevail in the end although it will be a long time. . . . It doesn't matter how long it takes . . . but it is [the poet's] intention to be completely revolutionary and to knock down all opposition in the end, if it takes him forever. He's going to win in the end, and it's a celebration of that" (from a tape recording of WCW reading nine poems at the home of Kenneth Burke, 21 June 1951; tape at the Rutherford Free Public Library).

The final version of this poem is a condensation and rearrangement of the first printed version in *The Old Line* (April 1943), reprinted below. This version was titled "A Possible Sort of Song":

> —through metaphor to reconcile
> (compose)
> the people and the stones. Compose
> (no ideas but in things)
> invent!
>
> Saxifrage is my flower, that splits
> the rocks—
> and harlequin and columbine.
> Let the snake wait under
> his weed
>
> for flies and spiders and the writing
> be of words
> slow and quick, sharp
> to strike, quiet to wait
> sleepless.

Although the poem contains language and concepts that become important in *Paterson,* in sending this first version to Norman Macleod for *The Old Line* on 5 January 1942, WCW commented: "as with so many other things I'm doing now it's so much smoke; maybe there's a fire under them somewhere, maybe not." The letter is reprinted in *Pembroke Magazine,* No. 6 (1975), 157.

CATASTROPHIC BIRTH   The first printing, in *VVV* (June 1942), is dated "April 22, 1942." The poem was originally written for *Paterson,* and intended at one stage for Book II, see Mariani 463 and Buffalo E4(s). The eruption described is that of Mt. Pelée in 1902, the eruption that "wiped out the last of my mother's family, the Hurrards" (A 71).

    32   to / for   (*VVV*)
    39   blocks / blots   (*VVV*)
    56   changes / change   (*VVV*)

PATERSON: THE FALLS   The poem describes a late stage in WCW's working out of the thematic and organizational format of *Paterson*. The first sixteen lines of the version in *View* (April 1943), printed below, contain a number of verbal and lineation differences:

> What common language, what to unravel?
> The Falls: combed into straight
> lines, hung from that rafter of
> a rock's lip, a clear speech.
>
> Begin; the middle of some trenchant
> phrase, some well packed clause,
> picked for the place. Then . . .
> answer! This is my plan.
>
> 4 sections: begin with
> the archaic persons of the drama—
> What drama? An eternity of
> bird and bush. An unraveling:
>
> the confused streams aligned, side
> by side, speaking! Sound
> married to strength, a strength of
> falling, from a height: Hear

23   Alexander / Alex   (*View*)
25-26   from that sea! and from a deeper sea!
        stopped cold   (*View*)

THE DANCE (IN BRUEGHEL'S GREAT PICTURE)   Although the poem describes Brueghel's *The Kermess* (at the Kunsthistorisches Museum, Vienna), the bagpiper in the painting has no "bugle and fiddles" to accompany him. These instruments are not traditionally associated with the kermess in sixteenth-century Netherlandish painting.

WRITER'S PROLOGUE TO A PLAY IN VERSE   Although not ever included with a published play, the poem's themes relate directly to WCW's interests in his two major plays of the 1940s, *Many Loves*, begun in 1941, and *A Dream of Love*, which he began in 1945.

The following is the first printed version, from *Calendar: An Anthology of 1940 Poetry* (1940), which contains many additional lines and other differences:

> In your minds you can jump from doors
> to sad departures, pigeons, dreams
> of terror, to cathedrals; bowed,
> repelled, knees quaking to the-closed
> without-a-key or through an arch
> to look out where an ocean races
> full of sound and foam to lay

a carpet for your pleasure or a wood
that waves releasing hawks
and crows or crowds elbow and fight
for a place or anything. You see
it in your minds and the mind at once
jostles it, turns it about, examines
and arranges it to suit its fancy.
Or rather changes it after a pattern
which is the mind itself, turning
and twisting the theme until it gets
a meaning or finds no meaning and
is dropped. By such composition,
without code, the scenes we see move
themselves or are moved and as
it may happen make a music, a poetry
which the poor poet copies if
and only if he is able—to astonish
and amuse, for your delights
in public, face to face with you
individually and secretly addressed.

We are not here, you understand
but in the mind, that circumstance
of which the speech is only poetry—
it would be unnatural to speak
otherwise. Or would you prefer
not to enter? Perhaps so. Sorry
to say there is a distorting mirror
which, with your permission, must
be broken at this place—we beg
your tolerance if we break it—
called, a stage. Ignore it, an accident
an impertinence, clumsy and in fact
lifeless. But look, we beg, try
and look rather within yourselves.
Yourselves! Tell me if you do not
see there, alive! a creature unlike
the others, something extraordinary
in its vulgarity, something
strange, unnatural to the world
that suffers the world poorly, is
tripped at home, disciplined
at the office, greedily eats money—
for a purpose: to escape the tyranny
of lies. And is all they can think
of to amuse you, a ball game? It
may be the Rodeo, Bailey's Beach or

skiing in Van Diemen's land in August—
to amuse you! Do you not come here
to escape that? For you are merely
distracted, not relieved in the blood,
deadened, defeated, stultified.

But this! is new. Believe it, to be
proved presently by your patience.
Run through the public appearance
of it—to come out, wearing . . .
to come out, let me not say stripped,
that's for the Turkish bath or
other thing with which we're not concerned
but, if you'll pardon me, something
which in the mind you are and would
be and have always been, unrecognized,
tragic and foolish, without a tongue.
That's it. Yourself, the thing
you are, is speechless. Do you think
so? Then it is because there is
no language for it—shockingly revealed.

Would it disturb you if I said
you have no other speech than poetry?
You, yourself, I mean. There is
no other language for it than the poem—
falsified by the critics until
you think it something else, fight
it off, something idle, a kind of lie,
smelling of corpses, that the practical
world rejects. How could it be you?
Never! without invention. That's
the courtesy of it—in which you're
mightily concerned. It is, if
you'll have patience, the undiscoverable
language of yourself, which you avoid,
rich and poor, killed and killers,
a language to be coaxed out of poets—
possibly, an intolerable language
that will frighten—to which
you are not used. We must make it
easy for you, feed it to you slowly
until you let down the barriers,
relax before it like students learning
trigonometry. But it's easy if
you will allow us to proceed, it
can make transformations, give it
leave to do its work in you.

Accept the conventions as you do opera,
provisionally; let us go ahead. Wait
to see if it may happen. It may not.
Or it may come and go, small bits
at a time. But even the chips of it
are invaluable. Wait to learn the
hang of its persuasions as it makes
its transitions from the common
to the undisclosed and lays it open—
where you will see a frightened face!
Don't be misled by old definitions,
that poetry is made of mediaeval
pageants. No. It is here, now
in your minds, struggling—not to
get out but to be hidden, hidden
from the one beside you—rightly. We
are few of us lovely naked. We do not
mean to bare you but with tact to
speak the language, let you make
the interpretation for yourself.

But believe! that poetry will be
in the terms you know, insist on that
and can and must break through everything
all the outward forms, to re-dress
itself humbly in that which you
yourself will say is the truth, the
exceptional truth of ordinary people,
the extraordinary truth. You shall see.
It isn't masculine more than it is
feminine, it is not a book more than
it is speech or speech more than
a book, inside the mind, natural
to the mind as metals are to rock
to be dug out and laid in their purity
for you—if you will open
your minds and let us tentatively dig
the metal which is there for our
construction—of a purpose to be
careful, as we are full of excuses,
confident of mistakes and misuses
in the material, a beginning
of discovery to make what is not seen
visible—in its own words, and, if
possible, a very broken image of
the music, pasting up what few passages
we can discern and interpret to our

purpose. These the puppets of your
minds which if they present distinction
it is from that hidden dignity
which they, by your leave, reflect
from you who are the play.

This is a play of a husband and a wife.
As you love your husband or your wife
or if you hate him or if you hate
her, watch the language, see if you
think that it expresses something of
the things, to your knowledge, that
take place in the mind and in the world
but seldom on the lips. This play
is of a woman and her lover, all
mixed up, of life and death and all
the secret language that runs through
those curious transactions, seldom
heard but in the deadest of presentations
now respectfully unnaturalized. This
play is of two races in a counterpoint
of feeling. This play is made of
words whose weighted meanings are
so many cues for you to disentwine,
secretly, to yourself, to see yourself
and to know covertly (as an actor
in that play in which we all
are actors wearing masks—hiding our
identity) the world today. Courteously,
respectfully, anonymously before
the confession both of music and of
what verse we can manage to pick up
from what we are and what you are
and to begin . . . .

For pleasure! pleasure, not for
cruelty but to make you laugh until
you cry, like General Washington
at the river seeing the travelers
who had had their clothes stolen and
did not know what next to do.
How he laughed! and how you shall
laugh, all naked. Have you never thought
you'd like to be on the stage?

66   it's / it   (*The Wedge*)

BURNING THE CHRISTMAS GREENS   "An occurrence in our home. Certainly no
one can escape the conclusion that this poem envisages a rebirth of the 'state'

perhaps but certainly of the mind following the destruction of the shibboleths of tradition which often comfort it" (Author's Note in *Modern Poetry*, ed. Kimon Friar and John Malcolm Brinnin [New York, 1951], p. 546).

WCW told Byron Vazakas on 30 March 1944: "As far as I know the Christmas poem was as good as anything I've ever written. . . . I also find the poem on the munitions plant ["The Semblables"] to be what I think worthwhile doing" (Yale).

12 the Omitted in *Poetry* (Jan. 1944).
18 brought / bought (*Poetry*)
26 above / about (*SP*)
58 flame / flames (*Poetry*)
69 of Omitted in *Poetry*.
75 that / the (*Poetry*)

IN CHAINS
5 us / it (*The Wedge*)
5-8 torture us we must perforce either
join arms with them or bend
to their designs while our thoughts
gnaw, bite and snap within us
(*Poetry*, Sept. 1939; *American Decade*, 1943)
10 we learn from that / from that we learn
(*Poetry*; *American Decade*)
13 we water / we will water (*Poetry*; *American Decade*)

THE OBSERVER
2 breath / death (*Poetry*, Nov. 1940; *The Wedge*)
4. death / breath (*Poetry*; *The Wedge*)

THE HOUNDED LOVERS
8 hard / hard-packed (*The New Yorker*, 25 Oct. 1941)
13 nor / Or (*The New Yorker*)
19-21 Jerk at their dead
stalks, signalling hieroglyphs
of grave warning. (*The New Yorker*)

THE CURE
12 flower-like / fragile (*Furioso*, Summer 1939)

TO ALL GENTLENESS
22 and 130-31 the anti-poetic WCW was annoyed at Wallace Stevens' use of this term in his preface to WCW's *Collected Poems 1921-1931* (1934), see the note to "The Entity" in CPI 535-36. "The Entity" was the final poem in the typescript of *The Wedge* sent to Harry Duncan at the Cummington Press. WCW sent Duncan instructions to delete the poem from the book on 5 October 1943 (Buffalo F1016).

49 Queen Blanche Blanche of Castille, wife of Louis VIII, mother of Louis X, and twice regent of France.

144 of thigh / of her thigh (*New Directions 8*, [1944]; *The Wedge*)

THREE SONNETS

2 is moving—ruled
  by an ungovernable determinant
    (*Calendar: An Anthology of 1942 Poetry* [1942])

6 rime-cupped / rim-cupped (CLP) Error in Harvard/Yale Za47 typescript. I have restored the reading of the two previous printings.

8-11 what was the mudbank now
  so sparkling
  with diamonds big as fists that
  it is unbelievable to witness (*Calendar*)

13-14 do not change their hieroglyphs
  of poise—the broken line (*Calendar*)

16 waken / wakens (*Calendar; The Wedge*)
18 in the half-light upon the ice-strewn (*Calendar*)
21 will / shall still (*Calendar*)

22-24 open my eyes with the morning
  even though my eye-lids have been closed
  faster with ice than stone. (*Calendar*)

23 be / have been (*The Wedge*)
24 by / with (*The Wedge*)
26 Dr. Kennedy Probably Dr. Foster Kennedy, whom WCW consulted about a neck injury to FW. She hit the roof of the car when WCW took a railroad crossing too fast.

29 court—the son of a bitch—
  that: (*Calendar*)

THE POEM A reworking of lines 10-20 of "The Poet and His Poems," see p. 5.

RUMBA! RUMBA!

8-11 to pull all after
  rather than to submit—
  and end in a burst of laughter
    (*The New Republic*, 19 Aug. 1940)

FIGUERAS CASTLE Mariani, p. 421, notes that the poem concerns "the imprisonment of Spanish Loyalists who had failed to turn over what was left of their government's jewels to the French consulate when they had fled across the Pyrenees into France to escape Franco's victorious forces."

5   people's enemies / enemy   (*Matrix*, October 1939)

10-20   check them in for us
at the Consulate
in Perpignan.

But some didn't
bother—like those who had
stolen them first
and were not

arrested for it as these were
in their need. Rhyme
that up right for us, will yuh,
Williams, ol' Keed?   (*Matrix*)

ETERNITY
2   country / county   (*The Wedge*)
25   Noah   one of the names for the central man/city/poet figure in *Paterson I* (p. 15).

THE HARD LISTENER   Also printed in CPI 463 as an example of the poems
WCW was writing and publishing in connection with the *Detail & Parody for
the poem Paterson* typescript. In *Hika* (March 1939) lines 6-10 read:

keep some relation
to the truth of man's
unhappiness, in poverty
lacking love. That
is what the late flowers
say to me, unspoiled

THE CONTROVERSY
5   away   Omitted in *The Wedge*.
8   *Apologia* / of the Apologia   (*The Wedge*)

A VISION OF LABOR: 1931
Title: "A Vision of Labor" in *The Nation*, 10 Feb. 1940.

11   exploded away—but in this case
a bomb of construction,   (*The Nation*)

20-23   That's the answer.
Alone made that possible there
in that place.   (*The Nation*)

25   the / an   (*The Nation*)

54-56   —till they threw the switch and
the pump stopped and
the bishop died   (*The Nation*)

58   flung / threw   (*The Nation*)

THE LAST TURN   See the first version, p. 27.

THE A, B & C OF IT   See the first version, p. 21.

THE SEMBLABLES   The monastery is in Secaucus N.J. near the Giants football stadium. Just south of it was a munitions works called "Black Tom." The garbage dump was the source of food for the biggest and most foul-smelling piggery on the East Coast.

1   The / That   (*Partisan Review*, Jan.-Feb. 1943; *The Wedge*; *The Clouds*; SP)

21-28   faces, all silent that miracle
        that has burst, four-square,
        hugging the ground on all sides,
        liturgically sexless   (*The Wedge*)

31   swaying / swaying lazily   (*Partisan Review*; *The Wedge*; *The Clouds*; SP)

THE STORM
Title: Storm   (*Palisade*, Summer 1943)

10-12   but drives violently
        the smoke from a few lean
        chimneys streaming southward   (*Palisade*)

THE FORGOTTEN CITY   WCW describes this drive with his mother through the hurricane of fall 1938 in A 303-04.

1-2   When I was coming down from the country
      with my mother, the day of the storm,
        (*Poetry*, Sept. 1939; *New Poems: 1940* [1941])

6   with / with the   (*Poetry*; *New Poems: 1940*)
8   sluices / sluiceways   (*Poetry*; *New Poems: 1940*)
9   what / any   (*Poetry*; *New Poems: 1940*)

THE YELLOW CHIMNEY
9   amber / bitter   (*American Prefaces*, Summer 1943)
12   pale sun / sun   (*American Prefaces*)
14-15   the satiric
        season   (*American Prefaces*)

THE BARE TREE
1   The / This   (*The University Review*, Spring 1944; *The Wedge*)

RALEIGH WAS RIGHT   WCW's contribution to the sixteenth-century exchange between Christopher Marlowe ("The Passionate Shepherd to his Love") and Sir Walter Raleigh ("The Nymph's Reply to the Shepherd"). See the first version, p. 17.

THE MONSTROUS MARRIAGE   "Flesh is weak but love is great—where there is daring. And the mind must sometimes resort to strange devices, guarding the too tender flesh, to protect love's advances. Obviously this is a romantic love story and only 'monstrous' in that all unions between mythological beasts and women were monstrous" (Author's Note in *Modern Poetry*, ed. Kimon Friar and John Malcolm Brinnin [New York, 1951], pp. 545-46).
12   him / it   (*The New Republic*, 23 Aug. 1943)
34   made off / flew   (*The New Republic*)

SPARROWS AMONG DRY LEAVES   See the first version on p. 15.

PRELUDE TO WINTER   First printed in *The New Yorker*, 14 Oct. 1939, p. 24.

SILENCE   First printed in *The New Yorker*, 7 Oct. 1939, p. 66.

*THE CLOUDS   WCW subsequently extended the poem to four sections, see p. 171.
29   blinds: / blinds: Relief!   (*Hemispheres*, Summer 1943)   WCW sent the printers of *The Wedge* instructions to make the change (Buffalo F1016).

A COLD FRONT
11   carved eyes as a cat does   (*Poetry*, Sept. 1939)

AGAINST THE SKY
7   the / its   (*The Broken Span*)

14-16   southward above the grave chickens
         walking gingerly upon
         the level of the tremulous lawn.
                    (*The Broken Span*)

*THE GENTLE NEGRESS (WANDERING AMONG THE CHIMNEYS)   The subject is the same as "The Gentle Negress" (No other such luxuriance), see p. 47. WCW told Reed Whittemore in 1939 that the book in which the poem "will appear and of which it is an essential part is to be called *Detail and Parody*." The poem "is a parody of Yeats' 'Down by the Salley Gardens'" (*New Directions 17* [1961], 264).
The version in *American Prefaces* (Summer 1943) is titled "Lillian" and contains a number of differences:

                    Wandering among the chimneys
                    my love and I did meet
                    I had a white skin
                    and she was brown as peat

                    Her voice was low and gentle
                    and full of surprise

that I should find her lovely
and search her eyes

with a longing hard to understand
from what she said
and sit by her and comfort her
lying in bed

TO FORD MADOX FORD IN HEAVEN   "I did erupt a poem to Ford Madox Ford in Heaven which I like but it's really the sort of occasional verse which I some-what mistrust. The subject makes such demands on a man that he is likely for the moment to forget the poem in the occasion—somewhat topical" (to James Laughlin, 23 Oct. 1939, Yale).

Ford died in Deauville 26 June 1939. WCW first met him in 1924 in Eu-rope; Ford published WCW in *the transatlantic review,* and the two renewed aquaintance when Ford moved to New York in 1935. In the first half of 1939 Ford founded "Les Amis de William Carlos Williams," a group that met monthly to hear readings from WCW's work, to lament his lack of recognition, and to have a good party (see Mariani 424-25 and A 299-300). WCW offered the poem to *The New Yorker* on 16 October 1939, noting that "I wrote it, to be frank, for some kids up at Yale running a mag they call *Furioso.* It's a good mag but I'd like to have people think about Ford—I thought I'd aim a pot-shot at you anyway" (*New Yorker* files). The poem did not appear in *The New Yorker.*

Lines 3-16 were omitted in *The Wedge* (and in SP) in response to the com-ments of Louis Zukofsky, who suggested that the whole poem be dropped from *The Wedge* typescript. WCW told Zukofsky on 5 October 1943 that he had adopted all his suggestions and "corrected all the errors you detected. I have deleted the poems entire which you found fault with, all except the Ford Madox Ford piece. In that I cut the first stanza, all except the first line, which has been left standing alone to the great improvement of the whole poem" (Harry Ransom Center, University of Texas, Austin). The lines were restored to CLP at a late stage, since they are not in the Harvard/Za47 typescript.

6   circumstances / circumstance   (*Furioso,* Spring 1940)

POEMS 1945-1948

THE PHOENIX AND THE TORTOISE
1   Calas   Nicolas Calas (see note on p. 451).

3   Rexroth   Kenneth Rexroth, who published his book of poems *The Phoenix and the Tortoise* in 1944. "I hear Bill has a poem about how me and Nicolas Calas don't get along. That's right, we don't" (Rexroth to FW, n.d. [1945?], Yale). In praising Rexroth's book to James Laughlin, WCW wrote: "I have long wanted some mind to write of the classics and to handle the classic Greek and Latin material in our language as against the English and English imitators—to whom flock the Pounds and Eliots—like blind fish and bats from the caves" (1 Nov. 1944).

22 affect / to affect (*Pacific*, Nov. 1945)

24-32 Calas published his *Confound the Wise* in 1942. The quotation in lines 25-32 is from page 116 and contains two slight changes from Calas' text: "so far said" for "said so far," and "monist and opposed" for "monist, and I am opposed."

33-34 Read of Miranda / the Portuguese torso WCW could be referring to one of two Portuguese 'advertisements' Calas describes in *Confound the Wise:* 'a headless mannequin,' p. 183, or a replica of the Venus de Milo holding a telephone, p. 185, or to the "exceptionally beautiful girl of ten" who "lost both her legs in an automobile accident" and whom Calas links to Iphigenia, both being necessary nightmares to provoke action. None of these figures are associated with the name "Miranda," and there is no "Miranda" in the book.

*THE YELLOW TREE PEONY William Gratwick, whom WCW met through Charles Abbott of the University of Buffalo Library, published this poem in his *My, This Must Have Been A Beautiful Place When It Was Kept Up* (New York, 1965) noting: "One summer when Bill Williams was here he watched me working on the plant form allegory shown on the opposite page. He wrote this poem, printed here for the first time. . . . The sculpture, eight inches high, is still in the original beeswax." Gratwick also reproduced the poem and sculpture in his *The Truth, Tall Tales and Blatant Lies* (1981). In addition, poem and sculpture are reproduced in Emily Wallace's "Musing in the Highlands and Valleys: The Poetry of Gratwick Farm" WCWR (Spring 1982), as part of a full discussion of the poetry that emerged from WCW's visits to the Gratwicks in the Genesee Valley. See also A 326-327.

WCW told Abbott on 29 July 1946 that his attempts to revise the poem for publication had come to naught, it "has too special an application for general reading; I was able to do not a thing with it" (Buffalo F898).

*TRANSLATIONS OF PAUL ELUARD—POET OF FRANCE These six translations appeared under this title in *New Directions 9* (1946). WCW originally intended to publish a seventh translation, "Trained by Famine," but was dissatisfied with the results. The poem appeared in *ND9* as translated by André du Bouchet. All of the poems are from Eluard's 1942 *Poesie et Vérite*.

Although generally critical of the French surrealists' lack of structure (to Pound in 1946: "a crappy and ignorant crew of something out of a dog's stomach. If there is sterility prevalent in the world today you'll find much of it just there" [*Grand Street*, Winter 1984, p. 114]), WCW admired Eluard's work, telling James Laughlin in May 1946 "even my own work seems stale to me after Eluard" (Mariani 520-21). In March 1949, writing to David Ignatow, he cautioned: "Eluard, the Frenchman, could teach you a lot. He is relaxed before his broken faith. He is loose jointed. You (and I) have a tendency to be tight. Too tight" (Kent State University Library).

*HEY RED! *The Harvard Wake* (Spring 1946).

DEATH BY RADIO Published without the dedication in *The Harvard Wake* (Spring 1946).

EAST COOCOO   T. S. Eliot's "East Coker" was first published in 1940, and appeared as one of *Four Quartets* in 1944.
15   locomotive / locomotives (*Yale Poetry Review*, Summer 1946)

AT KENNETH BURKE'S PLACE   The poem arose from a visit WCW and FW made to Burke's farm in Andover, 9 November 1945. The following day WCW wrote to Burke: "I saw the beginnings of many valuable conversations between us sticking their heads up as we passed them by yesterday—I particularly liked your manner of explanation when you lowered your voice and spoke quietly of the elementals that interest us both, the humane particulars of realization and communication" (Pennsylvania State University). See also Mariani 516.

*"THE ROCK-OLD DOGMA"   *Poetry*, The Australian International Quaiterly of Verse (June 1946).

APPROACH TO A CITY
20   braver / greater   (*Briarcliff Quarterly*, Oct. 1946)

*THE USURERS OF HEAVEN   *Harper's Bazaar* (Nov. 1946)

ROGATION SUNDAY   The poem was written for Harriet Gratwick, wife of William, who had requested a poem that could be set to music. It was read by a local farmer as part of the 7:30 p.m. "Rural Life Sunday" service of the Avon Methodist Church, Livingston County, N.Y. on 18 May 1947, and printed in the program for the service. On 13 August 1950 WCW read the poem at Gratwick Farm, and it was sung by the chorus of Harriet Gratwick's Linwood Music School to music composed by Thomas S. Canning.
2   unrest / the unrest   (Avon Church)
13   and to / and   (Avon Church)
19   and / with all   (Avon Church)

21-28   by our labor this springtime
        as we plant them in the May of the year!

        Who will reap the harvest?
        To whom shall praise be given?
        No man—but all men together
        in love and devotion! There is no richer
        harvest and no better praise!
        Let the seeds and the tubers be planted,
        and the rain and the sun
        and the moon add their wonder!   (Avon Church)

LUSTSPIEL   Sent by WCW to Norman Macleod for *Cronos* with the comment: "not perhaps so very *lustig* but it's what there is at the moment—I don't know if there's anything in it or not" (n.d. [1947], University of Maryland).
1 and 16   Volk / Folk   (*Cronos*, Fall 1947)

9-10   she likes to dance and sing!

—and given the meanest break
she'd lead them hell bent—
　　who likes to dance and sing!

until they'd chuck the racket   (*Cronos*)

13   the / their   (*Cronos*)

THE UNITED STATES   On a typescript of this poem at the University of Virginia is a note by Kitty Hoagland, WCW's friend and typist: "Bill told me this was written in praise of a certain woman." She dates the poem "Spring 1946," although it was not published until the end of 1947. On the typescript of another poem, "Design for November," which she dates from this period ("Nov. 1945"), she notes: "this Bill said was written about same woman as 'The United States.' Also he said 'Choral' [she almost certainly means 'Chanson'] was in praise of her."

*THE RESEMBLANCE   *Accent* (Winter 1947). "I was pragmatically putting things down. But I didn't know where I was going. I was turning away from free verse, but I was writing free verse" (recorded by Thirlwall beside this poem in his copy of *Accent*).

THE BIRTH OF VENUS
5   rock's / rocks'   (*Botteghe Oscure*, 1948)
26   old Ford   Ford Madox Ford
35   coasts / coast lines   (*Botteghe Oscure*)
40   heedless / needless (*Botteghe Oscure*)   WCW makes the change on the Harvard typescript.

SEAFARER
Title: "The Sea Farer" (*Interim*, 1948; *Modern American Poetry* [1950])

2-6   and the rocks—whether seen
　　by air, jagged ribs
　　riding the cloth of foam
　　or a knob or pinnacles
　　lined with gannets—
　　whose screams we may guess,
　　are the stubborn man.
　　　　(*Interim*; *Modern American Poetry*)

APRIL IS THE SADDEST MONTH   "April is the cruellest month" are the opening words of Part I of T. S. Eliot's *The Waste Land*. For WCW, Eliot, "gave the poem back to the academics" (A 146) and he became the figure against whom WCW defined his poetic concerns in many letters and essays for more than forty years.

FOR G.B.S., OLD.   In March 1948 WCW was reading Eric Bentley's biography of George Bernard Shaw, then 92 (Mariani 558).

1   As / When   (*Harper's Magazine*, Aug. 1948)
12   And by such / Until by   (*Harper's Magazine*)

*THE MODEST ACHIEVEMENT   *The Golden Goose* (Autumn 1948).

*NO GOOD TOO   *The Golden Goose* (Autumn 1948).

THE CLOUDS (1948)

AIGELTINGER   Aigeltinger had been a fellow student of WCW's at Horace Mann School, a mathematical genius who became a successful engineer until heavy drinking ruined his career. Nevertheless, his abilities made him a byword in New York, and he was regarded as indispensable for solving certain difficult technical problems. WCW heard a Rutherford neighbor remarking that he would have to consult an "Aigeltinger" in the city, and thus discovered the story. See Mariani 565-66.
Title: April 6   (*The General Magazine and Historical Chronicle*, Summer 1945; SP)
15   Jim will read the encyclopedia   Jim Hyslop, WCW's boyhood friend in Rutherford, wrote "for twenty years at his encyclopedia of noxious insects— only to be met at the end by a refusal on all sides to publish his magnum opus" (A 282).

LABRADOR
7   to the very thoughts   (*The Nation*, 22 Feb. 1947)
8   an / this   (*The Nation*)
9   that as it rises unmarred   (*The Nation*)

A WOMAN IN FRONT OF A BANK   Probably the National Community Bank, Rutherford, on the corner of Park and Ames.

THE NIGHT RIDER   In *The Clouds* lines 13 and 14 are reversed.

CHANSON   See the note to "The United States," p. 469.
11   or clever / nor clever   (*Yale Poetry Review*, Spring 1946)

THE VISIT   The poem is a response to a visit to Rutherford by Vivienne Koch on 30 September 1945 (see Mariani 510-11). She had been commissioned by New Directions to write a book-length study of WCW's work, which eventually appeared in 1950 titled *William Carlos Williams*. Koch began writing on WCW in the late 1930s, and WCW was initially enthusiastic about her work, writing to Norman Macleod on 6 November 1939 (she was Macleod's second wife): "Together the verse and prose constitute, I think, a marriage likely to prove fertile if cultivated. . . . I couldn't wish for a better style of prose as emphasis and explanation. It is a strong stimulus to me. I wish no one at all would discuss me but Vivienne Koch." But on 10 August 1945 he told Macleod that she should spend her time writing on younger poets—he preferred not to be "fussed over just now" (*Pembroke Magazine*, No. 6 [1975], 154, 159). And when the book finally appeared he found it "as a biography . . . unsatisfactory—even false I am sure in many instances in its interpretation of individual pieces" (to Babette Deutsch, 23 January [1950], Washington University, St. Louis).

20   rarely / barely   (*Briarcliff Quarterly*, April 1946; *The Clouds*; SP)

26   day / day but   (*Briarcliff Quarterly*; *The Clouds*)

58-60   You were kind to take so much
    pains with me and—thank
    you for the view.
        (*Briarcliff Quarterly*; *The Clouds*)

THE QUALITY OF HEAVEN   First published in *Poetry Quarterly* [London] (Winter 1946-47), p. 225.

16-18   the near hive, parched to drink
    at the bird-bath

overeager were drowned there   (*Poetry Quarterly*)

TO A LOVELY OLD BITCH
2   handmaiden / hand-matron   (*The Quarterly Review of Literature*, 1945)
11   Omitted in *The Quarterly Review of Literature.*

THE BITTER WORLD OF SPRING
5   desires / desire   (*Orígenes,* Fall 1944; *The Quarterly Review of Literature,* 1945); *The Clouds*)

LAMENT
5   struggling / straggling   (*The Quarterly Review of Literature,* 1945)

A HISTORY OF LOVE
17   ol' / old   (*The Quarterly Review of Literature,* 1945)
17-18   ol' Bunk / Johnson   The negro jazz musician whose music is the subject of "Ol' Bunk's Band," see the note on p. 474.

MISTS OVER THE RIVER
7   adjusting / adjustment   (*Wake,* Spring 1948)

EDUCATION A FAILURE   First published in *Poetry Quarterly* [London] (Winter 1946-47), p. 224.
Title: "Education is a Failure" (*Poetry Quarterly*)
5   two bridges   The Union Avenue and Rutherford Avenue bridges, crossing the Passaic.
17   threading / walk through   (*Poetry Quarterly*)

THE BANNER BEARER   This final version is a condensation of the first version,
printed in *The Harvard Wake* (Spring 1946), and reproduced below:

> In the rain, the lonesome
> dog (diagonal down
> the reflecting highway)
> comes running.
>
> Idiosyncratically he
> throws out
> the left forefoot, with each
> quadribeat, beyond
>
> the right, intent
> in his stride on some obscure
> insistence—from
> bridgeward whither
>
> he has crossed
> (repeating
> always the same gesture)
> into new territory.

LESSON FROM A PUPIL RECITAL   In 1946 WCW attended a piano recital in Buf-
falo in which Buffalo librarian Charles Abbott's daughter Agnes participated.
    16   who / that   (*The Kenyon Review*, Summer 1948)
    23   the good teacher   Warren Case, Agnes Abbott's piano teacher, whose
appreciative letter of response to this poem is filed with the poem's drafts at
Buffalo (A179).

VOYAGES   Emily Wallace in "Musing in the Highlands and Valleys: The
Poetry of Gratwick Farm," WCWR (Spring 1982) notes that this poem "de-
scribes an arrangement on the wall of a bathroom in the garage apartment,
'The Annex' (formerly occupied by the coachman, then the chauffeur, then
Mrs. William Henry Gratwick), where the Williamses always stayed from 1946
on when they visited the Abbotts" (p. 21).

THE MIRRORS   First printed in 1945. WCW was questioned twice by the FBI
about Pound's broadcasts from Italy during the Second World War (A 318).
His attitude toward Pound at this time as both man and writer is spelled out
in a 23 Feb. 1944 letter to Robert McAlmon reprinted in SL 220-223. Early
drafts of this poem, originally headed "Not For Publication," read "take some
traitor" for "take Ezra Pound," see Buffalo A208.

DESIGN FOR NOVEMBER   Kitty Hoagland dates this poem "Nov. 1945" on a
typescript. See the note to "The United States" on p. 469.

THE MANEUVER
    3   last, / last moment   (*The Harvard Wake*, Spring 1946)

5-8 turned in the air
and landed, together, back-
wards! that's what got
me—to face about
into the wind's teeth. (*The Harvard Wake*)

THE HORSE "Dashed off a fast one for the U. of Arizona Review" [*Arizona Quarterly*] (to Fred Miller, 30 Jan. 1946, University of Virginia).

HARD TIMES
Title: "The Statue" (*The General Magazine and Historical Chronicle*, Summer 1945)
16 fellows / brothers (*The General Magazine and Historical Chronicle*)

THE DISH OF FRUIT
8 contents / content (*The Quarterly Review of Literature*, 1945)

THE MOTOR-BARGE
2 the bridge Either the Union Avenue or the Rutherford Avenue bridge, both crossing the Passaic. WCW would cross one of these bridges on his way to the Passaic General Hospital. From the Union Avenue bridge he painted his *Passaic River* (c. 1912) now in the Beinecke Library, Yale University, reproduced in Mike Weaver's *William Carlos Williams: The American Background* (1971) opposite page 52, and in ARI opposite page 2.

RUSSIA This poem was one of those used against WCW in 1952 when he was appointed Consultant in Poetry to the Library of Congress. Mrs. Virginia Kent Cummins of the Lyric Foundation was quoted in the *Chicago Daily Tribune* of 20 Oct. 1952, under the headline "Poet Assailed As Unfit For His Praise Of Reds," as terming the poem "the very voice of communism." Subsequent publicity caused WCW's appointment to be delayed and in the following year withdrawn. See Mariani 651-59, 666-67.
WCW told Selden Rodman on 1 Dec. 1950: "The Russia piece ends on the note of empire in an ironic sense, bitterly. Russia whose avowed intent has been to free the world from capitalism (for which we tentatively praised her) has turned out to be an empire seeker of the most reactionary sort. It will be her downfall BUT in the meantime we shall all of us suffer. It is to Russians, not Russia that I am talking at the end of that piece, sadly pointing out to them how they have been deceived by their own leaders" (American Heritage Center, University of Wyoming).
46 idiot / the idiot (*The New Republic*, 29 April 1946)
54-55 Between these lines CLP prints an additional "Look." The Harvard/ Za 47 typescript reproduced the square bracketed catchword at the bottom of the page in *The Clouds* as if part of the poem.
56-57 a poet, a stupid, uninfluential poet, excluded
from anthologies, with no skill
(*The New Republic*)

59-71   WCW heard Vladimir Mayakovsky read at Lola Ridge's Greenwich Village apartment at 7 East 14th Street on 19 Sept. 1925, where his reading included "Willie the Havana Street Cleaner." Mayakovsky committed suicide in 1935. WCW again compares the reading to *The Odyssey* in A 163.

65   his voice came / it sounded   (*The New Republic*)

THE WELL DISCIPLINED BARGEMAN
2   on / upon   (*Harper's Magazine*, July 1948)
11-12   avidly into the gale. Only the bargeman upon
      his barge, amazed, seems like the shadow, sleeping.
                                    (*Harper's Magazine*)

OL' BUNK'S BAND   WCW's friend Fred Miller introduced him to the jazz of Bunk Johnson in 1945. Sharing Miller's interest in this 'native American' music—then at the center of the classical jazz revival of the forties—WCW purchased some records, and twice heard the band live in November 1945. "Well, I was so impressed that I came home and wrote a poem about Ol' Bunk Johnson" (in a 1950 interview, *Interviews with William Carlos Williams*, edited by Linda Wagner [New York, 1976] p. 21). See Mike Weaver, *William Carlos Williams: The American Background* (1971) pp. 71-73, and Mariani 512-515.

20   backs / back   (CLP)   I have restored the reading of all previous printings. The poem is not in the Harvard / Za 47 typescripts because it is one of the "mislaid" poems.
21   stomps / stamps   (*Yale Poetry Review*, Summer 1946)

SUZANNE   WCW's grandchildren Paul and Suzanne, the children of Paul and Virginia Carnes Williams, were born in 1942 and 1944.
6   What's / What is   (*The Clouds*)
7   Suzanne / Suzie   (*The Clouds*)

NAVAJO   This and the next two poems came out of WCW's journey through southwestern Colorado and northern New Mexico in the summer of 1947.

GRAPH
Title: "The Graph"   (*Yale Poetry Review*, 1948)

THE TESTAMENT OF PERPETUAL CHANGE   The first printing, in *Partisan Review* (Oct. 1948), identified the italicized lines as the opening of Robert Bridges' "The Testament of Beauty" (1929). "I think poetry has a technical future which old fumbling Bridges only 'goosed.' It is blocked by ordinary thinking and by all metaphysics" (to Kenneth Burke, Pennsylvania State University, [1947]).
9   a compass   Bridges' poem reads "the compass"

FOR A LOW VOICE
13   ha, ha, ha, ha, ha, ha, &c. / ha, ha, ha, ha, ha, ha, ha, etc.   (*Briarcliff Quarterly*, Oct. 1946)
24   more to / to more   (*Briarcliff Quarterly*)

THE WORDS LYING IDLE

7 curled / curled, brown (*The Quarterly Review of Literature,* 1945)

13 The / But the (*The Quarterly Review of Literature*)

15-16 be somewhat appeased against this dryness
and the death implied.
      (*The Quarterly Review of Literature*)

LEAR

25 earlier? / sooner? (*The Clouds*)

PICTURE OF A NUDE IN A MACHINE SHOP

11 the right / with the right (*The New Leader,* 1 March 1947)

14 beside / besides (*The New Leader*)

THE BRILLIANCE The poem appeared in both CEP and CLP. In CLP and earlier printings it is printed without a stanza division.

A UNISON FW and WCW told John Thirlwall [typescript of a taped conversation 23 July 1953] that the setting of the poem is a deserted pasture and farmhouse they visited—"pure Vermont"—on the camp site in Wilmington, Vermont "where the boys have gone for years. . . . In this pasture was a family graveyard. . . . The only thing that's left was this little stone of a child." The site is a quarter of a mile north of the "Molly Stark Trail" on the Bennington-Brattleboro Road.

3 the mountain Haystack, just east of Mount Snow.

16 down that way / down (CLP) I have restored the reading of all previous printings. The poem is not in the Harvard / Za 47 typescripts because it is one of the "mislaid" poems.

34 shed snake's / snake's shed (*The Clouds*)

45-46 through which, tomorrow, the great sun
will rise bejeweled—the
      (*The Nation,* 7 Dec. 1946)

THE HURRICANE

Title: "Address" (*The Quarterly Review of Literature,* 1945)

THE MIND'S GAMES

4-5 the famous / double sonnet Possibly the double sonnet by Wilfrid Scawen Blunt ("He who has once been happy is for aye / Out of destruction's reach") that is the subject of an article by Pound in *Poetry* of March 1914 which reprints the poem.

20 to bathe / bathe (*Contemporary Poetry,* Spring 1946)

26 "The world is too much with us" are the opening words of Wordsworth's famous sonnet.

NOTE TO MUSIC: BRAHMS FIRST PIANO CONCERTO

Title: "Brahms First Piano Concerto" (*The General Magazine and Historical Chronicle*, Summer 1948)

1-2   In a cavernous house we enjoy
         of music our humanity the more
             (*The General Magazine and Historical Chronicle*)

6-7   the Demuths, the Sheelers, / the Hartleys   The house at 9 Ridge Road held a number of paintings by Charles Demuth, Charles Sheeler and Marsden Hartley, all friends of WCW.

THE INJURY   In May 1946 WCW underwent a herniotomy at Passaic General Hospital. On 28 May he told Fred Miller: "Just sold a poem I wrote in bed at the hospital to *The Nation*" [where this poem first appeared] (University of Virginia). But he came to think the poem "weak," and it appeared in SP only at Randall Jarrell's insistence (WCW to James Laughlin, 6 Aug. 1948, Yale).

THE RED-WING BLACKBIRD   WCW wrote to Louis Zukofsky on 12 Sept. 1948 that he was glad he liked his recent poems "and also the one about the 'red-wing blackbird' which was, I suppose, autobiographic" (Harry Ransom Center, University of Texas).

A PLACE (ANY PLACE) TO TRANSCEND ALL PLACES   In Nov. 1945 WCW told Byron Vazakas that this poem was a reply to Wallace Stevens' "Description Without Place"—"which I didn't like at all." Stevens' poem appeared in the November 1945 issue of *Sewanee Review* (Mariani 517, 824).

40   tuberculin / tuberculous   (*The Kenyon Review*, Winter 1946)

73-74   Elsa / von Freytag Loringhofen   A Greenwich Village figure whom WCW calls "The Baroness" in A 164-69, noting: "Wallace Stevens at one time was afraid to come below Fourteenth Street when he was in the city because of her."

THE MIND HESITANT

17   sooty   Omitted in *Wake* (Spring 1948).

TRAGIC DETAIL

5   some work / some slight work   (*Wake*, Spring 1948; *The Clouds*)

PHILOMENA ANDRONICO

37   shoves / runs   (*The Clouds*)

48-49   Between these lines CLP prints an additional "Fall" as a fifth line to the stanza. The Harvard / Za47 typescript reproduced the square bracketed catchword at the bottom of the page in *The Clouds* as if part of the poem.

THE CLOUDS   "Part one was written first [see the first version p. 91]. At the suggestion of a friend the other parts followed in order. It is a question as between the mind and—those warm clouds which pass for mystery in our lives. The poet is constantly tossed about between one and the other—but in our day the mind claims supremacy, a minority, which seems to rule, from which the various priests peek grinning or thundering or using adding machines" (Author's Note in *Modern Poetry*, ed. Kimon Friar and John Malcolm Brinnin [New York, 1951], p. 545).

The early drafts of this poem center upon the death of WCW's father, who died on Christmas Day 1918, but the personal references are removed in subsequent revisions.

41 a onetime / an   (*The Quarterly Review of Literature*, 1945; *The Clouds*; *SP*; *Modern Poetry*)

49 Toulouse-Lautrec   WCW dedicated *Paterson V* (1958) "To the Memory of Henri Toulouse Lautrec, *Painter.*"

52 whom / who   (*Modern Poetry*)

68 it will / will it   (*Modern Poetry*)

78 (Scherzo)   Omitted in *Modern Poetry*.

78-93 WCW and FW visited the church of St. Andrew's in Amalfi in 1924 (Mariani 227).

90 such / such a   (*Modern Poetry*)

96 what / which   (*Modern Poetry*)

105 or / and   (*Modern Poetry*)

THE PINK CHURCH (1949)

Dedication: "to James Laughlin"

CHORAL: THE PINK CHURCH   The poem was originally intended to be included in *The Clouds* but was deleted at the insistence of Wells College, sponsors of the book. WCW sent these extended comments on the poem to Babette Deutsch: "As to The Pink Church. . . . I AM a pink, plainly and finally. I am *not* a red. I sympathize strongly with the blood, the thing that makes a communist whatever good he is capable of being. The 'pink' of life, of a pink cheek if you care to say it. I won't be put down because I sympathize with the life that at best the Reds symbolize. The rosy fingers of dawn opens the poem in the best Greek manner.

"Secondly the poem is anti-Catholic, anti all that the Bible damnation theorem symbolizes. It is anti-Eliot, anti-Church of England—anti all the biblical shit of the church and all the usual churches and anything that postpones the perfectibility to 'heaven' and all that heaven implies. Servitus, who was burnt to death for denying the damnation, Garden of Eden, original sin concept, is my saint. He is a Unitarian saint. I was raised a Unitarian—a rather barren tenet but with great virtues inherent in it.

"I particularly detest Eliot, the Catholic church and the Dictatorship not of the proletariat but of such rats as Stalin and all his kind.

"What else does the poem mean? Well, philosophy isn't a tea-table to be pushed around on castors to serve the guests. It (philosophy) over-reaches itself in the minds of the cosmologists, fails because it tries to grasp too much in its puny hands—but, rightly applied, to the modest task of the 'good' in the world: what is good and what is Eliot-Catholic-Stalinist excrement—it has its place and I respect it. There IS an understandable minimum of knowledge concerning what is good and what is bad. I'm for the good. It is NOT difficult to apprehend.

"HOWEVER, I think The Pink Church fails in that it speaks of a 'church.' It seems to want to present a formula for Heaven. In that I too find fault with it. It is, however, a protest poem, a protest against palpable abuses against reason. That was its main purpose" (August, [1947?], Washington University, St. Louis, and see Mariani 524-26, and IWWP 76-78).

Kitty Hoagland added a note to a typescript at the University of Virginia: "The Pink Church written by Bill upon my reminding him that Paderewski's sister was buried in the graveyard of the Polish orphanage at Lodi. 'Rose-colored,' I said. 'Pinkish,' said Bill. He there and then drove over to see the Lodi orphanage which in sunlight glowed rose-like—the Sisters of Perpetual Adoration. One afternoon he heard the orphans singing en masse, also answering the rosary in Polish. Betime, he sent the orphanage some money—"

WCW sent the poem to Celia Zukofsky on 22 May 1946 with the note: "Could music be made for it?" (University of Maryland), and her music was subsequently published with the poem in *Briarcliff Quarterly* (Oct. 1946).

93 new / new oak (*Briarcliff Quarterly; SP; The Pink Church; Modern American Poetry* [1950])

96-99 Matthew 5:48. "Be ye therefore perfect, even as your Father which is in heaven is perfect."

THE LION

11 apace / space (CLP) Printer's error. WCW changed to "apace"—the reading in all other printings—in his reading copy of CLP.

NEW MEXICO

1 transformed / transferred (*The Golden Goose*, Summer 1948; *The Pink Church*)

12 noon / moon (*The Golden Goose; The Pink Church*)

Both variants are printer's errors (Golden Goose Press also published *The Pink Church*). WCW commented to the publisher, Richard Emerson, regarding the error in the first line: "The poor little kitten won't mind, poetic license will I am sure be blamed" (University of Maryland, n.d. [1949]).

A ROSEBUSH IN AN UNLIKELY GARDEN

2 blown / blown, the pink bud (*The Pink Church*)

THE WORDS, THE WORDS, THE WORDS

4-8 The version in *The Pink Church* has a number of differences:

is enhanced by money

Sand does not chafe, with money.
Sheep fold, horse neigh but money

mollifies
and enhances

"I WOULD NOT CHANGE FOR THINE"   The title quotes the last line of the first
stanza of Ben Jonson's "Song, To Celia":
> The thirst, that from the soule doth rise,
> Doth ask a drinke divine:
> But might I of Jove's nectar sup,
> I would not change for thine.

THE LOVE CHARM   On a typescript of the poem sent to Richard Emerson
WCW insisted this be the last poem in the book (University of Maryland).

POEMS 1949-1953

MAY 1ST TOMORROW   This and the following thirteen poems first appeared in
New Directions 11. In asking that the poems be published in *ND11* in this
order, WCW told James Laughlin on 29 August 1949: "I've managed to pick
up a group of poems which rather surprises me; I didn't, even, know they were
there. And of course they weren't—until I started to work on them. One of
them gave me a terrific battle (day and night for a day and a half) but she
came through finally and well. All this shows that I will not write, seriously,
unless pushed to it. Your card set me off. Without the card the poems would
have still lain lost in the matrix. . . . And I'd like them to appear in the order
in which I have them, including the one that Poetry, Ireland has taken ["May
1st Tomorrow"] for it is necessary to the group" (Yale).
  14   shall / will   (*Poetry Ireland*, Oct. 1949)

SPRING IS HERE AGAIN, SIR.
1   Goffle brook   A tributary of the Passaic north of Paterson.

THE HARD CORE OF BEAUTY
5-6   at the swamp's center: the / dead-end highway   Paterson Plank Road,
which dead-ends at the Hackensack River. The site was at the heart of the
Cedar Swamps, and is now surrounded by the New Jersey Turnpike, the
Meadowlands Racetrack, and Giants Stadium.

CUCHULAIN   The legendary Irish hero, about whom Yeats wrote his early
poem "Cuchulain's Fight with the Sea," his late poem "Cuchulain Comforted,"
and several plays, including "The Death of Cuchulain." Kitty Hoagland pub-
lished a number of the Cuchulain poems from the twelfth-century Red Branch
Cycle in her anthology *1000 Years of Irish Poetry* (New York, 1947).

NUN'S SONG   Not in the group of poems that WCW first forwarded to James
Laughlin, but sent as a replacement for a discarded poem a few days later: "a

shocker—to take the place of the other shocker that we have just removed"
(2 Sept. 1949, Yale).

ANOTHER OLD WOMAN   The poem is one of several WCW wrote at this time
about his aged mother, Elena Hoheb Williams, who died on 7 October 1949.
She had moved from 9 Ridge Road to be cared for in a local nursing home.
  12-28   WCW described his mother's Mexico 'vision' to Louis Zukofsky, 19
Nov. 1948: "Poor soul, being unable to see or hear or walk she has invented
the most marvelous assembly of witches and whore-masters to entertain her.
The other day it was an endless column of Mexican cavalry riding bareback
'to show us how they ride.' There's a war on between Mexico and the U.S., you
know. She tells you all about it" (Mariani 592).
  23   lifeless / mileless   (*New Directions 11*, 1949)

WIDE AWAKE, FULL OF LOVE
  1   in / at   (*The Quarterly Review of Literature*, 1949)
  11   cello / heavy cello   (*The Quarterly Review of Literature*)
  17-27

> whose round brow seems
> to push it from the way
>
> I return upon the thought
> thinking to migrate
> to that south and hop about
> upon the still shining
> grass half ill with love
> and mope and will not startle
> for the grinning worm.
>   (*The Quarterly Review of Literature*)

SONG (RUSSIA! RUSSIA!)
Title: "No Song" (*Wake*, Autumn 1949)

  5-11   woven among the wire cables—
> (woven by growing in and out among
>   the 3 rusted guard-cables)
>
> —flowers daisy shaped, pink
>   and white in this
> September glare and the white
>   soapwort matted
> down: There will be soon a further
>   dispensation.   (*Wake*)

TRANSLATION   In an early draft at Buffalo (A 372) the poem is addressed to
"Kitty" [Hoagland].
  Title: "Imitation of a Translation"   (*Wake*, Autumn 1949)
  1   in / to   (*New Directions 11*, 1949; *Wake*)

Sweet / Chloe   (*New Directions 11*)
3   which / as   (*Wake*)
5   but / save   (*Wake*)
12   hide / keep   (*Wake*)

13-16   more than should be spoken, of love, uniting
        all flowers—beyond caresses,
    before our Mistress, the Queen of Love,
        whom we serve.   (*Wake*)

THE RAT
24   cost / costs   (*The Quarterly Review of Literature, 1949*)

THE HORSE SHOW
2   so / as   (*The Quarterly Review of Literature, 1949*)
10   life's / life is   (*The Quarterly Review of Literature*)
12   afterward / afterwards   (*The Quarterly Review of Literature*)
15   said / shouted   (*The Quarterly Review of Literature*)
28   talking to / talking now to   (*The Quarterly Review of Literature*)
32   when your / when   (*The Quarterly Review of Literature*)

TWO PENDANTS: FOR THE EARS   In late 1954 Parker Tyler wrote to WCW of this poem, and WCW returned: "You frighten me. No one has a right, I have always thought, to look at that poem—and I thought no one ever would. It's not a good poem. I myself seldom look at it—there is something about it that disturbs me, it comes from a part of my life which is forever past and forgotten. . . .

"The Elena of the poem is my mother and that is probably why I am disturbed by it. It is like resurrecting the dead. Undoubtedly I was closer to my mother than either she or I knew.

"I have just finished reading the rest of the poem. It makes me think of Eliot's Easter poem that I can't bear to hear read (Ash Wednesday). I know now why: it has no trace of life in it. Just death and more death no matter how he tries to beautify that mummy. My mother's grotesque gyrations approaching death are at least of the essence of life and so of art. God damn it, the essence of art is life, not death.

"Forget it ALL. If there is any virtue in the poem it is in the fierce desire of my mother to live and the immediacy of my transmission of that desire, my refusal to falsify anything that escaped from her lips" (1 Nov. 1954, Harry Ransom Center, University of Texas).

1   *more to be desired* / better   (*Botteghe Oscure, 1949*)
158   a friendly poet's   Dudley Fitts
194   she of the tropics   WCW's mother was born in Puerto Rico.
205 and 212   the old boy . . . his wife   Harry Taylor, the subject of "The Artist" (see p. 267), and his wife Ann. The Taylors ran the nursing home which cared for WCW's mother. WCW describes the colorful British couple in A 352-55.

233-40   This is the "fashionable grocery list" that became the subject of an exchange between WCW and Mike Wallace in 1957, and which WCW incorporated into *Paterson V* (pp. 224-25).

276-77   Jowles, from under the / Ionian sea   Perhaps a reference to Harry Taylor, who had enlisted in the navy in the First World War.

345   child / chi . (*Botteghe Oscure*)

410   Hulda   WCW's sister-in-law, wife of Edgar Williams.

ALL THAT IS PERFECT IN WOMAN

61   At five in the afternoon   A translation of the refrain in Lorca's elegy "Llanto por Ignacio Sánchez Mejías" (1935): "*a las cinco de la tarde*." Mejías was a bullfighter and friend of Lorca's who was killed in the arena. Bullfights in Spain begin at five p.m.

57-68   Fecund and jocund
             are familiar to the sea
             (Oh Lorca, shining singer,
             if only you could

             have remained alive for this,
             At five in the afternoon)
             and what dangles lacerant
             under the belly of

             The Portuguese-Man-O-War
             is also familiar
             to the sea, familiar
             to the sea, the sea
                  (*Zero*, Spring 1949)

AN ETERNITY   The version that appeared in *Wake* (Autumn 1949) is quite different:

        At ninety a strangeness is upon you! Come back,
        Mother, come back from the dead
        —where I cannot yet follow you. This
        winter moonlight is a bitter thing.

                           Had I been
        to all corners of the world, what gift
        could I have brought you but luxury and that
        you have taught me to despise. I turn my face
        to the wall . revert to my beginnings
        and turn my face also to the wall.

                           And yet,
        Mother, that's not the truth of it: the night,
        the night we face is no blacker than the day—
        the day we faced and were defeated
        and yet lived to face the night—in which

the fair moon shines, "naked"
a good word in that context   .   makes the night
light! light as a feather (in the night)

                      —but like Todhunter
let me give up rhyme.

              The soul, my dear, is paramount,
the soul of things that makes the dead moon
shine. Frankly, how can I love you?
by the moon's flames (whatever answer
there may be elsewise) *that* I know
is abandoned   .   I remember how
at eighty you battled through the crisis and
  .   survived. Desiring what?

It is the loveless soul, the soul
of things that has surpassed our loves. In this
you live, Mother, you live in me always.

8   Todhunter   The Irish poet and dramatist John Todhunter (1839-1916)
also practiced medicine.

14   At ninety   Elena's husband and sons had believed that she was born
in 1856 (and thus ninety when this poem was first drafted in December 1946),
but in 1956 WCW discovered that her birthdate was actually nine years earlier
(Mariani 596).

On page 123 of WCW's biography of his mother, *Yes, Mrs. Williams* (New
York: McDowell, Obolensky, 1959), he translates a poem by her from Spanish:

                      From My Window

              Look, look how they fall
              They are the dried leaves
                  of the inexorable Autumn
              No need to be sorrowful
                  they will relive
                  in the radiant Springtime

              Alas, for lost illusions
              they are leaves falling from
                  the tree of the heart
                  these will not relive
              But they are dead in the
                  Winter of human life.

THE THREE GRACES
12   there should / there   (*Poetry*, Nov. 1949)

3 A.M. THE GIRL WITH THE HONEY COLORED HAIR   In correcting Henry Wells'
reading of the second stanza, WCW commented "it is not she at the begin-

ning of the poem that staggers to the toilet but a male drunkard whom she observes as well as the poet and the others. She remains beautiful and remote, timidly aloof in her obvious pennilessness before the whole company" (27 July 1955: General Manuscript Collection, Rare Book and Manuscript Library, Columbia University).

In the first printing, in *Glass Hill* (Dec. 1949), the poem carries a dedication "For C.A." [Charles Abbott].

1-2 Everyone looked and revealed himself,
  passing,   (*Glass Hill*)

10 and / and in (*Glass Hill*)
16 protection and with / protection, with (*Glass Hill*)

THE SELF This poem, which is addressed to WCW's daughter-in-law Virginia Carnes Williams, replaced "Turkey in the Straw" in the revised edition of CLP (1963).

*POEM (LOOKING UP, OF A SUDDEN) *Gale* (Feb. 1950).

*THE END OF THE ROPE The poem was first published in *The Massachusetts Review* in Winter 1962 with the note: "Worn out after receiving an honorary degree [from Rutgers] in 1950, WCW called on Ben Shahn in Roosevelt, N.J., leaving some lines as 'payment' for an hour's sleep." Mariani, p. 608, dates this visit 10 June 1950. As Mrs. Shahn remembers it, WCW became bored while sitting for a Shahn portrait in the early 1950s and wrote the lines. The poem also appeared in Shahn's *Love and Joy about Letters* (New York, 1963), where the manuscript is reproduced on page 32. A mouse has nibbled at the bottom right-hand corner of the paper, devouring the "Williams" of WCW's signature, and possibly the final word of the poem [soon?]. I have printed the poem from this nibbled manuscript.

THE NON-ENTITY
7 janistically A non-word. Perhaps WCW intends "jansenistically," referring to Jansenism and its doctrines that deny free will.

CHILDE HAROLD TO THE ROUND TOWER CAME WCW's title conflates Byron's *Childe Harold's Pilgrimage* and Browning's "Childe Roland to the Dark Tower Came."

IO BACCHO!
4 Dr. Goldsmith Possibly a pseudonym for a local doctor for whom WCW sometimes administered anesthesia.
5 Mrs. Reiter A patient of WCW's.

THE R R BUMS This is the CLP text. The poem also appeared in CEP with the first line printed as the title.

INCOGNITO "Fordie" is Ford Madox Ford, who died in 1939.

TURKEY IN THE STRAW FW was displeased by this poem in 1948 when it was written, and had it removed from the revised edition of CLP in 1963 (it was replaced with "The Self").

WCW sent the poem to Louis Zukofsky on 17 Sept. 1948 (WCW's sixty-fifth birthday) with a suggestion that "maybe Celia will set it to music—notice the slow nostalgic line." Later that month WCW explained to Celia Zukofsky: "I guess I didn't exactly mean the same tune as Turkey in the Straw—but after that nature . . . I have no clear conception of what sort of music it might take. All I have in mind is a contrast between a residual sensuality and the romantic dreams of youth: both, however, somehow related. You know in popular music sometimes the time will change suddenly from fast to slow, from fast to half as fast—the same tune continuing. Something like that. Then it picks up again and finishes presto" (University of Maryland; the library holds a copy of Celia Zukofsky's music, as does the Harry Ransom Center, University of Texas).

4-5 These are the first two lines of WCW's "Portrait of a Lady" (CPI 129), although here an exclamation point replaces a period.

THE MARRIAGE OF SOULS Although included by Thirlwall in the section "The Lost Poems (1944-1950)" of the revised edition of CLP, this could be a much earlier poem.

*JUNE 9 *Spearhead* (Spring 1951).
22 roar / roars (*Shenandoah*, Summer 1951)

*STILL LIFE *Shenandoah* (Summer 1951).

*DECEMBER *What's New* (Christmas 1951).

*THE WRONG DOOR *Quarto* (Summer 1952).

*PATERSON, BOOK V: THE RIVER OF HEAVEN *Poetry* (Oct. 1952).
An early version of the opening lines of "Asphodel, That Greeny Flower," see the note on page 495. "Of Asphodel, though I have told no one, was to have been Paterson 5! Or rather the poem was begun with that in mind—but I changed my mind before Book 1 was no more than begun. . . . Now since the first of the year I have begun to write the final Paterson 5" (to William Wilson, 27 April 1956, University of Virginia).

WCW had originally conceived *Paterson* as having four books, and Book IV appeared in 1951, but he almost immediately began to consider a fifth. In late 1957, in connection with the opening lines of *Paterson V* as finally printed, WCW told Thirlwall: "When the river ended in the sea I had no place to go but back in life—I had to take the spirit of the river up in the air" (notes on a typescript of *Paterson V* at Yale).

*THE PROBLEM *Origin* (Summer 1953)

*THE CLOCK OF THE YEARS   *The New York Times Book Review*, 27 December 1981, p. 2. Published as part of a letter from Joseph Kahn, in which he explains: "I was privileged to care for Dr. William Carlos Williams during his long illness [see the note on *The Desert Music* following]. During our sessions together we would often speak of philosophy and worldly topics he loved. He seemed particularly interested in 'time,' since we each spoke of the passage of time in relative terms, rather than general.

"Dr. Williams wrote the enclosed poem for me, and typed it himself, actually as a measurement of his rehabilitative gains at that time (late 1953)."

THE DESERT MUSIC (1954)

Dedication: "To Bill and Paul" [WCW's sons William Eric and Paul]

The book as published in 1954 is divided into three parts, "Part One" containing all the poems up to "Work in Progress," "Part Two" containing "Theocritus, Idyl 1," and "Part Three" the long poem "The Desert Music." The division into parts was dropped when the book was reprinted in *Pictures from Brueghel* in 1962.

The mood and subject of many of the poems is influenced by the strokes WCW suffered in 1951 and 1952, and especially the severe depression he went through in 1952-53. He had told Robert Lowell on 11 March 1952 "I haven't written a poem in a year" (SL 312). But on 8 October 1953 he announced to Robert Creeley: "In the past year I have written ten or twelve poems along a new line stressing the importance of measure. By the way a Greek sculptor and amateur dancer, whom I have met but barely know, Lekakkas [perhaps the well-known wood sculptor Michael Lekakis, 1907-1987], has been of much help to me. Not that he knows anything about it but his knowledge of the dancing of the choruses from the Greek tragedies has been an inspiration to me" (Washington University, St. Louis).

THE DESCENT   The lines are included in *Paterson II* (1948), pp. 77-78. In asking James Laughlin's permission to reprint "The Descent" in *The Desert Music*, WCW explained: "I certainly want to include The Descent in the forthcoming book. Otherwise, if I exclude it, the train of thought which induced the present format of my poems will not be completely revealed" (16 Sept. 1953). And see IWWP 80-83.

When the poem appeared in the anthology *Poet's Choice*, ed. Paul Engle and Joseph Langland (New York, 1962), WCW appended a brief statement: "I write in the American idiom and for many years I have been using what I call the variable foot. 'The Descent' is the first poem in that medium that wholly satisfied me." (For WCW's concepts of "the variable foot" and "the American idiom" see the note on "Some Simple Measures in the American Idiom and the Variable Foot," p. 511).

12   toward / towards   (*Paterson*; *The Desert Music*; *Poet's Choice*)
30   awaken / waken   (*Partisan Review*, Feb. 1948; *Paterson*)

TO DAPHNE AND VIRGINIA   Daphne Spence Williams and Virginia Carnes Williams were the wives of WCW's sons William Eric and Paul.

113   an old farm   Gratwick Farm, see the note on "The Yellow Tree Peony," p. 467.

THE ORCHESTRA

79-81   FW wrote to Karl Shapiro of *Poetry*, 7 Nov. 1952: "Bill isn't *sure* that it is necessary to say that the Bertrand Russell quote must be acknowledged—so we'll leave it to you" (University of Chicago). The prose quotation receives no acknowledgement in the *Poetry* or any other printing. The central idea informs a number of Russell's chapters in his *New Hopes for a Changing World* (New York, 1951), a copy of which WCW owned, but the quotation itself is not in the book.

FOR ELEANOR AND BILL MONAHAN

Patients and friends of WCW's. Eleanora Monahan had successfully given birth in 1943 despite the extreme dangers caused by a low placental pregnancy, and WCW had been deeply impressed by her determined faith both during the ordeal and in subsequent years (see Mariani 655-57, and Kathleen N. Monahan, "Williams' 'For Eleanor and Bill Monahan,' " WCWR [Spring 1987], 14-23).

62-63   In the printings in *Poetry* (May 1953) and *The Desert Music*, the final version's lines 71-85 appear between these lines. WCW noted this printing as an error in a note to David McDowell, his editor at Random House, and in the Reader's Subscription Club edition of the book (1955) lines 72-85 were printed as in the final version, but line 71 remained misplaced between lines 62-63. WCW marks the correction in the dedication copy to FW of the Reader's Subscription Club edition now at the University of Pennsylvania.

63   lovers / lover   (*Poetry*; *The Desert Music*)   The change is marked on the Fairleigh Dickinson PB paste-up.

90   Dian's / Venus'   (*Poetry*; *The Desert Music*)   The change is marked on the Fairleigh Dickinson PB paste-up.

TO A DOG INJURED IN THE STREET

12-14   WCW echoes the opening lines of Keats' "Ode to a Nightingale."

16 and 58   René Char   "Do you know the work of René Char? . . . I wish I were more like him, but how he has survived the bruising existence he has been through and come out from it sweet in disposition with his love for humanity undimmed is more than I can say" (to Srinivas Rayaprol, 26 Oct. 1953, SL 321-22). Char fought with the French Resistance during the German occupation of France. For WCW's translation of Char's "Vers L'Arbre-Frère Aux Jours Comptés," see p. 344.

THE HOST

3   table separate / separate table   (*The Desert Music*)   This printer's error is corrected in the Reader's Subscription Club edition.

4   his / the   (*The Desert Music*)

58   they / we   (*The Desert Music*)

60   they / we   (*The Desert Music*)
         their / our   (*The Desert Music*)
All of these *Desert Music* variants are as in PB in the Reader's Subscription
Club edition.

59-61   or how dainty they may be
                             according to the way
           they have been bred.
                 how they put the food to
                     their lips, it is all
           (*The Kenyon Review,* Summer 1953)

62-63   between these lines *The Desert Music* has an additional line:

                 Say what you will of it,

WCW deletes the line in the dedication copy to FW of the Reader's Subscrip-
tion Club edition now at the University of Pennsylvania.

82   save only for / but solely for   (*The Kenyon Review*)

DEEP RELIGIOUS FAITH
48   or of a / or a   (*The Desert Music*)   WCW marks the correction in the
dedication copy to FW of the Reader's Subscription Club edition now at the Uni-
versity of Pennsylvania, and on the Fairleigh Dickinson PB paste-up.

THE MENTAL HOSPITAL GARDEN   From 21 February to 18 April 1953 WCW was
hospitalized for his severe depression at the Hillside Hospital, Queens, N.Y.
    Title: "The Garden"   (*The Desert Music*)
59   a last year's bird's / last year's   (*The Desert Music*) WCW marks the
correction in the dedication copy to FW of the Reader's Subscription Club
edition now at the University of Pennsylvania, and on the Fairleigh Dickinson
PB paste-up.
62   be / by   (*The Desert Music*; PB). Printer's error. The Yale "setting
typescript" Za61 has "be." WCW marked the error in the dedication copy to
FW of the Reader's Subscription Club edition now at the University of Pennsyl-
vania, and in a pamphlet, *The Griffin* (Jan. 1955), announcing this edition, but
not on the Fairleigh Dickinson PB paste-up.
    On 17 March 1953, in a letter now at the Lilly Library, Indiana, WCW sent
FW a poem he had composed for the patients' newspaper. No copies of the
newspaper survive in the hospital records:

                 In the darknesses, waken!
                 and who of us is not
                       in the dark?
                 Listen!
                 It is the piercing call
                       of the night hawk.
                 Dawn is at hand.

1 Mr. T. Harry Taylor, who with his wife ran the Rutherford physician exchange, as well as the nursing home in which WCW's mother boarded and where she witnessed this incident. WCW described "Mr. T." to Henry Wells as "an old professional dancer who had been reduced in the social scale to the position of being an assistant to his wife in a nursing home. He drank whenever he could get his hands on the stuff and when under the influence would sometimes let himself in some practical reminiscence that in this case forced him on his toes in an *entrechat* as described. . . . [my mother] was delighted at the show and applauded as described. The man's wife overhearing the rumpus came from the kitchen with the comment that ended the incident" (27 July 1955: General Manuscript Collection, Rare Book and Manuscript Library, Columbia University); and see the note to "Two Pendants: for the Ears" on p. 481, and A 354-55.

THEOCRITUS: IDYL 1 "The Idyls of Theocritus have always been a dream, an obsession of mine. I love everything that's pastoral. I read of Theocritus in Syracuse and I'd read [*sic*] translation. I'd always wanted to get a Greek text, which I never had in college. When I had my stroke at Charles Abbott's [in August 1952] I asked Charles for a translation of Theocritus by an Oxford don. While I was lying in bed, unable to talk, I indicated I'd like to hear the Theocritus, so Harriet Gratwick came to my room and read Theocritus—the first six or seven Idyls. . . . I was very interested in the divided line. In *Paterson* [Book II, section] III I happened to strike on this, and when I went back accidentally it seemed an excellent device, a flexible foot—three stresses to a line. If I could do it accidentally in *Paterson* [II] III, 'The descent beckons'—I was tremendously excited writing this and decided this was what I wanted to do and have used it ever since" (conversation notes by Thirlwall, 16 Oct. 1954, Yale).

"This was an experiment. I have always been interested in Theocritus. I don't know any Greek but the pastoral mode fascinates me. Theocritus . . . adopted a mode which was the Idyl . . . no one did it as well as Theocritus, and I have always wanted to know more about it, about him, so I came upon— searched for and found—a translation of Theocritus in the British tradition, but it was *terrible*—it had no more Theocritus, feeling of Theocritus, in it— well, it was Oxford not Theocritus. So I took that translation, stole it, took it to make it sound more of as I think Theocritus should sound. So I was led by this interest in the American idiom . . . to invent a translation, taken from a translation, a transliteration of Theocritus. You can judge yourself if you like it" (WCW introducing the poem at a reading at the University of Puerto Rico in April 1956, from a tape recording at the Rutherford Free Public Library).

WCW wrote to Charles Abbott on 10 February 1953 to ask for the loan of the book Harriet Gratwick had read to him from—"a thin little green book" (Buffalo F972), and Emily Wallace in "Musing in the Highlands and Valleys: The Poetry of Gratwick Farm," WCWR (Spring 1982) has identified this book as probably *The Greek Bucolic Poets*, trans. J. M. Edmonds, Loeb Classical

Library, No. 28 (WCW's term "Oxford" is a generic usage—Edmonds was a Cambridge don.) WCW's translation is only of the first half of Idyl 1.

In a letter to Cid Corman on 6 April 1955 WCW explained what he saw as the role of translation: "A translation from the classics is exactly the proper way to show how our present modes differ from the past by showing what in the present is *equivalent,* not the same, with what existed then. To attempt to adopt the ancient mode by a word for word rendition of the old mode is to acknowledge defeat before you start. You lose the whole thing, it becomes a lifeless imitation of a lively invention. An invention on your part has at least a chance of bringing the life into it again" (Harry Ransom Center, University of Texas).

Title: "Dactyls—from Theocritus" (*The Quarterly Review of Literature,* 1954)

4   water / waters   (*The Quarterly Review of Literature*)

7   shall / will   (*The Desert Music*) The change is marked on the Fairleigh Dickinson PB paste-up.

9   the goat / the he goat   (*The Quarterly Review of Literature*)

10   the / his   (*The Quarterly Review of Literature; The Desert Music*). As in PB in the Reader's Subscription Club edition. The change is marked on the Fairleigh Dickinson PB paste-up.

14   will / shall   (*The Quarterly Review of Literature*)

24   yonder / that   (*The Quarterly Review of Literature; The Desert Music*). The change is marked on the Fairleigh Dickinson PB paste-up.

58   let / and let   (*The Quarterly Review of Literature*)

67   let / give   (*The Quarterly Review of Literature*)

69   a goat that is the mother / from a goat that is mother   (*The Quarterly Review of Literature*)

70   even when / when   (*The Quarterly Review of Literature*)

71   sucked / suckled   (*The Quarterly Review of Literature*)

74-76   new made,
            a bowl of ivy-wood
                rubbed with bee's wax,
                    a two eared bowl
(*The Quarterly Review of Literature*)

81   flecked / strewn   (*The Quarterly Review of Literature; The Desert Music*). The change is marked on the Fairleigh Dickinson PB paste-up.

In the version published in *The Quarterly Review of Literature* the final 97 lines contain many differences:

                a tendril is twisted
                        joyful with the saffron fruit.
        Inside
                is drawn a girl,
                    as fair a thing

as the gods have made
        dressed in a sweeping
                gown,
her hair is done up
        in a snood.
                Beside her
two blond haired youths,
        first one, then the other,
                are contending,
but her heart is
        untouched.
                Now
she glances to the left,
        smiling,
                and now lightly
she flings the other a thought
        while by reason
                of love's sleepless nights
their eyes are heavy
        but their labors
                are all in vain.
Furthermore,
        there is fashioned there
                an ancient fisherman
and a rock,
        a ragged rock,
                on which with might
and main
        the old man poises a great net
                for the cast,
as one who put his whole heart to it.
        You would say
                that he is fishing
with the full strength of his limbs
        so big do the muscles about his neck
                stand out;
grey-haired though he be,
        he has the strength
                of a young man.
Now, separated
        from the sea-broken old man
                by a narrow interval
is a vineyard,
        heavy
                with fire-red clusters
and on a broken wall

a small boy sits
            guarding them.
Round him two she foxes
      are skulking.
                  One goes the length
of the vine-rows
      to eat the grapes
            while the other
brings all her cunning to bear
      against what has been set down
            and vows
she will never quit the lad
      until
                  she leaves him
bare and breakfast-less.
            But the boy is plaiting
                  a pretty locust-cage
with stalks of asphodel,
            fitting in the reeds
                  and cares no whit
for the vines
      but only for his delight
            in the plaiting.
All about the cup
      is draped the soft acanthus,
            a miracle of varied work,
a thing for you to marvel at.
      I paid
                  a Caledonian ferry-man
a goat and a great white
      cream-cheese
            for the bowl.
Still virgin for me,
      its lip has never touched mine.
                  To gain my desire
I would gladly
      give this cup
            if you, my friend,
will sing for me
      that delightful song.
                  Nothing will I hold back!
Begin, my friend,
      for you cannot,
            you may be sure,
take with you
      that which drives all things out of mind,
            to the other world.

91   by / in   (*The Desert Music*)

93   fair / blond   (*The Desert Music*). Both changes are marked on the Fairleigh Dickinson PB paste-up.

THE DESERT MUSIC   Note accompanying the poem in *The Desert Music*: "Poem given at the Harvard Assembly in June 1951, subsequent to which Dr. Williams was awarded an honorary Phi Beta Kappa membership."

To Norman Macleod, 11 June 1951, WCW wrote: "It has taken me a month or more to write it, transcribe it, have it typed, correct it and polish it. That took about all the drive I had" (SL 301). "From the faces of some (not all) of the faces of those on the platform I think they must have fumigated Memorial Hall after I left. The student body was, on the other hand, delighted and showed it by their tumultuous applause after I had finished my '15 minute' poem" (to Robert Lowell, 1951, SL 302).

WCW told Edith Heal in 1957 that "the other poems in *Desert Music* are more important than the title poem because they consciously use what I had discovered" (IWWP 89).

3   Juárez and El Paso   WCW and FW visited El Paso and Juárez for three days in 1950, after a trip to the West Coast, see A 388-89.

6   The others   FW, Robert McAlmon (see below), McAlmon's two brothers and their wives (Mariani 626).

33   dance / dancer   (*Botteghe Oscure*, 1951)

66   our friend   Robert McAlmon, the writer and publisher with whom WCW had edited *Contact* in the early 1920s, and who spent much of that decade in Paris.

151   the / that   (*Botteghe Oscure*)

239-240   bare can / buttocks   (*Botteghe Oscure*) WCW was prevailed upon to make the change by the editor of *Botteghe Oscure*.

327-28   and held a deep cello tone across Franco's
            lying chatter! and I am speechless
                (*Botteghe Oscure; Origin*, 1952)

The change is marked in the *Desert Music* galley at Yale.

JOURNEY TO LOVE (1955)

Dedication: "For my wife"

"At the last moment I wanted to change the title to Asphodel, that greeny flower, but it was too late . . . But the name of the title poem, I insisted, was not right. The name of the book had to be retained. The name of the long poem *was* however changed to be as I wanted it" (to Winfield Townley Scott, 27 Sept. 1955, Brown University).

THE IVY CROWN

40   wills / will   (*The Times Literary Supplement*, 17 Sept. 1954)

58   briars / the briars   (*The Beloit Poetry Journal*, Fall 1954; *The Times Literary Supplement*)

70   before / against the   (*The Beloit Poetry Journal*)
      before the   (*The Times Literary Supplement*)

VIEW BY COLOR PHOTOGRAPHY ON A COMMERCIAL CALENDAR   "I feel that the vein of poetry welling strong with 'Of Asphodel' is petering out, as evidenced by 'View by Color Photography'" (conversation notes by Thirlwall, 15 April 1954, Yale).
36   the / a   (*Chicago Review*, Spring-Summer 1954)
37   small church / small stone church   (*Chicago Review*)
48   accomplished. / completed   (*Chicago Review*)

THE SPARROW
128   of the breast   Omitted in *Journey to Love*. The lines are inserted in the Fairleigh Dickinson PB paste-up.

THE KING!   First published in *Art News Annual* (1955), p. 82.

TRIBUTE TO THE PAINTERS   The poem also appeared, with this title and in this form, in *New World Writing* (1955), but in *The Nation* of 3 May 1958 a version titled "The Satyrs" appeared among a group of poems "From *Paterson V*." This version contains six more lines at the beginning and omits the final fifteen lines. With two minor differences this later version appears in *Paterson V* (1958) on pages 221-24.
32   on / upon   (*New World Writing; Journey to Love*) The change is marked in the Fairleigh Dickinson PB paste-up.
54   5th / 9th   (*New World Writing; Journey to Love;* PB) "In the middle of Book 2 [of *Paterson V*] a symphony by Beethoven is referred to. It is the famous "elephantine scherzo." But that occurs in the FIFTH *Symphony, not the 9th!* Please make that change in the text" (WCW to New Directions, 11 Jan. 1958). Although the change was made in *Paterson*, WCW omitted to mark the change on the Fairleigh Dickinson PB paste-up.
70   had / has   (*New World Writing*)
91   put / and put   (*New World Writing; Journey to Love*) The change is marked in the Fairleigh Dickinson PB paste-up.

TO A MAN DYING ON HIS FEET
18   Whither? / Where?   (*New Ventures*, June 1954)

THE PINK LOCUST
54-55   "a rose is a rose / is a rose"   Gertrude Stein's famous phrase appeared in her "Sacred Emily" in *Geography and Plays* (Boston 1922).

CLASSIC PICTURE
16   seem / be   (*Folio*, Spring 1955)

THE LADY SPEAKS   This poem is printed between "The King!" and "Tribute to the Painters" in PB.

ADDRESS: "his son's [Paul's] face glimpsed in a mirror with a look on it of despair as his marriage began to fall apart" (Mariani 681).
46-47 The opening line of Burns' "Sweet Afton."

THE DRUNK AND THE SAILOR   Mariani dates the incident 1 Oct. 1954, at the Port Authority Bus Terminal in New York (Mariani 683).

A SMILING DANE   Mariani links the poem to "a photograph he'd seen in the newspapers and magazines of the Tolland Man, the recently exhumed corpse of an adult male who had been hanged and then thrown into a northern European bog a thousand years before only to be unearthed in the early '50s, the face incredibly preserved by the tanning qualities of the bog" (Mariani 680).

COME ON!   This poem appears between "To a Man Dying on his Feet" and "The Pink Locust" in PB. As in the case of "The Lady Speaks" (see above), the rearrangement is probably a result of the design for the page layout. The change is not sanctioned by WCW in the Fairleigh Dickinson PB paste-up.

SHADOWS
4   shadow / shadows   (*Pennsylvania Literary Review,* 1955)
5   presumes / presume   (*Pennsylvania Literary Review*)
45 and 46   concept / context   (*Pennsylvania Literary Review*)
81   the rose / a rose   (*Pennsylvania Literary Review*)

ASPHODEL, THAT GREENY FLOWER   The poem evolved out of WCW's initial plans for *Paterson V* (see the early version of the opening lines on p. 238). WCW appears to have changed his mind at the end of 1953. When discussing the printing of an extract in *New World Writing* with Richard Eberhart he directed him on 23 Oct. 1953 to go ahead with the subtitle "Paterson 5," but on 17 Nov. 1953 told him: "I have decided not to use that title at all in the finished work. Instead the sub-title should be ('Of Asphodel')" (Dartmouth College). In *New World Writing* the section was published as "Work in Progress," the title that Book 1 of the poem appeared under in *The Desert Music.*
13   were / are   (*New World Writing*)
102   tropics / topics   PB   Printer's error. I have restored the reading in all previous printings and in the Fairleigh Dickinson PB paste-up.
113   wakened / awakened   (*New World Writing*)
125   brink / edge   (*The Desert Music; Journey to Love*). The change is marked on the Fairleigh Dickinson PB paste-up.
149   attained / obtained   (*The Desert Music*). WCW marked the change in the dedication copy to FW of the Reader's Subscription Club edition now at the University of Pennsylvania. He had previously asked David McDowell at Random House to make sure to change the word in the edition.
358-64   WCW's poems "Between Walls" and "On Gay Wallpaper," in CPI.
369-81   WCW and FW had shared this experience in 1924.

382-400   WCW describes the incident, from his trip to Spain in 1910, in A 122-23.

551-52   the fire / at the Jockey Club in Buenos Aires   On 16 April 1953 a mob burned the Jockey Club in retaliation for a bombing at a Péron rally the previous night. The Jockey Club was an aristocratic stronghold of anti-Péron sentiment, and was world famous for its paintings, library and wine cellar.

559   treasured / treasure   (Poetry, May 1955)

562-64   the one / by the dead / Charlie Demuth   WCW and FW owned three paintings by WCW's friend Charles Demuth: Tuberoses (1922, see CPI 501), Pink Lady Slippers (1918), and the painting referred to in these lines, End of the Parade: Coatesville, Pa. (1920). (All three are reproduced in ARI between pages 130 and 131.) In an early draft of the poem (Yale Za196) the lines read:

> Charlie Demuth
> of the black chimneys
> at Cotesville?

575   came / come   (Journey to Love)

599-600   after winter's harshness / it comes again   The lines are reversed in Perspective (Autumn-Winter 1953).

603   in hell's despite   Omitted in Perspective.

609   it be / it not be   (Perspective)

611   also / for us also   (Perspective)

612-14   Omitted in Perspective.

623-30   WCW's strokes and depression had led him to confess his marital infidelities to FW, much to her distress, see Mariani 661-62, 670-71.

637   with / and with (Perspective)

641   again to / to (Perspective)

643-44   WCW had seen Verrocchio's statue of Bartolomeo Colleoni in Venice with his wife in 1924.

663-70   The "friend" is Marsden Hartley, on Rutherford station, see A 172.

847   come / comes   (The Kenyon Review, Summer 1955)

1008-10   "Sweet Thames, run softly / till I end / my song" The refrain in Spenser's "Prothalamion," and also quoted in T. S. Eliot's The Waste Land, Part III.

POEMS 1955-1962

*ON ST. VALENTINE'S DAY   The Literary Review (Autumn 1965)   "The poem was found by Mrs. Williams in November, 1964, folded inside a book" (note in Wallace 245). My dating here is a best guess. WCW started to become dissatisfied with his three-step line in 1955 (see Mariani 689), but he still used the form for some of the subsequent PB poems and for some of Paterson V. WCW was still uncertain of his next direction on 3 July 1957 when he told Cid Corman: "I realize that my arbitrary division of the line into my recent triple division is only an approximation to give my own mind something to cling to [to] indicate the necessity for the variable foot. It is not satisfactory even for that but must soon be discarded, something more comprehensive has to take its place" (Harry Ransom Center, University of Texas).

*HYMN AMONG THE RUINS   The translation was printed in Octavio Paz, *Early Poems, 1935-1955* (New York, 1973), pp. 95-99, with the Spanish text on facing pages.

In a general discussion of WCW and his work in the *London Magazine* (June / July, 1974), 33-43, Paz describes meeting WCW as a result of this translation: "In 1955, if I remember correctly, Donald Allen sent me a translation into English of a poem of mine, 'Hymn Among the Ruins.' The translation made a double impression on me: it was a magnificent translation and the translator was William Carlos Williams. I promised myself a meeting with him." The two met in Rutherford, and Paz comments, "I have never met a man less affected. Just the opposite of an oracle. Possessed by poetry, not by his role as a poet."

The quotation from Góngora is from line 25 of his poem "Polifemo of Galatea."

*TO FRIEND-TREE OF COUNTED DAYS   In *Hypnos Waking* (New York, 1956) with Char's French on the facing page. The volume also contains a prose translation by WCW, "Magdalene Waiting." WCW told Srinivas Rayaprol, of Char: "I am impressed with his completely relaxed address to the words, the luxuriance of his imagination, yet the sobriety of his intelligence and mood. He is a man who adopts any form or no form at all with perfect indifference, writing regularly lines which scan perfectly or not according to the occasion, whatever it is" (26 Oct. 1953; SL 321-22). Char also served as an example of fortitude under stress for WCW, see the note on "To a Dog Injured in the Street," p. 487.

*REVERIE AND INVOCATION   First printed in *The New York Times*, 17 Sept. 1956, p. 29. WCW wrote the poem to be performed with music at a ceremony commemorating the 75th Anniversary of Rutherford's incorporation. Professor Thomas Monroe (see "Ballad" below) conceived the idea of bringing together WCW and Professor Stanley Purdy, then a part-time faculty member of the Fairleigh Dickinson University Music Department. Professor Purdy recalls, "I . . . was presented with a piece of yellow-lined paper on which Dr. Williams had typed the poem for which I was to write the music. The poem had no title but because of the nature of the choral setting, I suggested the title 'Reverie and Invocation,' and Dr. Williams agreed" (letter to Christopher MacGowan, 1 Oct. 1987). The poem and music were printed together in 1964 as a pamphlet in the Fairleigh Dickinson University Choral Series (No. 302). The poem was reprinted in the program of the 1972 "A Symposium on William Carlos Williams" held at Fairleigh Dickinson (when the choral setting was again performed). The capital letters, repeated phrases and lineation differences in this 1972 printing result from the transcription for the program being taken from the musical setting. The *New York Times* version, which I print, was taken from the original manuscript—which is now lost.

*BALLAD   *The Poet* (Summer 1957). The "musician" of the poem is Professor Thomas Monroe, for many years the Supervisor of Music in the Rutherford school system, and subsequently the first full-time faculty member in music at Fairleigh Dickinson University. Professor Monroe was the Director of Music for Rutherford's 75th Anniversary Celebration (see "Reverie and Invocation" above). In sending the poem to Karl Shapiro on 5 Oct. 1956 for *Prairie Schooner*, WCW dismissed it as "only a second rate poem written off in a moment" (University of Nebraska—Lincoln).

The printing in *Prairie Schooner* (Winter 1956) has a slightly different final stanza:

> Lucky man and woman!
> Hymen, god of
> married lovers has blessed
> them and their house.

*THE BIRTH   *The Massachusetts Review* (Winter 1962). Written for Brandeis University's annual Spring Festival of Poetry and Music in 1957 (Mariani 732). WCW told Thirlwall on 22 June 1957 that he had written "about twenty verses, slaving over the birth of an Italian baby from my own past." The poem also appeared in *The Plumed Horn* (July 1963), pp. 8-10.

2   Navarra   A large Italian family resident in Guinea Hill, which is part of Lyndhurst, just south of Rutherford. WCW's short story "Ancient Gentility" describes the Italian families of Guinea Hill.

*THIS IS PIONEER WEATHER   *The Beloit Poetry Journal* (Summer 1957). A note on the Yale Za196 typescript identifies the speaker as "Mrs. Korwan." She was a patient of WCW's whose husband was the local jeweler, with a shop on Park Avenue, Rutherford, directly across from WCW's office.

3   Northfield   In Massachusetts.

*SAPPHO   *Poems in Folio* (1957). A translation of Fragment 31. The poem appeared with the following note: "I'm 73 years old. I've gone on living as I could as a doctor and writing poetry on the side. I practised to get money to live as I please, and what pleases me is to write poetry.

"I don't speak English, but the American idiom. I don't know how to write anything else, and I refuse to learn. I'm writing and planning something all the time. I have nothing to do—a retired doctor who can't use his right hand anymore. But my coco (my head, you know) goes on spinning and maybe occasionally I work it pretty hard. It goes on day and night. All my life I've never stopped thinking. I think all writing is a disease. You can't stop it.

"I have worked with two or three friends in making the translation for I am

no Greek scholar but have been veritably shocked by the official British trans-
lations of a marvelous poem by one of the greatest poets of all time. How their
ears can have sanctioned the enormities that they produced is more than I can
understand. American scholars must have been scared off by the difficulties of
the job not to have done better. Their prosy versions were little better—to my
taste. It may be that I also have failed but all I can say is that as far as I have
been able to do I have been as accurate as the meaning of the words per-
mitted—always with a sense of our own American idiom to instruct me."

In October 1956 Charles Abbott sent WCW a copy of a prose translation
of the poem by W. Hamilton Fyfe from *Aristotle* (*XXIII*), Loeb Classical Li-
brary, No. 199, page 157, and WCW owned a copy of *Longinus On the
Sublime*, trans. A.O. Prickard (Oxford, 1906) in which a translation appears
on page 23. For a discussion of these and WCW's other sources see Emily
Wallace, "Musing in the Highlands and Valleys: The Poetry of Gratwick
Farm" WCWR (Spring 1982), 31-32. For WCW's comments to Thirlwall on
Sappho see *New Directions 17* (1961), 291-292.

WCW also published this version in *Evergreen Review* (Fall 1957), but in
Spectrum (Fall 1957) the translation ends:

> of dying . . . . .
> I am another person

and carries a note by WCW on the line: "Why the poem ends as it does no one
seems to know. It seems reasonable to believe that the poem is not complete as
recorded and the little tab at the end is put there merely to continue the poet's
thought, not her words—but we cannot be sure of this."

Other differences:

Title: "Translation from Sappho"   (*Spectrum*)
1   Peer of the gods is that man, who   (*Spectrum*)
A version of the translation begins *Paterson V*, Section ii (p. 217) [1958].

*THE LOVING DEXTERITY, AT THE BRINK OF WINTER   *The Literary Review* (Au-
tumn 1957), where both poems are untitled and appear under the general title
"Two Sentimental Little Poems." For the later version of "The Loving Dex-
terity" see p. 396.

*GREEN EYES, NAKED, PIANO SOLO, THE INFINITE HORSES, ODE TO LAZINESS   *New
World Writing*, 14 (Dec. 1958). Yale Za198 contains typescripts of these trans-
lations as well as of the Spanish originals.

"I did not meet 'Bill' until I called on him to find out how many poems by
Latin American poets he would translate for my selection of contemporary
Latin American literature that would appear in *New World Writing*" (Jose
Vázquez-Amaral in *Rutgers Review* [Spring 1967], 23).

"Los ojos verdes" is from Chumacero's *Palabras en reposo* (1956); "Des-
nudo" is in Figueredo's *Mundo a la vez* (1956); "Piano Solo" can be found in
Parra's *Poems and Antipoems* (New York, 1967) where WCW's translation is

also reprinted on page 32; "Los caballos infinitos" is in Ocampo's *Espacios Metricos* (1945); Neruda's "Oda a la pereza" is in his *Odas Elementales* (1954).

*AN OLD-FASHIONED GERMAN CHRISTMAS CARD *East and West* (Autumn 1959). "I have a picture post card on my desk sent to me by a friend, a woman living in Brazil now, whom I met in the nut house when I was there. It shows four old musicians walking poorly clad in the snow from left to right between—or approaching a village no doubt somewhere in Europe. They are all scrunched together their instruments in their hands trudging along. I mean to keep the card there a long time as a reminder of our probable fate as artists. I know just what is going on in the minds of those white haired musicians" (to Louis Zukofsky, 30 Jan. 1956, Harry Ransom Center, University of Texas).

*WIDOWER'S MONOLOGUE, THE WANDERINGS OF THE TRIBE *Evergreen Review* (Winter 1959). The poems are from Chumacero's *Palabras en reposo* (1956).

TRIBUTE TO NERUDA THE POET COLLECTOR OF SEASHELLS First published in *Rutgers Review* (Spring 1967), and added to CLP in 1975 (the fifth printing of the 1963 revised edition).
   In the Introduction of his *Final Approach* (Woodstock, Vt., 1986) Roderick Townley describes the circumstances of Jose Vázquez-Amaral handing him the manuscript of this poem "which Dr. Williams gave me twelve years ago, to give to Pablo Neruda," but which had remained undelivered. (In a note accompanying the 1967 printing in the *Rutgers Review* Professor Vázquez-Amaral explains: "I have not seen Neruda for many years.") Professor Vázquez-Amaral charged Townley with the duty of delivering the poem the evening of the Chilean poet's upcoming April 1972 reading at the New York YMHA, and Townley describes the vicissitudes accompanying his ultimately successful delivery.
   WCW had recently returned from a winter vacation in Florida, where he too collected seashells (Mariani 754-55). Mary Ellen Solt describes WCW working on this poem in an account of her visit to 9 Ridge Road on the 18th and 19th of April 1960, WCWR (Fall 1983), 93.
   Title: "Tribute to Neruda the Collector of Seashells" (CLP) I have taken the title from the typescript and the *Rutgers Review* printing.
   1 WCW's strokes increasingly impaired his vision.

*MIDWINTER *Prairie Schooner* (Summer, 1960).

*THE CASSIA TREE *New Directions 19* (1966). The poems were headed by a note by David Wang: "These poems are not translations in the sense that Arthur Waley's versions are translations. They are rather re-creations in the American idiom—a principle to which William Carlos Williams dedicated his poetic career." The attributions and dates appeared in the original publication, although I have corrected a few spelling and dating errors. For the Chinese text of most of the classical poems see *Ch'üan T'ang Shih* [The Complete T'ang Poems].

David Wang [also Wand], 1931-1977, was a Chinese-American poet and scholar. Hugh Witemeyer discusses Wang's career, including his relationship with both Williams and Pound—and his mysterious death—in *Paideuma* (1986), 191-210.

WCW first became interested in Wang's work when seeing his Chinese translations in the February 1957 *Edge*. The two men met the following month, Pound and Noel Stock having put them in touch. By September WCW had agreed to work with Wang on a group of translations, and by January the following year they were discussing and exchanging manuscripts. But by the end of the month WCW began to feel that the project might be too ambitious for his now limited energies, and on 25 February he returned the translations to Wang admitting defeat: "I have struggled with the poems but I cannot get a replica of the ancient language. Certain what you have put down is not it. . . .

"You were very kind to have come out to read to me the wonderful old language which no one has been competent even faintly to reproduce. To my mind it is futile as Pound has done to reproduce the ideographs which are so beautiful in themselves. They can mean nothing to an English-speaking reader.

"The sound of the ancient language is lacking. . . . The only thing is to return the poems to you. It is an ancient poetry whose very feeling is too far away from us to be captured by us. If I should immerse myself, provided I could, in the language it would be an exhaustive job that would take me a lifetime. I haven't at my age the time for it" (Dartmouth College).

Wang nevertheless continued to send WCW his translations, and WCW worked on them for publication, although his changes became fewer and fewer, until the last translation sent to WCW—"The Knight" on 27 Jan. 1961—is printed without any changes from Wang's draft. Wang regularly kept WCW informed of the publication of the poems in periodicals, and confirmed that WCW had no objection to their publication or to his name appearing as joint author.

On the evidence of the correspondence (at Yale and Dartmouth College) two of the translations that WCW made significant contributions to were "The Peerless Lady" and "Spring Song." I reproduce below the versions WCW received from Wang of the two poems:

The Lady of Lo-Yang

The lady of Lo-Yang lives across the street.
By her looks she's about fifteen years of age.
Fitted with jade and silk her husband's horse is ready for parade.
In golden plates she is served sliced herring and caviar.

Her painted screen and roseate stairs rival in their hues.
The peach blossoms and willow shades spread outside her room.
Through gauze curtain she glides into her perfumed sedan chair.
'Midst feathery fans she enters her sequined mosquito net.

Her husband is a budding young, haughty millionaire;
His extravagance puts Mark Anthony even to shame.

Pitying her maids she teaches them the classic Chinese dance.
Tired of gifts she freely gives her corals and pearls away.

By her crystal screen she blows the light off her velvety lamp.
The green smoke rises like petals bourne upon the waves.
Filled with fun and laughter she has no regrets.
With her hair done up in a roll she sits by the candle case.

In her circle of friends are men of pedigree and wealth.
She visits only the king and aristocrats.
Can she recall the girl who was pure as ivory
And used to wash her clothings by the creek not very far away?

(Sent to WCW 27 Jan. 1958)

Spring Song

> A young lass
> Plucks mulberry leaves by the stream.
>
> Her white hand
> Reaches toward the green.
>
> Her rosy cheeks
> Shine under the sun.
>
> The hungry silkworms
> Are waiting for her.
>
> Oh, young horseman,
> Why do you tarry? Get going!

(Sent to WCW 10 July 1958)

*LAMENT OF A GRAYING WOMAN   Traditionally attributed to Cho Wen-chun, wife of the famous Han dynasty poet Szu-ma Hsiang-ju (died 118 B.C.), the poem is now considered to be an anonymous product of the first century.

*PROFILE OF A LADY
14   lies / lives   *San Francisco Review* (Dec. 1960)

*CONSTRUCTION   *Sparrow* (April 1961).

*CEZANNE   *The Nation,* 13 May 1961.
7-8   WCW had met the then unknown Ginsberg through the younger poet's correspondence in response to reading *Paterson* in the late 1940s and early 1950s (see *Paterson IV,* pp. 173-75, and Mariani 604-05), and despite some reservations WCW supported his work. A number of Ginsberg's letters are incorporated into *Paterson IV* and *V.*
"Overcome your aversion to the beatnicks and distaste for vulgar and profaned language and read the first part of Kaddish and if you aren't elevated

in spirit I miss my guess" (to Thomas Merton, 10 April 1961, Thomas Merton Studies Center, Louisville).

*BIRD SONG   *Poetry in Crystal* (New York, 1963). "In the Spring of 1961 the [Poetry] Society [of America], in cooperation with Steuben, invited a number of distinguished American poets to submit new, hitherto-unpublished poems from which our glass designers and artist associates might derive themes for designs in crystal. There were two specifications only: that the poems not concern crystal or glass and that they be no fewer than eight nor more than forty lines in length" (from *Poetry in Crystal*, p. 9, quoted in Wallace 159). A photograph of the glass design appears facing the poem.

*THE ART, GREETING FOR OLD AGE, STILL LIFES, TRALA TRALA TRALA LA-LE-LA These four poems appeared in *The Hudson Review* (Winter 1963-1964). In sending them to *The Hudson Review* James Laughlin told Frederick Morgan: "The other evening I was visiting with Mrs. Williams out in Rutherford, going over with her the proofs for the new complete paperback of *Paterson* and she showed me, and gave me copies of some little poems by Bill which she had found in going through his things" (8 July 1963, *Hudson Review* archives). FW told Morgan that "Trala Trala Trala La-Le-La" "was presented to me on my birthday—April 18, 1962—the last one that Bill and I had together" (24 Jan. 1964, *Hudson Review* archives).

*THE MORAL   *Poetry* (Jan. 1964). Found among WCW's papers after his death and sent to *Poetry* (with "Cézanne") 13 August 1963, by James Laughlin.

*THE ORCHARD   *Focus / Midwest* (Sept. 1962).
8   im wunderschoensten Monat Mai   WCW echoes a refrain in stanza 1 of Heinrich Heine's "Lyrisches Intermezzo" (1823) in his *Buch der Lieder* (1827).

> Im wunderschönen Monat Mai,
> Als alle Knospen sprangen,
> Da ist in meinem Herzen
> Die Liebe aufgegangen.
>
> Im wunderschönen Monat Mai,
> Als alle Vögel sangen,
> Da hab ich ihr gestanden
> Mein Sehnen und Verlangen.

WCW's change turns the line into the superlative—i.e. "In the most wonderfully beautiful month of May."

*STORMY   *Poetry* (Oct.-Nov. 1962). "In the special Fiftieth Anniversary number of *Poetry* there appeared the last poem Floss was sure her husband had written" (Mariani 766).
Title: "Stormy is the name of the Williamses' Shetland sheep-dog" ("editor's note" following the poem in *Poetry*).

PICTURES FROM BRUEGHEL (1962)

The part-title page printed the following:

" '. . . the form of a man's rattle may be in accordance with instructions received in the dream by which he obtained his power.'

Frances Densmore
The Study of Indian Music"

"He also wants the enclosed quotation used in place of a dedication. Frances Densmore died recently and Bill wants to honor her" (FW to James Laughlin, 29 Sept. 1961, Yale). Densmore's study first appeared in the Smithsonian Museum's *Annual Report of the Board of Regents, 1942*, pp. 527-550. The quotation is on page 545.

Pictures from Brueghel was awarded the 1963 Pulitzer Prize for poetry.

PICTURES FROM BRUEGHEL The poems first appeared in *The Hudson Review* (Spring 1960), and WCW initially considered publishing the poems with reproductions of the paintings (to Frederick Morgan, 21 Oct. 1959, *Hudson Review* archives). WCW and FW saw some of the paintings in Vienna in 1924, but WCW used Gustave Glück's *Peter Brueghel the Elder* (Braziller: New York, 1952) as a source for the illustrations (FW to James Laughlin 18 Dec. 1961 and 5 Sept. 1962, Yale), although he apparently consulted other sources, too. In the early 1970s FW separately told Joel Conarroe and Allen De Loach (the editor of *Intrepid*) that WCW had used Thomas Craven's *A Treasury of Art Masterpieces, from the Renaissance to the Present Day* (1939, rev. edt. 1952) for some of the illustrations.

In *The Hudson Review* printing some of the titles of the paintings are capitalized where they appear in a poem.

SELF-PORTRAIT The painting is not by or of Brueghel, but is a fifteenth-century portrait of the court jester Gonella who lived in Ferrara at the court of Niccolò III d'Este (1393-1444). The painting is currently ascribed to Jean Fouquet (see Otto Pächt, "Le Portrait de Gonella I: Le probleme de son auteur," *Gazette des Beaux-Arts* 123 [1981], pp. 1-4; infrared-reflectography shows the underdrawing and color-indications to be French), but in the 1960s the painting was ascribed to an anonymous follower of Jan van Eyck, and in the 1950s to van Eyck himself. For a number of years following the discovery of the painting in 1882 some scholars suggested Brueghel as the author. When WCW visited the Kunsthistorisches Museum in Vienna in 1924 the painting was still being ascribed to Brueghel, although the attribution had always been questioned and was no longer made in the 1928 catalog. Nevertheless, although Brueghel's authorship was no longer accepted by scholars after the middle 1920s, at least one popular volume, *The Elder Peter Bruegel* (New York: Willey Book Co., 1938) reproduced the work as by the painter, the reproduction serving as a frontispiece and titled *The Old Shepherd*—which is a part of WCW's title in *The Hudson Review* printing. The painting does not appear in Glück's study.

Joel Conarroe reproduces the portrait in his "The Measured Dance: Williams' 'Pictures from Brueghel,' " *JML* (1971), 570.
Title: "Self Portrait: The Old Shepherd" (*The Hudson Review*)

LANDSCAPE WITH THE FALL OF ICARUS   Two versions of this painting exist. Glück reproduces the painting in the Brussels Royal Museum.
Title: "Brueghel: 1" (*The Hudson Review*)

THE HUNTERS IN THE SNOW   In the Kunsthistorisches Museum, Vienna.
Title: "Brueghel: 2" (*The Hudson Review*)
9-10   a stag a crucifix / between his antlers   The inn-sign depicts the conversion experience of St. Hubert (or St. Eustace), both patron saints of hunters, and both converted by seeing a crucifix between the antlers of a stag while hunting.

THE ADORATION OF THE KINGS   The National Gallery, London.
Title: "Brueghel: 3" (*The Hudson Review*)
2   which I have already celebrated   Section III of *Paterson V* (1958) opens with a much longer description of this painting.
10-11   from the Italian masters / but with a difference   Glück notes the influence of Italian mannerism in the painting, but quotes Max Dvořák: "there is nothing Italian in Brueghel's painting which results mainly from the entirely un-Italian conception of the events described" (p. 42).

PEASANT WEDDING   In the Kunsthistorisches Museum, Vienna.
Title: "Brueghel: 4"   (*The Hudson Review*)
5   is   Omitted in *The Hudson Review*.
10   the bearded Mayor   Glück speculates on the identity of this figure on the extreme right of the painting: "the painter himself has been suggested . . . perhaps it would be more correct to assume the landowner himself or the judge or mayor of the village" (p. 49).

HAYMAKING   The details of this poem come from two paintings, *The Hay Harvest*, in the Prague National Gallery, and *The Corn Harvest*, at the Metropolitan Museum of Art, New York. The poem is titled "Composite" in early typescripts (Yale Za192).
Title: "Brueghel: 5"   (*The Hudson Review*)

THE CORN HARVEST   In the Metropolitan Museum of Art, New York.
Title: "Brueghel: 6"   (*The Hudson Review*)

THE WEDDING DANCE IN THE OPEN AIR   In the Institute of Arts, Detroit.
Title: "Brueghel: 7"   (*The Hudson Review*)
3   round / around   (*The Hudson Review*)
9   the market square   This detail is probably from the setting of *The Peasant Dance*, in the Kunsthistorisches Museum, Vienna.

THE PARABLE OF THE BLIND   In the Museo Nazionale, Naples.

Title: "Brueghel: 8" (*The Hudson Review*) The men are also spiritually blind. Glück quotes Matthew 15:14, "Let them alone: they are blind guides. And if the blind guide the blind, both shall fall into the ditch" (p. 47).

The version in *The Hudson Review*, printed below, contains a number of differences from the final version:

> The parable of the Blind
> without a red
> in the composition shows a group
>
> of beggars leading
> each other diagonally downward
> across the canvas
>
> from one side
> to stumble finally into a bog
> where the picture
>
> and the composition ends back
> of which no seeing man
> is represented
>
> the unshaven features of the des-
> titute with their
> few pitiful possessions
>
> a basin to wash in
> a peasant's cottage are seen
> and a church spire
>
> the faces are raised as toward
> the light no detail
> extraneous to the compos-
>
> ition one following the other
> tentative stick in
> hand triumphant to disaster

A letter from WCW to Louis Zukofsky dated 10 Aug. 1961 acknowledges his help with the revision (Harry Ransom Center, University of Texas).

5 beggars Glück suggests that Brueghel has in mind the men being led by "one of those wandering preachers, who at that time came from the lowest strata of society, or at best from the class of artisans, and who knew to gather around them large crowds of followers of certain sects" (p. 48).

CHILDREN'S GAMES   In the Kunsthistorisches Museum, Vienna. A large reproduction of this painting hung in 9 Ridge Road.

Title: "Brueghel: 9   Children's Games" (*The Hudson Review*)

1   a schoolyard   "A whole town has been allotted to the children for their

activities with scarcely an adult present" (Glück, p. 38). Glück identifies eighty-four games in the painting.

55-56 a swinging / weight Glück interprets this detail as the poaching game "I fish in my master's pond."

SONG (BEAUTY IS A SHELL)
4   has had / have (*The National Review*, 3 Dec. 1960)
        has (*Agenda*, Aug-Sept. 1963)

THE LOVING DEXTERITY See the first version, p. 348.

3 STANCES Elaine, Erica, and Emily were WCW's grandchildren, the daughters of William Eric Williams. Mariani gives their ages at the time of these poems as "the baby," "five," and "nine."

ERICA
10   my / in (*Poetry*, March 1960)

SUZY WCW's fifteen-year-old granddaughter, daughter of Paul Williams.
Sections II and III of the poem are very different in the first printing, in *The Galley Sail Review* (Winter 1959-60):

2

when the flower opens
you look trembling
into the traditional mirror

if you are not swept
off your feet
look again there will be

shimmering in the background
the ghost of
a guffawing old man

3

beyond which will be
a figure a
woman of awe inspiring

presence Suzy where both
the old man
and yourself will join

gripping hands agape
trembling
in grudging praise

"I have written another poem dedicated to Paul's sister SUZY an unsuccessful version of which has been already published in another magazine" (on sending the revised version to Frederick Morgan at *The Hudson Review*, 17 May 1960: *Hudson Review* archives).

PAUL   WCW's grandson Paul, then seventeen, the son of Paul Williams.
1   shall / will   (*The Hudson Review*, Autumn 1960)

SONG (I'D RATHER READ)
21   eat out / eat   (*Harper's Magazine*, June 1961)

THE CHILDREN
7   the cemetery   Hillside Cemetery, Rutherford, where WCW himself is buried.
stanza 5   PB and *Harper's Magazine* (June 1961) print as two lines:

> with lots of children's graves
> so we'd take

I have preferred the three-line stanza as in the first printing, *New Poems by American Poets*, No. 2 (New York, 1957), p. 176, and as in the Yale Za192 typescripts. The Fairleigh Dickinson typescript reproduces the *Harper's Magazine* lineation, which is possibly an error.

THE PAINTING   The painting, which hung in the living room at 9 Ridge Road, is by WCW's mother, Elena Hoheb Williams, who had died in 1949. It is reproduced opposite page 131 in ARI. WCW's mother had left Santo Domingo in 1876 to study art in Paris, but was forced to return after three or four years because of her brother's financial difficulties. She married William George Williams in 1882 and settled in Rutherford.

THE STONE CROCK   A note on the Fairleigh Dickinson typescript, probably by Thirlwall, identifies the two figures in the poem as Dorothy Norman and Alfred Stieglitz.
13   was / is   (*The National Review*, 3 Dec. 1960).

HE HAS BEATEN ABOUT THE BUSH LONG ENOUGH
2   Flossie, Mary, a chemistry prof   Mrs. Williams, Mary Ellen Solt, and Walter Moore, then professor of chemistry at Indiana University. From the 27th to the 29th of July 1960 WCW visited Indiana University with Thirlwall to attend a lecture by Mary Ellen Solt on "the American idiom." While some members of the English Department were unsympathetic to the ideas in the talk, and to WCW's work generally, Professor Moore was interested and supportive (see Solt's article "The American Idiom," WCWR [Fall 1983], 103-108).

IRIS   "I sold a poem to a magazine named EPOCH (no pay!). It's really a fine poem, really good for reasons that I privately must respect. It gave me a thrill even to see it again" (to James Laughlin, 11 Jan. 1961, Yale).

THE DANCE (WHEN THE SNOW FALLS)   In the printing in *The Hudson Review* (Winter 1961-62) the poem is numbered in groups of three stanzas. The numbers are omitted in the Fairleigh Dickinson typescript, and the poem was printed with double spacing in place of the numbers in PB.

17   whirls and glides / whirl and glide   (*The Hudson Review*)

18   leaves / leave   (*The Hudson Review*)

JERSEY LYRIC   Mariani dates the poem early October 1960, noting "a poem based on a lithograph called *Jersey Composition* [now in the WCW-Niese correspondence at Yale] which his young painter friend Henry Niese had sent him to announce an upcoming showing of his work" (Mariani 759).

8   6 / 7   (*The Hudson Review*, Winter 1961-62)

TO THE GHOST OF MARJORIE KINNAN RAWLINGS

26   new / the   (*The Virginia Quarterly Review*, Autumn 1960)

31   smells / smell   (*The Virginia Quarterly Review*)

37   and it / to you and   (*The Virginia Quarterly Review*)

TO BE RECITED TO FLOSSIE ON HER BIRTHDAY

6   persist / persisted   (*Inscape*, Winter 1960-61)

THE INTELLIGENT SHEEPMAN AND THE NEW CARS   First printed in *New Poems by American Poets*, No. 2 (New York, 1957), p. 173.

The "intelligent sheepman" is William Gratwick, see the note to "The Yellow Tree Peony," p. 467. The "girls" are his pure-bred ewes. Emily Wallace quotes a comment by Gratwick written on a photocopy of the poem: "I *did* pull the back out of a classy convertible Mercury and use it to take the girls to Staunton, Virginia" ("Musing in the Highlands and Valleys: The Poetry of Gratwick Farm," WCWR (Spring 1982), 26.

7   my "girls" / "the girls"   (*New Poems by American Poets*)

THE ITALIAN GARDEN   The formal garden at Gratwick Farm. William Gratwick reproduces a photograph of the entrance to the garden in his *The Truth, Tall Tales and Blatant Lies* (1981), n.p.

1   she   Emilie Mitchell Gratwick, mother of William Gratwick, "her son" (line 7).

11   is / was   (*Contact*, June 1960)

43-45   and verbena.   Courtesy has
          revived and
          visitors   (*Contact*)

61   we would / would we   (*Contact*)

66   hers / here   (*Contact*)

The reprinting in *Contact*, July 1962, contains the same variants.

A FORMAL DESIGN   The poem describes the final tapestry, "The Unicorn in Capitivity," in the "Hunt of the Unicorn" series at the Metropolitan Museum of Art, the Cloisters, New York. The series also figures centrally in *Paterson V.*

1　This / This is a　(*Yūgen*, 1959 or 1960; *The Massachusetts Review*, Winter 1962)

14　a / by a　(*The Massachusetts Review*)

BIRD
4　yet / and yet　(*Chicago Review*, Winter-Spring 1959)

THE WORLD CONTRACTED TO A RECOGNIZABLE IMAGE　This poem was written shortly after a brief hospital stay in August 1959. On 2 October 1959, WCW wrote to Cristina Campo in Italy, then translating his poetry for an Italian collection, asking her to consider including the poem "che riassume tutto il mio lavoro in un modo che non mi era mai riuscito raggiungere fino ad ora" [which I have just written and which sums up all of my work in a way which I haven't succeeded in achieving until now]. *Poesie*, tradotte e presentate da Cristina Campo e Vittorio Serini (Torino: Giulio Einaudi Editore, 1961), p. 311. Campo cites the letter in Italian without a translation.

8　as a fly　The first seven printings of PB printed "as to a fly" due to a typing error on the Fairleigh Dickinson typescript. The error was noticed by Michael O'Brien of Hunter College and corrected in the 1972 eighth printing.

THE FRUIT
10　into / to　(*Chicago Review*, Winter-Spring 1959)

14-15　fruit of the same tree
which separate

jointly
whatever we were thinking
we embrace
　　　　(*Chicago Review*)

POEM (ON GETTING A CARD)　The card was from E. E. Cummings. WCW expressed some initial uncertainty about this poem. When sending the poem to Mary Ellen Solt on 16 July 1959 for publication in *Folio*, to accompany Solt's article "William Carlos Williams: Poems in the American Idiom," WCW commented: "it's my most recent written in fact in the last two weeks after a 2 mos. lapse, I thought the party was definitely over," adding a P.P.S.: "Maybe this isn't a poem at [all]: not an image in the G. damn thing—EXCEPT the musical measure of its lines." Later the same day WCW sent instructions to "Hold everything! . . . . I [had] liked that poem until I LOOKED at it carefully and discovered its total lack of an image. I must be growing old." Then five days later he reversed his decision again, deciding that it was the ideal complement to the article, and that it "brings out just the image I wanted to emphasize" (the letters are printed in Mary Ellen Solt's "The American Idiom," WCWR [Fall 1983], 98-99).

TO FLOSSIE
3   was / is   (*Colorado Review*, Winter 1956-57; *New Poems by American Poets*, No. 2 [New York, 1957])

PORTRAIT OF A WOMAN AT HER BATH   WCW wrote this poem for Dore Ashton's anthology *Poets and the Past* (New York, 1959). In July 1957, after WCW had agreed to participate in the project—to explore the idea of "pastness"—Professor Ashton selected and sent him a photograph of a pre-Columbian Venus figure. WCW responded with the poem within a few days. The photograph, labeled "Girl and Obsidian Mirror, Tlatilco 1000 B.C." is reproduced opposite page 34 in the anthology, and also opposite page 64 of the March-April 1961 *Evergreen Review* printing.

The version that appeared in *Evergreen Review* in Fall 1957 is titled "View of a Woman at Her Bath" and contains only three stanzas:

> It's a satisfaction
> a joy
> to have one of them
> in the house
>
> When she takes a bath
> she unclothes
> herself. The sun
> is brighter
>
> glad of a fellow to
> marvel at
> the birds and flowers
> look in

12   is / is brighter   (*Poets and the Past*; *Evergreen Review*, March-April 1961)
15   and the / and   (*Poets and the Past*; *Evergreen Review*)

SOME SIMPLE MEASURES IN THE AMERICAN IDIOM AND THE VARIABLE FOOT   "In connection with 'Some Simple Measures' Dr. Williams writes: 'During the past ten years modern poetry has got completely over the "free verse" phase. Measure is the sine qua non of verse. But our recourse to loose meters which we adopted in the last fifty or sixty years had its uses. Whitman's practices were the practices of, at times, a great poet however much he went astray. He introduced to us a new spoken language, the American idiom, which brought in its train the variable foot. What conjunctions there are between that and the struggle antedating Shakespeare among the English who were giving up qualitative verse for accentual verse. This earlier struggle was decided for the latter. Campion and others still veered at times either way. But now there is occurring a profound revolution of taste. Present day practitioners of the art are dissatisfied with the cultured patter of the iambic pentameter, even at the hands of Shakespeare, and look toward wider horizons' " (a note with the first printing in *Poetry* [March 1959], 416). For a fuller account by WCW of these concepts see "Measure—A Loosely Assembled Essay on Poetic Measure," *Spectrum* (1959), 131-157, and WCW's essay "The American idiom" in *New Directions 17* (1961), 250-51.

PERPETUUM MOBILE
5 gabbing / gabbling   (*Poetry*, March 1959)

THE BLUE JAY

4-5 in the cinematograph—

in motion   (PB)

I have restored the *Poetry* printing, which is also the reading in the Yale Za 192 typescripts. The Fairleigh Dickinson typescript has "in" for "ic" and an erroneous correction marked, changing the hyphen to a dash.
13 art / the art   (*Poetry*)

A SALAD FOR THE SOUL
Title: "A Salad to the Soul"   (*Poetry*)
1 peasant / pleasant   (PB)
I have restored the *Poetry* printing, which is also the reading in the Yale Za 192 typescripts.

CHLOE
5 lithely / lightly   (*Poetry*)

THE COCKTAIL PARTY
12 ears / eyes   (PB)
I have restored the *Poetry* printing, which is also the reading in most of the Yale Za192 typescripts. The change occurs during a retyping and is reproduced on the Fairleigh Dickinson typescript.

THE HIGH BRIDGE ABOVE THE TAGUS RIVER AT TOLEDO   WCW witnessed this scene while visiting Spain in 1910, see A 123.
16 day long / day   (*Edge*, Oct. 1956; *The Quarterly Review of Literature*, 1957; *Evergreen Review*, Fall 1957; *Spectrum*, Winter 1957)
20 and still / and will still   (*Edge*; *The Quarterly Review of Literature*; *Evergreen Review: Spectrum*)

15 YEARS LATER   WCW had begun working on his play *Many Loves* in 1941. The play received its first production on 13 Jan. 1959, performed by Julian Beck's and Judith Malina's Living Theatre in New York, ran for 216 performances, and was revived the following season. WCW traveled in to see the production on the 18th of January, writing to Julian Beck that although the production was "not perhaps a finished performance" it was nevertheless "a performance in which you were all interested and showed your interest in the intelligent reading of the lines" (Mariani 745-46).

12   there / here   (*The Massachusetts Review*, Oct. 1959)

THE TITLE   Gauguin's painting is in the Chrysler Collection, Norfolk, Virginia.
4   breast / breasts   (*The Hudson Review*, Winter 1956-57; *The Poet*, Summer 1957)
5   there / where   (*The Hudson Review; The Poet*)

MOUNTED AS AN AMAZON   The version printed in *The Grecourt Review* (Dec. 1957) is titled "The Swivelhipped Amazon" and has a number of other differences:

> She rides her hips as
> if it were
> a horse such women
>
> frighten me a pat ans-
> wer to philosophy
> or high heels would
>
> put them on their
> asses were it
> followed up but for-
>
> tunately more pliant
> we come of a
> far different race

THE SNOW BEGINS
6   fallen / the fallen   (*Monmouth Letters*, Spring 1959; *Genesis*, Spring 1962)

CALYPSOS   WCW offered all three sections to *The New Yorker*, which subsequently published sections I and II in a heavily punctuated form and with the title "Puerto Rico Song." Section III appeared in *The Hudson Review*.

AN EXERCISE   In a 6 Dec. 1958 letter to Ruth Witt-Diamant WCW described this poem as "composed in the Brooklyn subway on my return from a trip to the Zukofskys. . . . It has to do with a huge . . . negro who sat directly before me, really frightened me" (University of California, Berkeley).

THREE NAHUATL POEMS   First published in *The Muse in Mexico: A Mid-Century Miscellany*, ed. Thomas Mabry Cranfill (Austin: Univ. of Texas Press, 1959), pp. 90-91. WCW translates from the Spanish versions of Angel Maria Garibay, published in the first volume of his *Historia de la Literatura Nahuatl* (Editorial Porrua: Mexico, D. F., 1953). "One by one I proclaim your songs": "Tus cantos reúno" is on page 181, and is from Song 52, Folio 34; "Where am I to go": "¿Adónde habré de ir," is on page 196; "Will he return": "¿Vendrá otra vez," is on page 200, and both are from Song 53, Folio 35. For the original

Nahuatl text and a commentary on the songs see John Bierhorst, *Cantares Mexicanos: Songs of the Aztecs* (Stanford, 1985).

THE GIFT In 1962 Hallmark selected "The Gift" to accompany a reproduction of Giotto's *Adoration of the Magi* for a Christmas card, but the fresco is not the "old print" that is the subject of WCW's 1956 poem as some critics have suggested. WCW was not involved in the decision to pair his work with the Giotto.
52 this / that   (*The Hudson Review*, Winter 1956-57)

SAPPHO, BE COMFORTED
15 shows / shows me   (*New Poems by American Poets*, No. 2 [New York, 1957, p. 176])

TO MY FRIEND EZRA POUND   "As for Pound I have every confidence in him. . . . Sometimes he gives me a pain in the ass, he also, with his pretensions. When he goes off the deep end he's just as bad as any mediocre as any other bum poet but when he is good he's a world beater. I love him deeply.
"On that score I have a poem for your next issue of *Neon* when you get around to it. It's about Pound written in one of my periods of disgust with him" (to Gilbert Sorrentino, 31 May 1956, University of Delaware).
Lines 10-11 are reversed in *Neon* (1956).

TAPIOLA   WCW published the first (1957) version of this poem in PB, although after writing this version he had subsequently written and published a revision. Publishing delays caused the revised version to appear a year before the first.
In October 1957 WCW promised Gilbert Sorrentino a poem for *Neon* within a week—"a triumphant lament for the great Finnish composer Sibelius who has just died." Calling the poem "the only serious poem I have written in months" WCW noted "it is not in the triple division I used in *Journey to Love*—essentially it follows that pattern, the measure can be counted similarly." In a later note he told Sorrentino that "the extension of the line by an extra syllable, more or less, [is] to accord with Sibelius' musical measure." On 4 March 1958, wondering at the delay in publication, he advised Sorrentino that he had now written a "second version" of the poem—the first was "too hurried tossed off" (all three letters are at the University of Delaware). This revision, printed below, appeared in *Audience* in the Summer 1958 issue (with "Second Version" beneath the title), while the issue of *Neon* printing the first version did not appear until 1959.

> He is no more dead than Finland herself is dead
>   under the blows of the mass-man who threatened
>   to destroy her
> until she felled her forests about his head ensnaring
>   him to his own downfall.

Finlandia! thundered in his ears! Finlandia!
    echoed the ears I celebrate have heard the
    icy wind time out of mind lovingly
and with a smile!

The power of music, of composition, the placing of
    sounds together, edge to edge, Moussorgsky
    the half mad Russian had it, and Dostoyevsky
who knew the soul of music.

In such style whistled the winds grateful to be
    tamed, we say, by a man! Whee! yaugh!
    He stayed up half the night
in his attic room under the eaves, composing secretly,
    setting it down, period by period, as the
    wind whistled!

Lightning flashed! the roof creaked about his ears
    threatening to give way! but he had a
    composition to finish that could
    not wait!

The storm entered his mind where all good things
    are secured, written down, for Love's sake and
    to defy the Devil—of emptiness.

Children are decked out in ribbons, bunting
    and with flags in their hands to celebrate
    his birthday! they parade to music.
Sibelius has been born and continues to live in all
    our minds, all of us, forever.

WCW apparently continued to work with the poem, and among the papers found after his death was an unpublished revision of the poem subtitled "final version":

He is no more dead than Finland herself is dead
under the blows of that mass-man who threatened
to destroy her until they felled the forests about
his head ensnaring him to his inevitable doom.

But, children, the power in your own song, Finlandia!
held you up while you were waiting but no more so
than the music of him I celebrate knows the
wintry blasts, his familiars, and defied them
all lovingly and with a smile.

The power of music, of composition, the placing
of sounds together, edge to edge, Moussorgsky the

half mad Russian had it and Dostoyevsky who
knew the soul as the wind may be called.

In such wise whistled the wind, grateful to be tamed,
we say, by a man. Yeough-waugh!

You stayed up half the night in your attic room
under the eaves, composing, secretly, setting
it down, period by period, as the wind whistled,
lightning flashed! the roof creaked about
your ears threatening to give way! but you had a
composition to finish that could not wait!

The storm entered your mind where all good things
are secured, written down, for love's sake
and to defy the devil of emptiness.

The children are decked out in colored ribbons and with
flags in their hands to celebrate your birthday!
They parade to music! a joyous occasion!
Sibelius has been born! and continues to live
in all our minds, all of us, forever . . .

6 It holds / holds (Neon)
7 had / has (Neon)

POEM (THE PLASTIC SURGEON) First printed in *The Massachusetts Review*
(Summer 1961), 632.

HEEL & TOE TO THE END "He read the TIMES out—went upstairs and wrote
this (Floss)" (note in Thirlwall's copy of PB). The front page of *The New
York Times* on 14 April 1961 carried a headline quoting the Soviet astro-
naut: "I Could Have Gone On Forever," followed by the sub-head: "Gagarin,
in Ecstasy, Says He Floated, Ate and Sang."

THE REWAKING "Composed April 10, 1961, expressly for the first issue of
Symposium" (note with the poem in *College Music Symposium*, Fall 1961).

Appendix C: Tables of Contents

THE COLLECTED LATER POEMS (1950)

An asterisk (*) indicates poems included in Volume I rather than the present volume.

THE WEDGE

BALLAD OF FAITH

ALL THAT IS PERFECT IN WOMAN

THE RAT

Nun's Song
Turkey in the Straw [replaced by "The Self" in the 1963 revised edition]
Another Old Woman
Wide Awake, Full of Love
Song (Pluck the florets)
Song (Russia! Russia!)
Convivio

TWO PENDANTS: FOR THE EARS

The Lesson
Two Pendants: for the Ears
To Close

THE ROSE

The Rose (The stillness of the rose)
The Visit
Ol' Bunk's Band
Lear
A Unison
The Quality of Heaven
The Province
The Injury
The Brilliance
The Semblables

[The following section was added in the 1963 revised edition, prefaced by "An Editorial Note" by John C. Thirlwall]

THE LOST POEMS (1944-1950)

The Rare Gist
Death (So this is death)
To a Sparrow
To the Dean
At Kenneth Burke's Place
Sunflowers
Death by Radio
East Coocoo
Rogation Sunday
The Marriage of Souls
Threnody
Translation
Period Piece: 1834
The Sale

[The following poem was added to the section with the fifth printing of the revised edition (1975)]

Appendix D: Four Additional Poems

The four poems below are additions to Emily Wallace's *A Bibliography of William Carlos Williams* (1968), and are added to this volume with the sixth printing. They are poems that Williams evidently intended for local special occasions. The first three are preserved in clippings that form part of the Williams collection at the Rutherford Public Library, while "To Oritani, our first Indian statesman" was printed on a dinner menu. Apparently none of the four poems were reprinted. "The Old Steps of the Passaic General Hospital" probably dates from the 1940s. "My Nurses" has a handwritten date "August 1946" beside the library's clipping, and stems from Williams' unsuccessful hernia operation at the Hospital in May of that year (and see his poem "The Injury" pp. 161–163 on this same event). "While there," the clipping records, "his nurses teased him into writing some verses commemorative of his immobilization in bed." Evidently Williams was not behind the printing of either poem, both of which found their way into the hands of local columnists writing on Rutherford's celebrity poet. Which of the region's local newspapers is the source of the clipping is not recorded in either case. Williams himself submitted "Early Days of the Construction of Our New Library" to *The South Bergen News*, where it appeared on the front page on September 5, 1957. The library is the Rutherford Public Library, across the street from Williams' home. The poet's brother Edgar Williams was the architect for the project. The fourth poem appeared in the printed program for a "Dinner in Honor of Dr. Peter Sammartino," held on April 11, 1959, in Teaneck, New Jersey, to celebrate the fifth anniversary of the Teaneck campus of Fairleigh Dickinson University. Dr. Sammartino (1904–1992) was founder and President of the university. For "Oritani," also known as Oratam and Oratamin, who died c. 1667, see Geraldine Huston, *Oratam of the Hackensacks* (Teaneck, N.J., 1950).

THE OLD STEPS OF THE PASSAIC GENERAL HOSPITAL

With bowed head, walking toward the old steps
I ran into a wall. The old steps were gone.
The new start from another quarter, more
convenient, safer, more protected from
the north wind and Summer sun, and the old
that led broadly to the carriage way from
the open porch above them are no more. There
chestnut branches leaned at one time and in
Autumn brown nuts would fall. Vanished now
with the men who mounted, heads often enough
bowed, to be led without twist, turn or
obstruction, discretely, straightaway upward.

MY NURSES

I can hear the rattle of their skirts
as I watch their minds
struggling to maintain the discipline
—of kindness—put to the test;
girls, that's all they are
softening their voices to
the adult necessity of their lives,
tickling my toes but attentive
to the need but watching always—not
only the need but what I might be—
me, jagged stalagmite in this curious
cavern of a sick room for their wonder.
Asking, asking and wanting to seem
not to ask; full of caresses—withheld.

EARLY DAYS OF THE CONSTRUCTION
OF OUR NEW LIBRARY

the young man is French
only a Frenchman—
rather than the Sicilians
we have mostly
around here among
our skilled artisans—
would have placed
his drawingboard exactly
in the center of the pit
his hair neatly combed
ready to start the
new library construction
I liked him at once
I had an ancestor came from
the South of France—
no one more appropriate
to entrust our library to
under my polyglot brother's
Direction I expect to see
a first-rate job come
of it . . .

TO ORITANI, OUR FIRST INDIAN STATESMAN
(DEDICATED TO PETER SAMMARTINO)

Oritani, lord of the
Hackensaki, you never knew
what happened to your people,

learning, sponsored by
a new world, or let's say
a drive for information

under the aegis of a
curious man who gathered
ignorant men about him

and drove them to acquire
learning. More power
to him, without his drive

the whole country would
still be frightened
to accept the forms by which

ignorance in a pretty dress,
charming enough, Oritani,
is still accepted among us.

Acknowledgments

Volume II of this edition, like Volume I, has benefited from the generosity of many individuals and institutions. James Laughlin kindly provided materials that proved invaluable for textual decisions and for annotations. The staff at New Directions could not have been more helpful, and the manuscript benefited particularly from the careful, intelligent editorial work of Peggy Fox.

A. Walton Litz, my co-editor for Volume I, was extremely generous with his time, knowledge, and experience during my work on this book, and I am very grateful to him. I am also indebted to the following scholars and poets who kindly responded to my queries: Dore Ashton, Mary Ann Caws, Joel Conarroe, Stephen Cushman, Robert E. Daggy, Terence Diggory, Carl Dolmetsch, Scott Donaldson, David A. Fedo, Glen MacLeod, Clare Mather, Paul Mariani, Jerome Mazzaro, Stanley Purdy, Karl Schültz, Peter Schmidt, David Schoonover, Mary Ellen Solt, A. Wilbur Stevens, Gilbert Sorrentino, Dickran Tashjian, Rod Townley, Ted Weiss, Eliot Weinberger, Peter Wiggins and Hugh Witemeyer. My particular thanks to Stephen Field for his help with the annotations to "The Cassia Tree" sequence, and to Catherine Levesque for her assistance with art historical matters.

This volume, like Volume I, owes a deep scholarly debt to Emily Wallace for her *A Bibliography of William Carlos Williams*. Paul Mariani's *William Carlos Williams: A New World Naked* again provided a rich source of helpful detail, while the catalogue of the SUNY Buffalo collection compiled by Neil Baldwin and Stephen L. Meyers proved once more a reliable, informative guide.

My special thanks to William Eric and Paul Williams, who again provided helpful information on their father's life as well as information on local geography, and to Thomas C. Thirlwall for permitting me to study his late father's richly annotated collection of WCW's books and periodical publications. I am also very grateful to Frederick Morgan, who generously allowed me to read the correspondence that accompanied WCW's submissions to *The Hudson Review*, and to Vickie Karp of *The New Yorker* for providing me with copies of WCW's correspondence with that magazine. Frederick Manfred, Selden Rodman, and Robert Creeley gave me permission to study their correspondence with WCW on deposit in libraries, and Kate Donahue provided permission for me to read WCW's correspondence with John Berryman.

Carol Linton of inter-library loan at the College of William and Mary's Swem Library was a tremendous help to me in helping to track down the printings of the poems, as were my research assistants Hilary Holladay and Cindy Currence. I am also indebted to the staff of the Beinecke Library, Yale University, to Cathy Henderson and the staff of the Harry Ransom Humanities Research Center at the University of Texas, and to Robert J. Bertholf and the staff at the Poetry/ Rare Books Collection at SUNY Buffalo.

Other libraries that assisted my research are: The Free Public Library, Rutherford, New Jersey; The New York Public Library; The Library of Congress; Newark Public Library; Park Memorial Public Library; Miller Library, Colby College; The Rosenbach Museum and Library; Thomas Merton Studies Center, Bellarmine College; The Starr Library of Middlebury College; The Newberry Library; The John Hay Library, Brown University; The Joseph Regenstein Library of the University of Chicago; The Huntington Library; The Lilly Library, Indiana University; the Rare Book and Manuscript Library, Columbia University; Mungar Memorial Library, Boston University; Olin Library, Wesleyan University; The University of Iowa Library; Fales Library, New York University; Washington and Lee University Library; The University of Florida Library; University Library, University of Illinois at Urbana-Champaign; Olin Library, Cornell University; the Francis Bacon Library; Wayne State University Library; The Golda Meir Library, University of Wisconsin-Milwaukee; Firestone Library, Princeton University; Fairleigh Dickinson University Library; the Houghton Library, Harvard University; Kent State University Library, Dept. of Special Collections; The Alderman Library, University of Virginia; the University of Arkansas Library, Special Collections; The Bancroft Library, University of California, Berkeley; Tufts University Library; The University of Wyoming, Archive of Contemporary History; The Milton S. Eisenhower Library, Johns Hopkins University; the Morris Library, Southern Illinois University at Carbondale; Temple University Library; the Amherst College Library; the Rare Books Room, University of Colorado at Boulder; Northwestern University Library; the Kenneth Spencer Research Library, University of Kansas; Pattee Library, the Pennsylvania State University; the University of Minnesota Library; the University of Saskatchewan Library; Department of Special Collections, University of California Library, Los Angeles; the University of Delaware Library; The George Arents Research Library, Syracuse University; Special Collections, the Library of Washington University in St. Louis; the University of Washington Library; the Dartmouth College Library; Special Collections, Van Pelt Library, University of Pennsylvania; The University of North Carolina at Chapel Hill, Southern Historical Collection.

The College of William and Mary and the National Endowment for the Humanities both provided financial assistance in the form of summer grants. My work was also facilitated by the generous support towards the research costs of Volume I contributed by the Marguerite Eyer Wilbur Foundation.

The poems printed in this volume originally appeared in the following journals, magazines and books: *The New Yorker, Furioso, The New Republic, Poetry World, Poetry, The University Review, Fantasy, Compass, The Nation, Diogenes, Matrix, Decision, The Providence Sunday Journal, Partisan Review, Harper's Bazaar, The Harvard Advocate, VVV, American Prefaces, Palisade, The Old Line, Hemispheres, Circle, Rocky Mountain Review, Experiment, Orígenes, The Quarterly Review of Literature, Tomorrow, The General Maga-*

zine and Historical Chronicle, Briarcliff Quarterly, Pacific, Yale Poetry Review, Arizona Quarterly, The Harvard Wake, Contemporary Poetry, Poetry (Australia), The Kenyon Review, The New Leader, Cronos, Accent, Botteghe Oscure, Interim, Wake, The Tiger's Eye, The Golden Goose, Imagi, Harper's Magazine, Zero, Glass Hill, Gale, Janus, Kavita, Spearhead, Shenandoah, What's New, Quarto, Origin, Calendar: An Anthology of 1940 Poetry, Calendar: An Anthology of 1941 Poetry, Calendar: An Anthology of 1942 Poetry, Chicago Review, Art News Annual, New Ventures, The Beloit Poetry Journal, Pennsylvania Literary Review, New World Writing, Folio, Neon, East and West, The Atlantic Monthly, Edge, Prairie Schooner, The Hudson Review, Colorado Review, Spectrum, Evergreen Review, The Literary Review, The Grecourt Review, Audience, Delta, San Francisco Review, Monmouth Letters, The Massachusetts Review, The Galley Sail Review, Yūgen, Approach, The Transatlantic Review, Selection, Agenda, Contact, The Poet, The Virginia Quarterly Review, Now, The Minnesota Review, Inscape, The Hasty Papers, Poems in Folio, The National Review, Inland, Sparrow, The Saturday Review, College Music Symposium, Epoch, The New England Galaxy, Focus / Midwest, The New York Review of Books, The New York Times Book Review, Rutgers Review, New Poems by American Poets, Poetry in Crystal, . . . and Spain sings (New York, 1937), My, This Must Have Been a Beautiful Place When It Was Kept Up (New York, 1965), Poets and the Past (New York, 1959), The Muse in Mexico: A Mid-Century Miscellany (Austin, 1959), New Directions 9, New Directions 16, New Directions 19, René Char's Hypnos Waking (New York, 1956), Yvan Goll's Jean Sans Terre (San Francisco, 1944), Yvan Goll's Jean Sans Terre (New York, 1958), Poesie (Torino, 1961), Octavio Paz's Early Poems 1935-1955 (New York, 1973).

Wherever possible permission from the original poet (or his publisher or estate) has been obtained for the translations included in this volume: Yvan Goll by permission of Fonds Goll; Nicolas Calas by permission of the author; Paul Eluard by permission of Editions Gallimard; Alí Chumacero by permission of the author; Nicanor Parra by permission of the author and New Directions Publishing Corporation; Silvina Ocampo by permission of the author; Pablo Neruda by permission of Agencia Literaria Carmen Balcells; Octavio Paz by permission of the author and New Directions Publishing Corporation.

INDEX OF TITLES

[This index lists titles in both Volume I and Volume II. Boldface indicates poem and sequence titles and page numbers in Volume I. The numbered poems of *Spring and All* are indexed under their titles in *Collected Earlier Poems* (see Volume I, pp. xi-xii). The untitled poems in *The Descent of Winter* are not included in this index, but are listed in the Index of First Lines. Titles of poetic sequences are in capital letters.]

INDEX OF FIRST LINES

[This index lists first lines in both Volume I and Volume II. Boldface indicates first lines and page numbers in Volume I. Although in some of Williams' poems the title is syntactically the first line, this index is confined to the lines that follow titles. When a first line is very short, usually one or two words, the following line or lines are supplied.]